I WILL REPAY

I Will Repay

A Cinematic Theology of Atonement

Dennis Oh

WIPF & STOCK · Eugene, Oregon

I WILL REPAY
A Cinematic Theology of Atonement

Copyright © 2018 Dennis Oh. All rights reserved. Except for brief quotations in critical publications or reviews, no part of this book may be reproduced in any manner without prior written permission from the publisher. Write: Permissions, Wipf and Stock Publishers, 199 W. 8th Ave., Suite 3, Eugene, OR 97401.

Wipf & Stock
An Imprint of Wipf and Stock Publishers
199 W. 8th Ave., Suite 3
Eugene, OR 97401

www.wipfandstock.com

PAPERBACK ISBN: 978-1-5326-3855-8
HARDCOVER ISBN: 978-1-5326-3856-5
EBOOK ISBN: 978-1-5326-3857-2

FEBRUARY 1, 2018

Contents

Acknowledgements | vii
Abbreviations | ix

1. Introduction | 1
2. Atonement Trends, Models, and Options | 12
3. Film as Theological Resource | 64
4. The Cinematics of Vengeance | 78
5. Scripture and Cinematic Vengeance in Dialogue | 112
6. Narrative Configurations of Atonement Dogmatics | 133
7. Conclusions: *Christus Ultor* as Cinematic Soteriology | 176

Bibliography | 187

Acknowledgements

THE DISSERTATION FROM WHICH this book has arisen and the degree toward which it was completed was made possible by the faculty, staff, and supporters of the Global Institute of Theology at Yonsei University in Seoul, Korea. I extend my gratefulness to its directors, present and past, Drs. Samuel Pang and Young-min Paik for their work and oversight in launching this program for the centenary celebration of Yonsei's College of Theology. Rev. Dr. Hana Kim and the dear folks at New Song Myungsung Church provided generous support and opportunities to serve in ministry during the coursework portion of my studies.

I especially thank my dissertation advisor, Dr. Ho-hyun Sohn for his patient supervision of the research project as well as Dr. Jaeseung Cha, who along with sharing his deep expertise in atonement theology also offered many words of encouragement and blessing in the months he served as an engaged reader and dissertation committee member. Thanks also to my reader, Dr. Nathan Shannon, for his committed faithfulness throughout the evaluation process and especially for his friendship and fellowship in our common confession. He also put me in touch with Dr. Ted Turnau, whose work in theology and culture was a great help.

I would also like to thank my fellow classmates with whom I shared so much of life during our short time in Incheon: my "session" mates, Russell Ocampo and Augustine Monoke; classmate, Mary Kihuha; roommate, George Okoth. Thank you to Alex Gattogo and Yabibal Teklu for their acts of brotherly kindness at critical junctures of submitting the drafts. A deep thanks also to my close friends in Seoul, who remind me of the precious joys and struggles of life outside of school: Aric Allen, Tim Lee, Mijito Chishi, Eugene Rhee, Ah Young Choi, Sarah Jun, and Derek Forbes.

Finally, a big thanks to my family: my brother, Dave, for his wise encouragements, and my parents, Peter and Catherine Oh, for their love, support, and constant prayers.

This work is dedicated to my spiritual family, Seoul Grace Community, for whom although the congregation and leadership may change, the gospel we love so much never will.

Soli Deo Gloria.

Dennis Oh
August, 2017
Seoul, Korea

Abbreviations

ABD	Anchor Bible Dictionary
ATR	Anglican Theological Review
CCEL	Christian Classics Ethereal Library
CBQ	The Catholic Biblical Quarterly
CR	Covenant of Redemption
CTM	Concordia Theological Monthly
ESV	English Standard Version
ET	The Expository Times
IJST	International Journal of Systematic Theology
JETS	Journal of the Evangelical Theological Society
JJKC	Journal of Japanese and Korean Cinema
JRF	Journal of Religion and Film
JTS	The Journal of Theological Studies
LXX	Septuagint
MAJT	Mid-America Journal of Theology
NASB	New American Standard Bible
NIV	New International Version
NICNT	New International Commentary on the New Testament
NICOT	New International Commentary on the Old Testament
NT	New Testament
NTS	New Testament Studies
NZSTh	Neue Zeitschrift für Systematische Theologie und Religionsphilosophie
OT	Old Testament

PSA	Penal substitutionary atonement
RTR	*The Reformed Theological Review*
SJT	*Scottish Journal of Theology*
ST	*Summa Theologiae*, by Thomas Aquinas
WCF	Westminster Confession of Faith

The NRSV translation of the Bible is used throughout except where indicated.

1.

Introduction

> "It is mine to avenge; I will repay. In due time their foot will slip; their day of disaster is near and their doom rushes upon them." The Lord will vindicate his people and relent concerning his servants when he sees their strength is gone and no one is left, slave or free.
> —Deuteronomy 32:35–36 (NIV)

> "If you let my daughter go now, that'll be the end of it. I will not look for you. I will not pursue you. But if you don't, I will look for you. I will find you. And I will kill you."
> —Bryan, *Taken*

Debating Atonement

CONTEMPORARY SOTERIOLOGY IS BECOMING increasingly uncomfortable with following the Apostle Paul's pronouncement to *glory* in nothing except the cross of our Lord Jesus Christ (Gal 6:14). A century ago, theologians debated finer points of the doctrine, matters of scope, mechanism, and terminology, but the breadth of discussion remained relatively restrained. In a series of articles contributed to *The Christian World* during the winter of 1899–1900, which came to be published as *The Atonement in Modern Religious Thought: A Theological Symposium*, eminent European theologians discussed atonement theology from a wide variety of perspectives. In the opening article, Adolf von Harnack declared, "While modern knowledge has rudely shaken the *form* of the doctrine in which earlier generations laid down their belief in the redemption and in the Redeemer, the thing itself has not been shaken."[1]

---

1. Adolf Harnack, et. al., *The Atonement in Modern Religious Thought: A Theological*

In the current theological milieu, however, significant concerns have arisen about the nature, process, and goal of redemptive violence in soteriology, especially the dominant Protestant model of penal substitution that posits a direct connection between Christ's execution and the Father's wrath. The impetus to disavow God's involvement and complicity in violence has driven many to rethink and revise what is meant by atonement, leaving the broader Christian world in what might be considered a state of impasse amidst a host of divergent positions.

In his 1931 classic, *Christus Victor*,[2] Gustaf Aulén sets forth a history of atonement that attempts to correct the misinterpretation and neglect of the "classic" (or "dramatic") type over the more well-known Latin and subjective types, championed by Anselm and Abelard, respectively. He questions the status of Anselmic satisfaction theory as the beginning of a truly robust theology of the atonement and argues that the assumption of this history is the result of tracing the theory through the conflicts between orthodoxy and liberal Protestantism in post-Enlightenment thought. He concludes his study persuaded that "no form of Christian teaching has any future before it except such as can keep steadily in view the reality of the evil in the world, and go to meet evil with a battle-song of triumph."[3] Aulén's survey reveals how historic models of atonement address the broad paradox of God's relation to sin, death, and the devil.

Recent atonement debates pick up from Aulén's reservations regarding the so-called "Latin model" but have been shaped by the atrocities of WWII and thereafter. Violence is not only fresh in history's memory but looms over the present and the future as we grapple with global terrorism, the threat of nuclear war, and the rapid depletion of earth's resources. It is within these contexts of violence that recent theological critiques of classical Protestant thought have been issued. Christian unity on the essentially positive view of the death of Christ (i.e. "Good Friday") has been replaced with proposals that not only question the mechanism of redemption, but the very need of redemptive sacrifice in the first place.

A new and recent symposium on atonement reflects the objections of present-day theologians, who manifest a resistance to the retributive punishment, redemptive violence, and individualistic ideology inherent in doctrines that support God's agency in violent judgments, of which penal

---

Symposium (Miami: HardPress, 2013), 5.

2. Gustaf Aulén, *Christus Victor: An Historical Study of the Three Main Types of the Idea of Atonement*, trans. A. G. Herbert (Eugene, OR: Wipf & Stock, 2003).

3. Ibid., 159.

substitution is the enduring model among evangelicals. One contributor, Steve Chalke, writes:

> The greatest theological problem for penal substitution is that it presents us with a God who is first and foremost concerned with retribution for sin that flows from his wrath against sinners. The only way for his anger to be placated is in receiving recompense from those who have wronged him, and although his great love motivates him to send his Son, his wrath remains the driving force behind the need for the cross.[4]

Criticisms such as these are extensive and sustained across denominational lines and academic fields. Some have followed Aulén in believing that recovering ancient models avoid the distasteful problems in penal substitution. Others call for a wholesale reconfiguration of the notion of salvation altogether. A typical strategy has been to retreat in the direction of one of the other two historic proposals (*Christus Victor* and moral exemplar). To help classify the various alternatives to the doctrine that have surfaced, I suggest a taxonomy that distinguishes positions according to the role that Christ's suffering and death plays in redemption:

1. duality—the cross as enmity between God and Satan;
2. solidarity—the cross as divine partnership with human pain; and
3. invalidation—the cross as deconstruction of sacrificial scapegoating.

Each of these approaches takes issue with the mechanism of atonement as held by traditional Protestant theology, and the tendency has spilled over into discomfort over violent biblical texts in general.[5] Evangelical soteriology, once a dominant means of explaining redemption by the cross, is fast becoming pushed to the fringe. Chalke concludes:

---

4. Steve Chalke, "The Redemption of the Cross," in Derek Tidball, David Hilborn, and Justin Thacker, eds., *The Atonement Debate: Papers from the London Symposium On the Theology of Atonement* (Grand Rapids: Zondervan, 2008), 39.

5. For example, see David R. Blumenthal, *Facing the Abusing God: A Theology of Protest* (Louisville: Westminster/John Knox Press, 1993); Jerome F. D. Creach, *Violence in Scripture: Interpretation: Resources for the Use of Scripture in the Church* (Louisville: Westminster/John Knox Press, 2013); John Dominic Crossan, *How to Read the Bible and Still Be a Christian: Struggling with Divine Violence from Genesis Through Revelation* (New York: HarperCollins, 2015); William W. Emilsen and John T. Squires, eds., *Validating Violence—Violating Faith? Religion, Scripture and Violence* (Adelaide: ATF, 2008); Eric A. Seibert, *Disturbing Divine Behavior: Troubling Old Testament Images of God* (Minneapolis: Fortress, 2009) and *The Violence of Scripture: Overcoming the Old Testament's Troubling Legacy* (Minneapolis: Fortress, 2012).

> A weakness of penal substitutionary theory is that it is culturally sluggish or even disconnected and, as such, fails to engage with or challenge our society and its macro values . . . If the church could rediscover a deeper understanding of the cross, we could once again speak prophetic power to a global society caught in the grip of the lie that violence can be redemptive. The church's inability to shake off the great distortion of God contained in the theory of penal substitution, with its inbuilt belief in retribution and the redemptive power of violence, has cost us dearly.[6]

The debate is believed to have sociological implications as well. Timothy Gorringe perceives a correlation between the satisfaction model of the atonement and historic penal practice in Europe and especially Britain, arguing that Anselm's theory lay behind the justification and perpetuation of retributive modes of punishment.[7] While this does not take into adequate consideration the fact that retribution is endemic to virtually all societies, not just those influenced by Judeo-Christian tradition,[8] Gorringe's attempt does illustrate the extreme caution that modern minds have against bringing the divine will and violence too closely together.

On the evangelical side, there has been little attempt to revise the existing model. On the contrary, recent publications have tended to defend penal substitution in large part due to a reaction of what are considered "caricatures" of the historic Protestant doctrine. A commitment to biblical fidelity and essential gospel truths demand an unwavering commitment to a doctrine for which the stakes are so high. As the writers of *Pierced for our Transgressions: Rediscovering the Glory of Penal Substitution* state in their introduction:

> In brief, we argue that penal substitution is clearly taught in Scripture, that it has a central place in Christian theology, that a neglect of the doctrine will have serious pastoral consequences, that it has an impeccable pedigree in the history of the Christian church, and that all of the objections raised against it can be comprehensively answered.[9]

---

6. Steve Chalke, "The Redemption of the Cross," in *The Atonement Debate*, 41.

7. Timothy Gorringe, *God's Just Vengeance: Crime, Violence and the Rhetoric of Salvation* (New York: Cambridge University Press, 1996). See also a recent study which argues that Protestant Fundamentalists are more likely to hold to retributive punishment, in Harold G. Grasmick et. al., "Protestant Fundamentalism and the Retributive Doctrine of Punishment," *Criminology* 30, no. 1 (March 2006): 21–46.

8. See G. W. Trompf, *Payback: The Logic of Retribution in Melanesian Religions* (Cambridge: Cambridge University Press, 1994), 2–6.

9. Steve Jeffrey, Michael Ovey, and Andrew Sach, *Pierced for our Transgressions: Rediscovering the Glory of Penal Substitution* (Wheaton: Crossway, 2007), 31.

In specific response to the charge of violence, much is made of God's foreordained plan and Christ's willingness to undergo redemptive suffering at the Father's hand, but there seems to be no desire to significantly reformulate the model along a nonviolent path. This "doubling down" is understandable in light of the polemical spirit of evangelicalism in general, but it also means that it should be of no surprise if conservative Protestants are relegated by their opponents to the enclaves of a sectarian and dangerous "fundamentalism."

Into this polarized theological terrain I endeavor to explore whether the atonement could be construed in a way that establishes a greater distance between divine intention and human violence while remaining consistent to evangelicalism's core convictions.

Challenges in Atonement Theology

Atonement theology has typically taken as its starting point biblical metaphors that point to God's activity of restoring or saving sinful humanity. Most prominent are the images of ransom, redemption, sacrifice, and victory. Critics of a single, dominant model of the atonement, like Peter Schmiechen, are quick to point out that "while the church officially adopted creedal statements regarding Trinity and Incarnation, it did not adopt one official theory of atonement. There is something inherently complex and diverse about the subject that resists the restriction of a single answer."[10] This has led some to conclude that the atonement is relatively unimportant in Christian dogmatics so as to provoke the level of theological articulation seen in the christological formulations of the first five centuries of the church.[11]

Paul may be said to be the first theologian to substantively deal with atonement metaphors and attempt to distill an essence. His approach, as Stephan Finlan observes, was to mix cultic and legal metaphors in such a way that the bottom line "is not metaphoric consistency but saving

---

10. Peter Schmiechen, *Saving Power: Theories of Atonement and Forms of the Church* (Grand Rapids: Eerdmans, 2005), 5; cf. Mark D. Baker, ed., *Proclaiming the Scandal of the Cross: Contemporary Images of the Atonement* (Grand Rapids: Baker, 2006), 16.

11. Against such a view, John McIntyre makes the compelling case that the centrality of the Eucharist in early Christian worship had already so clearly and so constantly brought to the Christian community a consciousness of Christ's work on the cross that further reflection and development seemed unnecessary. Furthermore, the understanding of the atonement as interpreted by the Eucharist, especially the institution narrative, was remarkably stable and remained more or less uncontested by the type of heretical opposition that tend to trigger sophisticated debates resulting in formal dogmatic categories. John McIntyre, *The Shape of Soteriology: Studies in the Doctrine of the Death of Christ* (Edinburgh: T&T Clark, 1992), 8-10.

outcome."[12] Finlan argues that this conflation of images, while effective, inevitably changes the meaning of metaphors and takes on a life of its own. What began in Paul as an almost haphazard blend of different motifs came to be developed, Finlan laments, into the theory of penal substitution that dominated Western Christianity. Like many modern critics of this traditional understanding, Finlan wishes to recover the variety—and even contradiction—of biblical expressions against the tendency to literalize the metaphors on the one hand and distort them on the other.

The flexible nature of biblical metaphor leads to a question of how it can or should be used when developing a theological system. Against the Enlightenment critique of the inadequacy and vagueness of Christian symbols, Colin Gunton defends that metaphors are epistemically successful for providing referentiality, for "telling things as they are."[13] He validates the metaphors of victory, justice, and sacrifice as communicating truly and relevantly the actuality of the atonement even if the mode of description is, admittedly, "indirect."[14] While this desire to uphold the primacy of the traditional biblical metaphors is commendable, the attempt to juggle and harmonize the various images is not without its difficulties. Furthermore, Gunton (like many others) is reluctant to permit God's anger and wrath to factor into the atonement, but while he looks disapprovingly upon penal substitution, he cannot deny the necessary function of the model.

> To conceive Jesus as primarily the victim of divine punitive justice is to commit three sins: to treat one metaphor of atonement, the legal, in isolation from the others; to read that metaphor literally and personalistically; and to create a dualism between the action of God and that of Jesus. Yet to ignore the fact that Jesus is shown in scripture as bearing the consequences, according to the will of God, of our breaches of universal justice—to forget that he was bruised for our iniquities—is again, to trivialise evil and to deny the need for an atonement . . . [15]

Two contrasting ironies in Gunton's method are worth observing here. First, in order to avoid "isolating" the forensic metaphor at the expense of others, the metaphor itself must be targeted and downplayed to fit his preconceived standard of what is acceptable as an atonement metaphor.

---

12. Stephen Finlan, *Options on Atonement in Christian Thought* (Collegeville, MN: Liturgical Press, 2007), 26.

13. Colin E. Gunton, *The Actuality of Atonement: A Study of Metaphor, Rationality and the Christian Tradition* (London: T&T Clark, 2003), 25.

14. Ibid., 65.

15. Ibid., 165.

Second, in order to affirm and not trivialize evil, which the victory metaphor supposedly achieves, one should, it would seem, affirm and not trivialize the forensic metaphor.

Some other attempts have been made to fully appreciate the atonement as a multifaceted reality and hold the various biblical images in tension. Joel B. Green's "kaleidoscopic view" proposes two "nonnegotiable points" of Jesus' historic execution and God's eternal purpose between which lies a multitude of possible explanations of how the cross effects salvation. As for the rationale, he writes:

> At the interface of the particular moment of Jesus' crucifixion and the eternal mission of God, we can find not one but many models of the atonement. So limited is the ground on which we walk and so infinite the mystery of God's saving work that we need many interpretive images, many tones, many voices.[16]

However, like Gunton, Green's refusal to permit propitition as an interpretation of OT ritual sacrifice betrays the convictions inherent in a kaleidoscopic approach.[17] John McIntyre offers greater balance by understanding the metaphors (or "models," as he prefers to use) as possessing a "constellational richness" or "nuclear profusion" that emphasizes their distinct qualities as well as their interpenetration and mutual influence and coherence.[18] Rather than illustrative after-thoughts, the metaphors "are all involved in, and part of, what happened when Jesus died . . . [They] share in the reality of that which they, in a very real sense, embody."[19]

It is now generally accepted that the theologian's experience of the world and how it should be inevitably leads her to select and interpret biblical material according to an underlying ideology. In discussing the use of metaphor for religious discourse, Janet Martin Soskice rightly argues that Christian claims are made on the basis of experience, be it one's personal encounter with God, or natural experiences of contingency that inform metaphysical postulation.[20] These experiences are accessed "in the categories

---

16. James Beilby and Paul R. Eddy, eds., *The Nature of the Atonement: Four Views* (Downers Grove: IVP, 2006), 185.

17. Ibid., 174. He writes, "It is crucial that we not confuse that we not confuse the wrath of Yahweh with the retributive, begrudging and capricious dispositions of the Greek and Roman gods to whom sacrifices were offered in order to both placate the deities and to solicit their favor . . . What is clear is that the God of Israel is 'slow to anger and abounding in steadfast love' . . . "

18. McIntyre, *Shape of Soteriology*, 82–83.

19. Ibid., 83.

20. Janet Martin Soskice, *Metaphor and Religious Language* (Oxford: Clarendon Press, 1987), 150.

used by a particular community of interest and within a particular tradition of evaluation."[21] In approaching biblical texts, readers have come to admit to a cyclical pattern of understanding (hermeneutical circle/spiral), in which we interpret texts and texts interpret us. Soskice continues, "It is not simply that texts interpret us, they interpret our experiences; and it is not simply that we interpret texts, for we also interpret the experiences which they more or less obscurely chronicle."[22]

While Gunton is correct that redemptive metaphors speak rightly and relevantly to our understanding a doctrine of salvation, it remains that their aesthetic quality and cultural distance to us leaves them open to interpretation. Furthermore, by remaining as particularized word-images, they resist being gathered into a comprehensive picture with a set of implications that flow therefrom. In practice, I suspect that theologians choose the metaphor(s) that are most meaningful and relevant to them and downplay others, thus, reducing the diversity and complexity that eclectic approaches purport to foster. McIntyre's image of a "nuclear profusion" of soteriological metaphors, though promising, inevitably produces the urge to identify the very *nucleus* of meaning from which metaphors branch out. For a faith that makes much of communicating and living *the gospel* as a single, unbroken message of the blessings wrought in Christ, it seems only natural to strive for unity of witness as a demonstration of the solidarity that ranks high among our values. Systematic theology can and should do more than simply catalogue exegetical givens in the biblical texts or proliferate contextual interpretations of those texts. Something can be said not only of what salvation is *like*, but also *how it works* and to do so in a way that makes the most sense. This study aims to show how it may be possible to encapsulate an account of the atonement and arrive at a comprehensive story that stems from (rather than avoids) one of Scripture's most ubiquitous themes: violence.

A Cinematic Approach to Theology

Besides the use of metaphors, many of Scripture's redemptive expressions are cast in terms of sequences of action, or "scenes," which are not metaphorical in the sense that they correspond to concepts outside themselves. Rather, they are concrete movements taking place within a frame of time, making the motivations and outcomes clear as aspects contained within a story's arc. Our own experiences aid us in achieving this clarity. Paul Ricoeur argues that human living is practiced in a narrative mode and that narrative

21. Ibid., 151.
22. Ibid., 159.

finds its full meaning as a condition of temporal existence.²³ In the initial stage of organizing and finding meaning in our lives through narrative is a "prefiguration" of the world of action in which we effortlessly understand our language and conventions of our society. Some narratives crystallize and become part of a collective consciousness. They find repeated expression in all forms of religious and cultural texts and are widely recognized. Insofar as universal narratives might be discerned in both Scripture and cultural artifacts, we come upon a resource for "fusing horizons" and the possibility of meaningful two-way dialogue and discovery.

Among the narratives common to our experience and redemptive history, I submit, is the sequence of offense and retaliation we call "vengeance." I understand this as an intuitive category describing *physical acts of retaliation issued against an offender for a perceived personal offense*. Probing deeper for the sake of clarity, these acts are physical—that is, bodily—and, thus, underscore the most basic notion of violence as infliction against material flesh; they are retaliatory, which is to say, motivated by, and performed subsequently in reaction to, some previous act; and, the effect of the offense touches the offended party on a personal level. These elements are multifaceted and are expressed in various permutations, but as a category, vengeance is capable of encapsulating much of Scripture's acts of divine retributive violence in a direct and recognizable way. If it is granted that violence in the retaliatory mode is God's means of dealing with sin, then this paradigm, as demonstrable and ubiquitous as it is, could warrant its use as a conceptual framework for atonement in general.

The resurgent interest in *Christus Victor* in part demonstrates the relevance of narrative and drama in the current theological milieu. Of the original, patristic version, Alister McGrath suggests that it represents an intermediate stage between narrative and doctrine in which New Testament metaphors were expanded and reconstructed to form a narrative account of redemption.²⁴ The concept of the *ius diaboli* was developed as a substructure "to make sense of the narrative at its more perplexing points;" this was later criticized by Anselm and the theory replaced with a "doctrine" of redemption.²⁵ In short, the ransom motif was unable to bear the weight of further doctrinal concerns. "Doctrine provides the conceptual framework by which the scriptural narrative is interpreted. It is not an arbitrary framework,

---

23. Paul Ricoeur, *Time and Narrative, Vol. 1*, trans. Kathleen McLaughlin and David Pellauer (Chicago: University Of Chicago Press, 1984), 52.

24. Alister E. McGrath, *The Genesis of Doctrine* (Grand Rapids; Vancouver: Eerdmans; Regent College Publishing, 1997), 57.

25. Ibid.

however, but one which is suggested by that narrative, and intimated (however provisionally) by scripture itself."[26]

But can narrative function as doctrine in its own right? While he emphasizes its origin in the scriptural narratives themselves, McGrath's idea of doctrine consists of highly developed assertions forged through debate and reinforced by the worshiping community,[27] But he also recognizes that "a narrative engenders a network of relations, demanding intrasystemic consistency."[28] Taken together with the tendency of revenge narratives to unfold according to expected patterns, a conceptual framework is indeed possible. In order to speak meaningfully to the full array of doctrinal considerations within the idea of salvation, the narrative should not be forced to depend on a single metaphor or motif (like ransom) but must be expanded.

To achieve this within the present work, two preliminary operations are in view: First, many biblical and theological motifs do not immediately register as properly belonging to an idea of revenge but could very well be brought into the wider story. Second, biblical passages require a narrative-structuring framework to bring the various components into a whole. Both of these considerations suggest a role for cinema to serve as a theological resource. Because the premise and structure of typical revenge films are stable and predictable, this offers a mechanism for organizing seemingly unrelated images and motifs into a recognizable and plausible story. This is essentially Ricoeur's notion of "emplotment," the capacity of otherwise disparate events to be enjoined into a meaningful story in such a way that motivation and causality become evident. Narratives of divine retribution at the level of biblical theology can, thus, through the help of cinema, be expanded into a model or theory at the level of systematic theology.

---

26. Ibid., 58–59.

27. He cites the Athanasian and Arian controversy as example: "The frameworks proposed by both Arius and Athanasius were sufficiently internally consistent to necessitate their evaluation on other grounds: those grounds included the degree of correlation with both the scriptural narrative itself, and the evaluation of that narrative within the community of faith as expressed in its prayer, worship and adoration," ibid., 58.

28. McGrath, *The Genesis of Doctrine*, 60. He uses Lindbeck's example that "if 'Denmark' is identified by the narrative of *Hamlet* as being 'the land where Hamlet lived', intrasystemic consistency demands that 'Denmark' shall not suddenly assume some other meaning." This example refers to a setting that is intrinsic to the story's plot. However, in a remarkable jump, McGrath makes his own analogous example, "If Jesus of Nazereth is defined as 'God,' then consistency demands that traditional monotheism either recognizes that there are at least two gods, or begin rethinking the question of just who the 'God' implicated within this narrative might actually be." While his point to establish doctrine as a "regulative discourse" is well taken, his analogy that moves from 'Denmark is the land where Hamlet lived' to 'Jesus is God' is a strained one. A story's setting is considerably more basic in determining narrative consistency than a dogmatic assertion.

Thesis and Thematic Outline of this Book

In both judgment and redemption, God deals with sin consistently in a retributive, vengeful mode. As such, narratives of vengeance mirror narratives of salvation. Bringing contemporary film into dialogue with biblical and systematic theology, it is my aim to make a case for a sufficiently positive vision of this mode of divine agency that runs throughout redemptive history and which culminates with the suffering and death of Christ. I will argue that certain narrative and cinematic elements in the revenge film genre are congruent with biblical motifs of retributive punishment, and, when employed as a hermeneutical lens for approaching biblical texts, can stimulate a positive appreciation for these scenarios as the bases for an atonement paradigm. Through collaboration with contemporary theological discussion, a revised and robust narrative model emerges that amends the problems that traditional Protestant soteriologies face. Rather than Christ being afflicted by God on account of humanity's debt of sin, atonement can be understood as Christ—or, *Christus Ultor* (Christ the Avenger)—actively issuing a vengeful "repayment" *to sin* for its offenses and damages upon God's creation and, especially, upon God's beloved people. A retributive framework that targets sin as an objective villain within the story of salvation is violence-dependent, yet it redirects the intentionality and force of divine aggression one step removed from creaturely flesh. This dissociation helps to avoid, albeit narrowly, the implication that the divine hand *directly* inflicts violence upon the God-man at the cross. I will show how this framework is distinct from current atonement models while at the same time responsive to their theological concerns.

In chapter 2, I will provide a survey and analysis of the current trends in atonement theology that underscore the impetus of this thesis. Chapter 3 explores theology's relation to film and proposes a methodological framework that establishes film as a hermeneutical resource for a narrative theology. In chapter 4, I will analyze the elements in film that constitute cinematic revenge in its various permutations. Chapter 5 compares cinematic and biblical portrayals of violent retribution and the ways they distill a narrative of redemption. In chapter 6, I will propose several syntheses of biblical and cinematic insights and make the argument for key themes in the atonement story as they relate to issues in systematic theology. My final chapter relates the model with contemporary theories, suggests points for further discussion, and offers some practical implications of this reformulated doctrinal emphasis.

2.

Atonement Trends, Models, and Options

THIS CHAPTER SURVEYS SOME of the ideas in contemporary theology that are relevant to our exploration on atonement. I begin with a brief sketch of the theory inherited from the Reformation, which, though it varies in certain respects within traditions, has enough common agreement to constitute what we might call "Protestant Orthodoxy." I will show how criticisms of this framework serve as the basis for subsequent revisions and/or calls for complete abandonment. I have grouped these into three categories that emphasize their distinctive orientations *vis-à-vis* their appraisal of the violence of the cross: duality, solidarity, and invalidation. My evaluation of the available options will attempt to delineate in greater detail the impasse that soteriology currently faces and the theological task before us.

Penal Substitutionary Atonement as Protestant Orthodoxy

Aulén categorized the theology of the Reformers—with the exception of Luther—as falling within the "Latin-type" paradigm, tracing its pedigree to Anselm. This move is obvious in light of the proliferation of the language of "satisfaction" issuing forth from the Reformers and later post-reformation scholastics in regard to the atonement.[1] If Calvin's use of the term, for example, is in any way typical of how the Reformed used it to speak of the atonement, we might well conclude that "satisfaction" in Protestant theology is

---

1. For example, Augsburg Confession (1530), article IV; Scottish Confession (1560), chapter 9.7, 9.8; Second Helvetic Confession (1566), chapter XV; Thirty Nine Articles (1572), XXXI.

a general term rather than a technical one.² Thus, it follows and should be noted that penal substitution is distinct from Anselmic satisfaction.³

The confessional documents of the Reformation churches are good starting places for defining a Protestant doctrine of atonement. As consensual statements, historically often presented and defended before magisterial authorities, the confessions enshrine a standard of belief agreed upon by whole worshiping communities.⁴ Chapter VIII, sections III–V of the Westminster Confession of Faith (1647) is perhaps most familiar:⁵

> III. The Lord Jesus, in His human nature thus united to the divine, was sanctified, and anointed with the Holy Spirit, above measure, having in Him all the treasures of wisdom and knowledge; in whom it pleased the Father that all fullness should dwell; to the end that, being holy, harmless, undefiled, and full of grace and truth, He might be thoroughly furnished to execute the office of a Mediator and Surety. Which office He took not unto Himself, but was thereunto called by His Father, who put all power and judgment into His hand, and gave Him commandment to execute the same.
>
> IV. This office the Lord Jesus did most willingly undertake; which that He might discharge, He was made under the law, and did perfectly fulfil it; endured most grievous torments immediately in His soul, and most painful sufferings in His body; was crucified, and died, was buried, and remained under the power of death, yet saw no corruption. On the third day He arose from the dead, with the same body in which He suffered, with which also he ascended into heaven, and there sits at the right hand of

---

2. See Robert A. Peterson, *Calvin's Doctrine of the Atonement* (Philipsburg, NJ: Presbyterian and Reformed Publishing, 1983), 91–93, in which he argues the coverage of Calvin's use of "satisfaction" is wide, including Christ's obedience, sacrifice, propitiation, legal fulfillment, and the cost of redemption in general.

3. See Steven D. Cone, "Non-Penal Atonement and Anselm's Satisfaction Theory," *Stone-Campbell Journal* 18, no. Spring (2015): 27–44; Rachel Erdman, "Sacrifice as Satisfaction, Not Substitution: Atonement in the Summa Theologiae," *ATR* 96, no. 3 (2014): 461–80; Bernard Lonergan, *Philosophical and Theological Papers, 1958–1964: Volume 6*, ed. Robert C. Croken, Frederick E. Crowe, and Robert M. Doran (Toronto: University of Toronto Press, 1996), 8–20.

4. Of course, debate was commonplace among divines. See for example, George Gillespie, *Notes Of Debates And Proceedings Of The Assembly Of Divines And Other Commissioners At Westminster: From February 1644 To January 1645* (Edinburgh: Robert Ogle and Oliver and Boyd, 1846); John Owen, *The Death of Death in the Death of Christ: A Treatise of the Redemption and Reconciliation That Is in the Blood of Christ, with the Merit Therof, and Satisfaction Wrought Thereby*, Reprint ed. (Carlisle, PA: Banner of Truth, 2013).

5. The footnotes in the document (scriptural proof texts) have been removed.

> His Father, making intercession, and shall return, to judge men and angels, at the end of the world.
>
> V. The Lord Jesus, by His perfect obedience, and sacrifice of Himself, which He through the eternal Spirit, once offered up unto God, has fully satisfied the justice of His Father; and purchased, not only reconciliation, but an everlasting inheritance in the kingdom of heaven, for those whom the Father has given unto Him.

Three features are immediately observable and fare prominently in expositions of the doctrine issuing from the Reformation. First, the atoning work of the cross is set within a trinitarian framework wherein the Father sets the Son on a course to complete the specific charge of serving as the Mediator and Surety of his people in the power of the Spirit; or, in other words, initiated by the Father, accomplished by the Son, and applied by the Spirit.[6] Again, the language of "satisfaction" is the anchoring metaphor in confessional articles on Christ's saving work and appears frequently. Lutheran theologians regarded Christ's entire life as "a series of satisfactions rendered to the violated justice of God."[7] Reformed confessions and catechisms understand the atonement as falling under Christ's priestly (or mediatorial) office while readily employing the language of Christ "fully satisfying" the justice and wrath of God.[8] This satisfaction involves an exchange in which Christ's offering of himself bestows upon the believer reconciliation and eternal life. This impartation is often described using the commercial terminology of a "purchase." The redemptive work of Christ was one in which sinners were reconciled to God. This is an important Reformed distinction, which, following Anselm, names God as the ultimately offended party. The Puritan, Stephen Charnock, writes:

> As the Father is the principal person wronged, and declaring his anger against us, the reconciliation is principally made to him; in which sense we are said to have "access to the Father," Eph.

---

6. See for example, John Owen's exposition of this theme in his 1684 classic, Owen, *The Death of Death in the Death of Christ*, 51–69.

7. Jaroslav Pelikan, *The Christian Tradition: A History of the Development of Doctrine, Vol. 4: Reformation of Church and Dogma* (Chicago: University Of Chicago Press, 1985), 360. He cites Johann Gerhard, *Meditations*, 1633.

8. See WCF VIII.5 and Belgic Confession chapter 21. Some early expositions of satisfaction from Reformation theologians like Luther and Bugenhegen regard the payment to be directed toward the law of God and the justice of God respectively, but this should be viewed in light of the "polemical opposition to the notion of a satisfaction wrought by human acts of penance" rather than as significant theological distinctions in themselves, Pelikan, 161.

ii.18, through Christ, and by the Spirit. The Son brings us to the Father, and the Spirit directs us to the Son.[9]

The mechanism of penal substitution

Within historic Protestant thought, the violence inflicted upon Christ is directly related with divine displeasure and wrath. Reformed theology has generally understood the death of Christ as a "substitutionary suffering of punishment."[10] Calvin arguably proffers the harshest form of this view,[11] and his influence may lie behind some of the modern backlash. The motif of Christ as punished and cursed in order to appease the wrath of God upon sinners is the result of humanity's status as lawbreakers. Crucial for Calvin is that "sinners, until freed from guilt, being always liable to the wrath and curse of God, who, as he is a just judge, cannot permit his law to be violated with impunity, but is armed for vengeance."[12]

Conveniently, we notice that "vengeance" is an apt term for God's disposition where sin is concerned. The difficulty, however, is the way Calvin unflinchingly closes the gap between divine wrath and Christ's person. This is because Christ "suffered death not because of innocence but because of sin"; in him is represented "the person of a sinner and evil-doer."[13] Calvin brings the narrative of Pontius Pilate's sham of a trial to bear on the argument as providing a positive, pedagogical function: ". . . to teach us, that the punishment to which we were liable was inflicted on that just One . . . "[14] The method of his execution—death on a cross—thus becomes "necessary" for satisfaction, for only in the context of condemnation by an earthly judge does the notion of punishment work. Calvin quickly recognizes the cross as fulfilling the symbolism of Deuteronomic curse,[15] but this curse is not to be

---

9. Stephen Charnock, "A Discourse of God's Being the Author of Reconciliation" CCEL, accessed May 26, 2016, http://www.ccel.org/c/charnock/reconcil/reconciliation.html.

10. Jan Rohls, *Reformed Confessions: Theology from Zurich to Barmen* (Louisville: Westminster John Knox Press, 1998), 91.

11. See Jaeseung Cha, "Calvin's Concept of Penal Substitution: Acknowledgement and Challenge," in *Restoration through Redemption: John Calvin Revisited*, vol. 23, Studies in Reformed Theology (Boston: Leiden, 2013).

12. Calvin, *Institutes* II.xvi.1.

13. Calvin, Commentary on II Corinthians 5:21; cf. Commentary on Luke 22:37.

14. Calvin, *Institutes* II.xvi.5.

15. Deut 21:23; cf. Calvin, *Institutes* II.xvi.6, Commentaries on Galatians 3:13, 5:1, and Luke 2:22.

understood in a passive way. Rather, God is personally involved in Christ's death. He imagines that it was "the sight of the dread tribunal of God" in which God was, once again, "armed with vengeance beyond understanding" that horrified Christ at Gethsemane.[16]

To be fair, Calvin's atonement theology constantly circles back to the love of God[17] and briefly attempts to steer clear of the insinuation that the Father could ever be hostile to, or angry with, the Son: "How could he be angry with the beloved Son, with whom his soul was well pleased?"[18] He goes on to say that the Son "bore the weight of the divine anger, that, smitten and afflicted, he experienced all the signs of an angry an avenging God."[19] How one can experience "all the signs" of divine displeasure yet having the opposite be true, therein lies a critical, missing component of the mechanism that makes the model seem so problematic, especially for contemporary audiences.

Related to this is how Calvin attempts to reconcile the apparent inconsistency in God's disposition toward sinners before and after the cross. If God was our enemy prior to the atoning work of Christ (Rom 5:10), then this seems to imply that his love for us was somehow activated by and conditioned on the cross. "How could he have given us in his only begotten Son a singular pledge of his love, if he had not previously embraced us with free favor?"[20] Calvin, in wanting to affirm God's love as the ground of our salvation, provides the rather unsatisfying answer that the language of verses like Romans 5:10 are "accommodated to our capacity, that we may the better understand how miserable and calamitous our condition is without Christ."[21] Andrew Hay rightly finds inadequate the interpretive logic that dissociates what God does from who God is. He helpfully explicates the problem facing Calvin's doctrine of atonement:

> We must show *how* the divine love is demonstrated precisely in the outpouring of wrath and judgment. If we fail to do this, we introduce a contradiction in the being of God between God's mercy and his righteousness. We confine God's mercy, so to speak, until such time as righteousness has been completely satisfied.[22]

16. Calvin, Commentary on Matthew 26:37.

17. This is one of the central theses of Peterson's work, *Calvin's Doctrine of the Atonement*.

18. Calvin, *Institutes* II.xvi.11.

19. Ibid.

20. Calvin, *Institutes*, II.xvi.2.

21. Ibid.

22. Andrew R. Hay, "The Heart of Wrath: Calvin, Barth, and Reformed Theories of Atonement," *NZSTh* 55 no. 3 (2013): 373. Emphasis in original.

Even for its time, the strong language of the doctrine was not without other softening strategies that perhaps anticipated the distasteful tone it exudes. Francis Turretin provides refinements to the legal apparatus of the Reformed model through his characteristic pedantic method. He begins by first drawing on legal language, distinguishing pecuniary and penal debt, the former as a payment that frees the debtor, and the latter as requiring not only a payment but also a personal punishment.[23] A judge may enact "relaxation" such that the guilty is freed of personal punishment by another's "vicarious satisfaction."[24] Turretin grounds this act of remission on the "forbearance" of the judge, who by his "rights of majesty" may dispense the manner of punishment "either in relation to time by the delay of punishment; or in relation to degree by mitigation; or in relation to persons by a substitution."[25] It is as this point that Christ takes on a substitutionary role and the language of "punishment" upon sinners makes its transition to the language of "satisfaction" toward God.

In submitting that two demands are required to satisfy God's justice, namely,

1. that sin be paid by one having the same nature as the one who sinned, and

2. that the payment be of infinite value to remove sin's infinite demerit,

Turretin sees the necessity of Christ's two natures to procure a satisfaction of infinite value.[26] He anticipates the objection of injustice that such a penal arrangement might warrant and argues that Christ perfectly meets the conditions for legitimacy in that he

1. is of a common nature with the guilty;

2. willingly consents to bear the burden;

3. has power and dominion over his own life so as to raise it up again (John 10:18);

4. has the power of bearing and removing the punishment due to us; and

---

23. Francis Turretin, *Institutes of Elenctic Theology, Vol. 2*, ed. James T. Dennison, Jr., trans. George Musgrave Giger (Phillipsburg, NJ: P & R Publishing, 1994), 419.

24. Ibid.

25. Ibid., 420. He stresses once again the quality of such a judge that may rightfully dispense this form of justice by "exempting sinners from the due punishment and transferring it to a substitute" is one who is supreme, accountable to no one, and who relaxes the extreme rigor of the law by "his infinite wisdom and unspeakable mercy."

26. Ibid., 421.

5. possesses "holiness and immaculate purity" so that the sacrifice might not be for himself but for us.[27]

Up to here, the Reformed do not find it problematic that Christ will endure excruciating suffering *at the Father's hand*. His altruistic disposition, willingness to undergo his torments, and future-oriented expectation of rising again is enough to dispel any qualms regarding the violence itself and its Ultimate Dispenser.

Going even further, Turretin also reinforces an earlier Protestant distinction that Christ's sufferings extends to his "active obedience" by which he fulfilled the law in his whole life, in contradistinction to the notion that only he suffered only on the cross.[28] Though the cross marks "the last and most piercing of all his sufferings, without which all the other antecedent sufferings would have been insufficient," he reasons that Christ's identity as priest, victim, and mediator necessitates that he be so *throughout* his life instead of commencing at some point there along.[29] These sufferings, though varying in their "degrees and acts," are effective in two ways: they free us from the punishments incurred by sin, and they merit the right to eternal life.[30]

---

27. Ibid. He writes: "On the basis of these conditions, it was not unjust for Christ, the righteous, to substitute himself for us, the unrighteous. For thus no injury is done to anyone. Not to Christ himself, both because he willingly took the punishment upon himself and because he had the power to determine concerning himself and the power to raise himself from the dead. Not to God, the Judge, because he willed and ordered it; nor to his natural justice, for this was satisfied by the punishment of the surety. Not to the empire of the universe, deprived of its best citizen by the death of an innocent person; for Christ, freed from death, lives for evermore. Nor by the life of the surviving sinner injuring the kingdom of God, because he is converted and made a new creature by Christ. Not to the divine law, for the most perfect fulfillment of all its demands made by Christ was foreseen and our twofold union with Christ (natural and forensic and mystical) by which, as he becomes one with us and we with him, so he may justly take our sins and evils upon himself and impart to us his righteousness and blessings. And thus there is neither an abrogation nor a derogation of the law, but an explication according to forbearance (*kat'epiekeian*), so that what was due to us in strict justice is transferred to Christ by the special grace of God," 420–21.

28. Already seen in Luther, Calvin, etc. Some Lutheran and Reformed theologians held to the minority view.

29. Turretin, 446–47. There is some seeming inconsistency on this point when compared to some of the Reformed confessions asserting that only the death of Christ effected satisfaction e.g. Canons of Dort, whereas the Heidelberg Catechism suggests satisfaction as procured through Christ's whole life. Turretin frames satisfaction as having begun with his birth, continuing through his whole, and *consummating* at his death (Q13); cf. Rohls ,98.

30. Ibid., 447. This two-fold benefit is distinguished but indissolubly connected. They arise from the law as having two aspects: precept (which prescribe duties) and sanctions (which regulate rewards and punishments). This correlates to a twofold

Supplementary discussions concerning the doctrine

Further refinements of the tradition down the centuries continue to anticipate the defensive stance that the doctrine would soon have to adopt. Charles Hodge stresses the necessity of satisfaction, arguing that the work of Christ accomplished satisfaction by virtue of its intrinsic worth and not on account of its gracious acceptance by God.[31] He also helps to clarify the terms vindicatory and vindictive, the former belonging to retributive justice, or "that form of moral excellence which demands the righteous distribution of rewards and punishments which renders it certain,"[32] and the latter connoting an attribute which pits God as a "malicious murderer" who is "thirsty for revenge"—an idea, he repudiates.[33]

Modern defenses of the penal model take a renewed interest in relating the atonement to the attributes of God. For P.T. Forsyth, the holiness of God is that which incites the wrath of God and must be satisfied.[34] He affirms the personal nature of law and denies its detachment from God and highlights that love is inextricably bound to God's holiness thus attempting to neutralize the conflict between God's love and holiness. Stott, on the other hand, resists this attempt at neutrality and, echoing Emil Brunner, instead posits a simultaneous expression of both holiness and love in a "dialectical" fashion.[35]

Stott's more controversial suggestion lays in his idea of "God in Christ" in his sixth chapter of *The Cross of Christ*, "The Self Substitution of God." The argues "the righteous, loving Father humbled himself to become in and through his only Son flesh, sin, and a curse for us."[36] Not surprisingly, this is in the context of Stott denying that the cross was "a punishment of a meek Christ by a harsh and punitive Father; nor a procurement of salvation by a loving Christ from a mean and reluctant Father; nor an action of the Father which bypassed Christ as mediator."[37] The statement is brief and he

---

relation to God which Christ fulfills: as one obliged to obey, and as one liable to punishment. He writes: "On this account, it cannot be said that the same debt is paid twice. A penal debt is one thing, arising from past transgression; an obediential debt is another thing, arising from the indispensable obligation of the creature ...," 449.

31. Charles Hodge, *Systematic Theology Vol. 2*, Reprint ed. (Peabody, MA: Hendrickson, 1981), 487–88.

32. Ibid., 489.

33. Ibid.

34. Peter Taylor Forsyth, *The Cruciality of the Cross* (Eugene, OR: Wipf and Stock, 1997), 5.

35. John R. W. Stott, *The Cross of Christ* (Inter-Varsity Press, 1986), 130–31.

36. Ibid., 159.

37. Ibid.

does not unpack it or perhaps immediately recognize the subtle modalism inherent in bringing the distinct personas of the Father and Son too closely together, which later finds its full-blown expression in Moltmann's theology of the cross. What it does indicate is the pressure felt by evangelicals to make urgent (in this case hasty) apologetic responses that reconcile the apparent disunity between the Father and Son when Christ's suffering is thought to proceed from the wrath of God.

In defense of the doctrine as historically understood, J. I. Packer, in his lecture, "What Did the Cross Achieve: The Logic of Penal Substitution," tackles the issue between the use of the term "substitution" against its more palatable counterpart, "representation." He calls this a "distinction with a difference,"[38] claiming that "substitution" is "a broad idea that applies whenever one person acts to supply another's need, or to discharge his obligation, so that the other no longer has to carry the load himself."[39] Proponents of the language of "representation," according to Packer, tend to discount the possibility of substitution in the penal realm, for they fear that substitution obscures Christ call to die and rise with him in sanctified living.[40] He asserts that repentance *presupposes* our identification with Christ, which is made available through substitution as the "basic category."[41] Packer's main agenda, however, is to simplify the doctrine by returning to a kerygmatic, or dramatic explanation of atonement in contrast to "defensive formula-models" frayed in centuries of debate.[42] His modernized restatement of penal substitution is as follows: "Jesus Christ, our Lord, moved by a love that was determined to do everything necessary to save us, endured and exhausted the destructive divine judgment for which we were otherwise inescapably destined, and so won us forgiveness, adoption and glory."[43]

---

38. He writes: "In this broad sense, nobody who wishes to say with Paul that there is a true sense in which 'Christ died for us' (*huper*, on our behalf, for our benefit), and 'Christ redeemed us from the curse of the law, having become a curse for us' (*huper* again) (Rom. 5:8; Gal. 3:13), and who accepts Christ's assurance that he came 'to give his life a ransom for many' (anti, which means precisely 'in place of', 'in exchange for' 16), should hesitate to say that Christ's death was substitutionary. Indeed, if he describes Christ's death as vicarious he is actually saying it."

39. J. I. Packer and Mark Dever, *In My Place Condemned He Stood: Celebrating the Glory of the Atonement* (Wheaton: Crossway, 2008), 69.

40. Ibid., 74. He cites P.T. Forsyth's terminology of "solidary reparation" as an example of this tendency in *The Work of Christ* (London: Hodder and Stoughton, 1910), 163; Cf. I. Howard Marshall, *Aspects of the Atonement: Cross and Resurrection in the Reconciling of God and Humanity* (London: Paternoster, 2007), 36.

41. Packer and Dever, *In My Place*, 77.

42. Ibid., 68.

43. J.I. Packer, "What Did the Cross Achieve? The Logic of Penal Substitution,"

In conclusion, the tradition which I have named Protestant orthodoxy is claimed by conservative evangelicalism on its cardinal point, namely, the vicarious death of Christ by which the cross satisfies God's wrathful judgment against sinful humanity. Refinements to the doctrine can be seen as apologetic attempts to smooth out the language from its more influential framers like Calvin, as well as to rationalize aspects that might portray God in a negative light. The Protestant tradition, then, seems tacitly aware of some of the problems that its theory now faces. While contemporary defenders have echoed many of the factors that mitigate against an essentially violent view of atonement (but not without some softening of language), many modern minds remain nonetheless unsatisfied. Critics of the Protestant model see an urgent need to dispense with such a violence-dependent view, and their efforts have led them to revisit other historic options, which I will now address.

Duality: the Cross as Enmity Between God and Cosmic Forces

One of the prevailing metaphors used to describe Christ's work on the cross is that of victory of the powers of darkness. Aulén champions this particular understanding of the atonement as the "classical" or "dramatic" view, in which "Christ—*Christus Victor*—fights against and triumphs over the evil powers of this world, the "tyrants" under which mankind is in bondage and suffering, and in Him God reconciles the world to Himself."[44] These forces are hostile to God but are at the same time "executants of God's will." Therefore, for Aulén, a dualism is in view but not one that is absolute in nature.[45] The key idea here is that Christ's passion and death are the means for his decisive victory over the enslaving power of the demonic realm. How this is achieved is not entirely obvious and depends on some necessary doctrinal precursors and creative "dramatic" narration. I will first survey some of the main component themes developed throughout the history of the theory that relate to our inquiry. Next, I will trace the main arguments of contemporary reappropriations of the theme that touch on the relationship of antagonism between God and the forces of evil.

TynBul 25 (1974): 25.

44. Aulén, *Christus Victor*, 4.
45. Ibid., 59.

The devil's ransom: historic doctrinal foundations

Patristic reflection over the atonement tended to lack the technical distinctions that marked medieval and modern theories of redemption, and seldom was Christ's death and resurrection bracketed as a distinct category from the incarnation. In fact, it is argued that an atonement theory that takes seriously the dualistic contrast between God vs. evil and heavenly vs. earthly cannot function without, nor be separated from, a robust theology of the incarnation.[46] The working out of christological dogma against heretics on the part of the early church fathers had salvation fully in view. Salvation could only be accomplished by God, for mere humans were incapable. Incarnation was central to Irenaeus' concept of recapitulation, in which the incarnation was an act of raising humanity to God while we await the renewal of all things at the Second Coming.[47] Likewise, Gregory Nazianzus, arguing against the Apollonarians, famously declared, "What has not been assumed has not been healed."[48] Although it cannot be denied that the patristic writers insisted God alone works salvation, it was in his work *as man* that made it possible for Christ to defeat death. As Irenaeus writes, "If man had not defeated the enemy of man, the enemy would have been fairly overcome."[49]

This leads us to consider the precise identity of the "enemy" who ancient Christians believed held the world in bondage. For the Eastern Fathers, sin and death were inseparably associated; sin leads to death and serves as the "wall of partition" that impedes communion and life with God. The devil is the lord of sin and death, in whose dominion humanity is cast and remains enslaved until victory is wrought in Christ, especially by his resurrection.[50] Within patristic discourse, sin, death, and the devil are often treated as though they were synonymous terms, although for Aulén, Irenaeus regards the devil as possessing an ontological reality with an existence independent to that of sin and death.[51] The language of "belonging" to the one to whom

---

46. Ibid., 20.
47. Irenaeus, *Against Heresies*, V.1.1.
48. Gregory Naziansus, *Epistle 101*.
49. Irenaeus, *Against Heresies*, III.18.6, quoted in Aulén, *Christus Victor*, 33.
50. Origen is famously credited for speculating that the ransom is paid to the devil. He writes: "But to whom did He give His soul as a ransom for many? Surely not to God. Could it, then, be to the Evil One? For he had us in his power, until the ransom for us should be given to him, even the life (or soul) of Jesus . . . ," *In Matthaeum, xvi. 8*, quoted in ibid., 49.
51. Ibid., 26. In fact, sin and death are also regarded by Irenaeus as "objective powers" and in some measure "personified," 20, 23.

one is in bondage is revealing along this line of thought. If a precise enemy were to be named, it would be the devil. Nicholas Lombardo notes that the early church practice of baptism reinforced this theology. It was believed that baptism exorcized demons from newly converted neophytes, and infant baptism in particular presumed that one was born into the world already belonging to the devil.[52] This led to the idea of the devil's "rights," a topic that drew varied responses and fanciful narratives from patristic writers, who speculated about how the devil came to have a claim on humanity and how the atonement reverses or forfeits this claim. [53] Understandably, there was reluctance on the part of theologians to grant the devil too many "rights." In many cases, the devil is often described as a "robber" and "usurper," who overreached his claim on humanity. Nevertheless, one can discern the idea that humanity's fall into sin resulted in the devil obtaining some sort of claim upon humanity that necessitated a rescue effort on Christ's part.

The "dramatic" nature of the narrative forced theologians to explain how humanity came to be released from the devil's enslavement. The predominant metaphor used is that of "ransom," drawn from military conquest, in which vanquished soldiers were taken captive and later sold back to their families or rich citizens for a price. Patristic authors drew on the language of "record of debts" (*chirographum*) from Col 2:14–15 to imagine the "accounts" that were owed to the devil. For Origen, sin was the "coin" with which he purchases humanity and enslaves them.[54] Drawing on passages such as Acts 20:28, 1 Pet 2:0, and Rev 12:11, the value of this "payment" that liberates sinners finds its focus in the blood of Jesus, once again tying back to the necessity of his incarnation. For those who understood the devil as improperly usurping "rights" that were not his, the value of the blood finds its basis in Jesus' innocence. As Augustine writes:

> The devil was holding on to our sins, and using them to keep us deservedly fixed in death. He who had none of his own discharged them, and was undeservedly led away by the other to death. Such was the value of that blood, that he who killed Christ even with a momentary death he did not owe would no longer have the right to hold anyone who had put on Christ in an eternal death he did owe.[55]

---

52. Nicholas E. Lombardo, *The Father's Will: Christ's Crucifixion and the Goodness of God* (New York: Oxford University Press, 2014), 187–88.

53. For a detailed discussion on this, see ibid., 189–98.

54. See quote from Origen, *Homilies on Exodus,* 6.9, in Ibid., 190–91. This is balanced by other authors like Eucherius of Lyons, who imagined the document as written by sinners, "with the hand of iniquity," ibid.

55. Augustine, *On the Trinity,* 13.21, quoted in ibid., 195.

Because the devil had absolutely no rights over the blameless Jesus, his crucifixion, orchestrated by the devil, disarmed his ability to hold anyone captive. That the devil works to undo his own work, like a house divided against itself, is a prominent theme among the Fathers.

Still operating within a "dramatic" framework, one idea that gave fuller expression to how this transaction led to the devil's demise imagined God as securing victory through deception. Although, the metaphor was employed by several patristic authors,[56] the analogy of the "fish-hook," as expounded by Gregory of Nyssa, is perhaps the most famous. It envisions the devil being baited into falling upon the easy prey of Jesus' humanity not realizing that immortal deity was hidden within his flesh. He writes:

> Since the hostile power was not going to enter into relations with a God present unveiled, or endure his appearance in heavenly glory, therefore God, in order to render Himself accessible to him who demanded of Him a ransom for us, concealed Himself under the veil of our nature, in order that, as happens with greedy fishes, together with the bait of the flesh the hook of the Godhead might also be swallowed, and so, through Life passing over into death, and the Light arising in the darkness, that which is opposed to Life and Light might be brought to nought. For darkness cannot endure when the Light shines, nor can death remain in being where Light is active.[57]

While the Latin church also had its corresponding metaphors, such as Augustine's "mousetrap" analogy, the popularity of the fish-hook image lay in its source in allegorical interpretations of Scripture, namely, Job's allusion to Leviathan (Job 41:1–2) and the story of Jonah. Jonah, it can be said, serves as a "hermeneutical key" to patristic redemption narratives given Matthew's

---

56. For example, Rufinus of Aquileia, who makes a closer connection between the analogy and purpose of the incarnation, ". . . that the divine virtue of the Son of God might be like a kind of hook hidden in the form of human flesh . . . to lure on the prince of this world to a contest; that the Son might offer him his human flesh as a bait and that the divinity that lay underneath might catch him and hold him fast with its hook . . . Then, just as a fish when it seizes a baited hook not only fails to drag off the bait but is itself dragged out of the water to serve as food for others; so he that had the power of death seized the body of Jesus in death, unaware of the hook of divinity that lay hidden inside. Having swallowed it, he was immediately caught. The gates of hell were broken, and he was, as it were, drawn up from the pit, to become food for others, *Exposition of Apostle's Creed*, 14.

57. Gregory of Nyssa, *Great Catechism*, chapter 24, quoted in Aulén, *Christus Victor*, 52.

relating him with Jesus' entombment as well as the natural connection it makes with the Christian ritual of baptism.[58]

To sum up, we find in patristic formulations of redemption a kind of narrative theology that describes atonement in terms of humanity's fall under bondage to the devil and Christ's victory through an ingenious ransom payment that destroys the devil's work and liberates humanity. The cross, once again, is inextricably linked to the incarnation and resurrection, as might be expected within a dramatic framework that prefers integration over compartmentalization. The end goal of these expositions surrounding the cross seems to have been motivated by a desire to highlight God's wisdom and justice.[59] Rather than using violence, God wisely employs the cross to enter into humanity's predicament to demonstrate that humanity could be saved without relying on brute force or divine *fiat*.[60] For Lombardo, the crux of the victory lies in God's "*deliberate provocation of evil*" such that he "absorbs" violence into himself and vanquishes it with his death.[61] This is not to say, however, that Jesus' passion and death are to be understood as passive. While it is true that victory is secured through a Lamb that was slaughtered (Rev 5:6), it is vital to have in view Jesus' active participation in a *battle*, even if it is won primarily by guile rather than force. If the analogy of the hook trapping the "greedy fish" and becoming food for others is to have any explanatory force, we should be willing to admit that violence is inflicted *in some sense*, not upon human souls, but upon the forces of evil as objective realities.

I will now proceed to trace the main lines of argument from contemporary theologians who have appropriated and adapted the *Christus Victor* theme in attempts to propose atonement models that respond to various criticisms of penal violence.

Recapitulation and reconstitution: Hans Boersma

Among ecumenically-minded theologians working to critique—and provide a response to—Protestant theology's complicity with abuse and brutality, Hans Boersma is perhaps most sympathetic to traditional Protestant

---

58. Lombardo, *The Father's Will*, 212–21. Notably, the thrice-fold immersion into water was linked to the three days Jesus spent in the tomb.

59. Aulén insists that the emphasis on justice should not in any way be construed to mean that the view of Irenaeus, in particular, is "juridical" like that of the Latin theory, *Christus Victor*, 27–28.

60. Lombardo, *The Father's Will*, 191.

61. Ibid., 229.

conceptions of atonement theology. Part of his theological project, therefore, involves defending the use of violence as an expression of divine "hospitality"—the prevailing metaphor he chooses to describe God's love expressed historically.[62] By violence, he means, "any use of coercion that causes injury, whether that coercion is positive or negative," and, for the sake of "consistency," he includes nonphysical and systemic problems, like racism and poverty, as well acts that are morally acceptable, like restraining someone from attempting suicide.[63] His underlying thesis is that hospitality necessarily involves violence yet retains its hospitable character.[64] Drawing from Derrida's interaction with the work of Levinas, Boersma concludes that "pure" hospitality, regarded as "unconditional openness," is eschatological in nature and impossible in this world.[65] Therefore, "All activities that we undertake in our present historical circumstances are indeed necessarily accompanied by inhospitality, by a kind of violence."[66]

One major instance of unnecessary violence he sees in theology is the principle of exclusion that undergirds its doctrine of election in the Reformed tradition, to which Boersma admittedly belongs but also critiques on several fronts. The strong version of the doctrine, "double predestination," is particularly problematic because it "draws divine violence from history into the heart of God and thereby undermines his unconditional hospitality."[67] Affirming insights from N.T. Wright, he repackages this doctrine in an historical mode as a form of "preferential hospitality" in which God's elects Israel for the purpose of covenant relationship. This has a number of benefits, including safeguarding monotheism, condemning the immorality of Israel's surrounding nations, and demonstrating God's preferential option for the poor. Through these ends, election becomes an *instrumental*, divine act of hospitality. This hospitality is extended when one considers Israel's role as "missionary" to the nations through which blessing is offered to the whole world. Rather than attempting to remove biblical violence, his aim is to "lessen its tension."[68]

Boersma's constructive theological reformulation of the doctrine of the atonement relies heavily on the concepts of recapitulation and reconstitution

---

62. Hans Boersma, *Violence, Hospitality, and the Cross: Reappropriating the Atonement Tradition* (Grand Rapids: Baker, 2006).

63. Ibid., 17, 45, 47.

64. Ibid.

65. Ibid., 30.

66. Ibid., 35.

67. Ibid., 56.

68. Ibid., 94.

in the writings of Irenaeus and N.T. Wright, respectively. Using these as the "paradigmatic framework" on which to locate his theory, he believes the three traditional atonement models can be incorporated into what he calls a "modified Reformed view."[69] He rather ingeniously categorizes the traditional theories under the Reformed doctrine of the three-fold office of Christ: prophetic (Abelardian), priestly (Anslemian), and kingly (*Christus Victor*).[70] Scripturally, the term *recapitulation* finds its source in Eph 1:10, in which everything is brought together under Christ. As the second Adam, Christ is representative of humanity and nullifies Adam's disobedience through his obedience. Thus, the incarnation and life of Christ is of utmost importance while not denying the role of the cross, upon which our record of debt is fastened for the remission of sins.[71] Irenaeus' view of Christ's recapitulation, according to Boersma, is a "retracing and reversing" of Adam's disobedience. The image of *Christus Victor*, within which recapitulation is understood, is manifested through Christ's obedience. As Boersma states: "Christ gains the victory not by employing counterviolence but by faithful obedience in the face of satanic temptation."[72]

Because of the broad scope of Irenaeus' soteriology, Boersma finds the notion of recapitulation an apt means of harmonizing the three atonement models. Christ's work involves battling the devil (*Christus Victor*), modeling obedience (moral influence), and suffering the curse of the law (penal representation). It is important to note his deliberate deviation from the traditional nomenclature "penal *substitution*" here. Christ becomes the new humanity, not only representing Adam's flesh, but that of all humanity. This explains the necessity in Irenaeus for Christ to have experienced every stage of human existence (infancy, youth, old age, etc.). For Christ to function as a "corporate personality" in this way provides the link to his role as reconstituted Israel. This idea, for which Boersma credits N.T. Wright, places redemption within the course of human history and avoids the "juridicizing, individualizing, and de-historicizing" tendencies of traditional Protestant atonement theology.[73] The curse of the law described in Gal 3:6–14 is to be understood within the covenant context of Deuteronomy 27–30 that anticipates restoration and redemption. Boersma quotes Wright:

69. Hans Boersma, "Violence, the Cross, and Divine Intentionality: A Modified Reformed View," in *Atonement and Violence: A Theological Conversation*, ed. John Sanders (Nashville: Abingdon, 2006), 54.

70. Boersma, *Violence, Hospitality, and the Cross*, 200.

71. Boersma, "Violence, the Cross, and Divine Intentionality: A Modified Reformed View," 55.

72. Boersma, *Violence, Hospitality, and the Cross*, 124.

73. Ibid., 173.

> Christ, as the representative Messiah, has achieved a specific task, that of taking on himself the curse which hung over Israel and which on the one hand prevented her from enjoying full membership in Abraham's family and thereby on the other hand prevented the blessing of Abraham from flowing out to the Gentiles. The Messiah has come where Israel is, under the Torah's curse . . . , in order to be not only Israel's representative but Israel's *redeeming* representative.[74]

In the cross, then, Christ suffers Israel's exilic punishment and in rising from the dead the people of God are reconstituted. This idea, in turn, funds Boersma's practical application of the doctrine to champion restorative justice and liberation in the public sphere.

In the end, Boersma sees in Irenaean recapitulation the finest expression of the *Christus Victor* theme for its ability to incorporate the Anselmic and Abelardian emphases while avoiding the moral ambiguity of the "fish hook" motif on the one hand, and the potential antinomianism that might result from neglecting Jesus' incarnation and life of obedience on the other. Because of its source in military metaphors, Boersma recognizes the difficulty in escaping the image of divine violence. While he recognizes that "the *Christus Victor* theme cannot function without at least some degree of metaphysical or cosmic dualism as part of the Christian heritage,"[75] Boersma does not wish to emphasize this point. However, he finds in Irenaeus a recognizable distancing from the language of violence to that of "persuasion" that reaches out to embrace elements in moral influence theory.

Evaluation

Boersma's main contribution is to defend the ubiquity and necessity of violence and its instrumental use within God's working of redemption in history. He rightly insists that any atonement theology that involves the cross must deal with the issue of violence.[76] His strategy to "remove blood from God's hands," as it were, requires bringing soteriology out of the decretive and eternal and into the historic and temporal: because violence can be used instrumentally in situational contexts, atonement dogmatics need not belabor the difficulties inherent in violence. Furthermore, in an effort

---

74. N. T. Wright, *The Climax of the Covenant: Christ and the Law in Pauline Theology* (Minneapolis: Fortress, 1993), 151, quoted in Boersma, *Violence, Hospitality, and the Cross*, 176.

75. Boersma, *Violence, Hospitality, and the Cross*, 199.

76. Ibid., 40.

to minimize exclusivistic theologizing, one can only praise Boersma's effort to engage in critical dialogue with a wide range of theological perspectives with which he aims to arrive at a conclusion that is both sensitive to tradition as well as ecumenical.

Does Boersma's proposal succeed in lessening the tension of divine violence? Assuming that the atonement is foreknown by God, attempting to steer clear of its eternal and decretive aspects is extremely difficult. Cornelius P. Venema questions: "How does Boersma propose to account for history without an appeal to God's eternal purposes or decrees, unless he believes history occurs *ex nihilo*?"[77] The criterion by which Boersma determines relative degrees of violence is far from clear or obvious. This becomes more pronounced in light of the fact that he criticizes J. Denny Weaver for defining non-physical acts of resistance (e.g. boycotts, protests) as nonviolent, asking "by what standard" are acts judged as violent or nonviolent?[78] From this, it is odd that he seems justified in favoring historical and corporate decrees over eternal ones as though they arose from different places or had different ends whereas basic Reformed convictions understand the unity of God's character and his actions.[79] In fact, some interpretations of Reformed covenant theology, like that of Meredith Kline,[80] for example, already offer robust and convincing arguments for understanding the corporate, national, and redemptive character of Israel's election *vis à vis* the land promises and threats of exile without adopting the presuppositions of N. T. Wright and the New Perspective," whose scholarship is far from uncontested.[81]

---

77. Cornelis P. Venema, "Violence, Hospitality, and the Cross: Reappropriating the Atonement Tradition," *MAJT* 16 (2005): 184.

78. Boersma, *Violence, Hospitality, and the Cross*, 46–47.

79. As the seventeenth century Dutch Reformed divine, Wilhelmus à Brakel puts it: "The decree of God, being an intrinsic act of His will, is not incidental to God, but is the decreeing God Himself." Wilhelmus à Brakel, *The Christian's Reasonable Service*, ed. Joel R. Beeke, trans. Bartel Elshout, vol. 1 (Rotterdam: D. Bolle, 1999), 196.

80. For example, he writes: "The Sinaitic Covenant in itself, as a covenant ratified by Israel's oath, made law obedience by the Israelites themselves the way of life-inheritance, and yet in the Mosaic revelation as a whole, law was accompanied by promise sealed by divine oath and offering an alternative way of inheritance. Thus the Deuteronomic law covenant mediated through Moses, though not ratified by divine oath in the covenant-making ceremony itself, contained a divine oath sealing the promise of ultimate and eternal restoration of a remnant by the grace of God," in Meredith G. Kline, *By Oath Consigned: A Reinterpretation of the Covenant Signs of Circumcision and Baptism*, First Edition edition (Grand Rapids: Eerdmans, 1968), 32–33. See also Meredith G. Kline, *Kingdom Prologue: Genesis Foundations for a Covenantal Worldview* (Eugene, OR: Wipf & Stock, 2006).

81. For example, see D. A. Carson, Peter T. O'Brien, and Mark A. Seifrid, eds., *Justification and Variegated Nomism: The Paradoxes of Paul* (Grand Rapids: Baker, 2004);

Similarly, the Reformed idea of the active obedience of Christ closely mirrors Irenaeus' notion of recapitulation. Again from à Brakel:

> The active obedience of Christ in subjecting Himself under, and fulfilling, the law is not only a necessary requisite for Him who would be Mediator (all of which is true for Christ), but this active righteousness of Christ is a part of His satisfaction for His own. As He delivered them from all guilt and punishment by His passion, by His active obedience, fulfilling the law on their behalf, He has also merited a right unto eternal life for them. These two aspects coalesce in Christ and neither may nor can be separated from each other. Christ has merited salvation atoningly and has made atonement meritoriously. Likewise the elect, in being delivered from guilt and punishment, receive a right to eternal life, and in receiving that right are delivered from guilt and punishment.[82]

The most significant issue Boersma raises is how violence fares within the heart of God prior to any redemptive work in time. He points to the exclusivistic character of predestination as marking a lamentable moment of violence and attempts his doctrinal modification from that starting point. However, the Reformed doctrine of the covenant of redemption, as we will explore in chapter 6, offers an earlier and more relevant starting point that imagines divine violence as exerted outwardly toward sin itself rather than created beings. Thus we have a means for clearing God of creaturely violence from the very outset of redemption. In light of the rich and extended treatment of this and other related themes already present in Reformed theology, one is forced to wonder whether a modification is really necessary at all.

Christus Victor through penal substitution: Jeremy R. Treat

Where Boersma is critical of many aspects of the Reformed tradition, Jeremy Treat is a staunch defender. In his book, *The Crucified King: Atonement and Kingdom in Biblical and Systematic Theology*,[83] Treat aims to synthesize the themes of kingdom and atonement by integrating *Christus Victor* with penal substitution. His main argument is that "Jesus bears the penalty for sin by taking the place of sinners, thereby defeating Satan and establishing

---

Aaron O'Kelley, *Did the Reformers Misread Paul?: A Historical-Theological Critique of the New Perspective* (Eugene, OR: Wipf & Stock, 2014).

82. à Brakel, *The Christian's Reasonable Service*, 1:610.

83. Jeremy R. Treat, *The Crucified King: Atonement and Kingdom in Biblical and Systematic Theology* (Grand Rapids: Zondervan, 2014).

God's kingdom on earth."[84] By tracing themes such as sacrifice, covenant, exodus, and temple throughout the Old and New Testaments, and tying them together under the rubric of kingdom, Treat attempts a unified and coherent account of atonement that includes forgiveness, ransom, and victory, all of which find their fulfillment in the cross.

Before attempting to reconcile *Christus Victor* and penal substitution as atonement theologies, the author undertakes to tackle the question of how Christ might be regarded as a majestic king while suffering on the cross. Unlike traditional Lutheran and Reformed theology that view Christ's exaltation as subsequent to his humiliation on the cross, Treat makes the bold proposal that "the proper view is exaltation *in* humiliation within a broader progression of exaltation *through* humiliation."[85] He makes his case on two main fronts: first, by observing the overlap that exists between Christ's humble and exalted states before and after the cross; that is, "Christ is exalted before the resurrection and humble after the crucifixion;" and second, by invoking the paradoxical character of God's wisdom compared with that of the world, which only faith can fathom.[86]

As far as his engagement with systematic theology, Treat critiques Aulén's dichotomizing of victory and satisfaction and embarks upon the task of arguing for *Christus Victor through penal substitution*. Treat's view of sin is thoroughly conventional in its Godward orientation. He argues that "humans are in bondage to Satan *because* they have rejected God as king; they are in the kingdom of Satan *because* they have been banished from the kingdom of God. Enmity with God—entailing God's wrath on humans and human guilt before God—is the root problem."[87] Satan's work is to tempt, deceive, accuse, and bring death; and he does so primarily through words.[88] God's victory against Satan, his influences, and effects, therefore, is accomplished by dealing with sin, and that through penal substitution. By foregrounding sin as the true archenemy, and a battle that is primarily legal, penal substitution becomes the "silver bullet" that secures God's victory.

Treat quarries various New Testament texts in order to scripturally ground the central metaphor of Christ's defeat of Satan. Among them include depriving him of the power to strike fear (Heb 2:15), disarming him

84. Ibid., 39.
85. Ibid., 156.
86. Ibid., 161. Entailed is the idea of Christ's "veiled" glory. "The servant form of Christ both hides and reveals his kingship. It veils his majesty because people look at a man dying a criminal's death and would never assume him to be a king. Yet his servant form also reveals his majesty, for his sovereignty can be expressed in servitude."
87. Ibid., 199.
88. Ibid., 200–202.

through the "legal-demand-satisfying death on the cross" (Col 2:13–15), and undoing his accusatory power (Rev 1:5–6, 12:11).[89] Echoing the Reformed emphasis on the "active obedience of Christ," Treat sees the fulfillment of the law and the penalty of breaking it as "paid off." Obedience serves as the crucial link between both the life and death of Christ, and between *Christus Victor* and penal substitution,[90] for it is in his life of faithful obedience as the "suffering Word" that a proper counter-attack to Satan's deceiving and destructive "word" is enacted.[91] This work of obedience is wrought within Christ's humanity as the "Second Adam," thereby rendering his human nature essential to the work of salvation and challenging the notion that his victory is *purely* a divine one.[92] Additionally, Treat claims that Satan is defeated "through Christ *and* Christians"—not in the sense that humans contribute to his atoning work, but that the victory is "appropriated and consummated" by believers.[93] Interestingly, despite the strong affirmation of the role of Christ's human nature in the atonement and the appropriating of victory on the part of the saints, Treat avoids allowing Jesus' incarnation, life, and resurrection to pull the efficacy of the atonement away from the centrality of the crucifixion.[94] He writes:

> We need an expansive view that encompasses all of Christ's work, but in a way that still upholds the particular significance of each aspect through integration, order, and rank. The cross must be upheld as central within the broader framework of Christ's work and related to each of these various aspects.[95]

This "broader framework" is God's kingdom and the glory that marks its goal. The vicarious sacrifice of penal substitution is the means by which Christ is victorious, and because of its explanatory power to explain how Satan is conquered and its "directness" in addressing the problem between God and humans, Treat grants it theological priority.[96]

---

89. Ibid., 205–207.
90. Ibid., 210.
91. Ibid., 204.
92. Ibid., 213.
93. Ibid., 214. He cites Rom 16:20, 1 John 2:13–14, Eph 6:10–20, and Rev 12:11, which speak of believers conquering Satan. Elsewhere, he writes: "Though the final defeat is yet to come, Christians continue to conquer Satan, exposing his deception by witnessing to Christ's obedient life and the true efficacy of his death," 127.
94. His position is thus markedly opposed to contemporary proponents of "solidarity," as will be seen in the next section.
95. Treat, *The Crucified King*, 218.
96. Ibid., 222–23. In the end, Treat's desire is for integration, not subordination, of

Evaluation

Jeremy Treat's attempt to build an account of the kingdom of God that places the cross at the center and reconciles two atonement theories thought to have little in common with each other is a commendable one. That kingdom is a prominent motif in Scripture cannot be denied, so it serves well as a unifying theme that runs through many genres and biblical subplots and is capable of drawing together many seemingly unrelated motifs into its domain. His unflinching resolve to maintain a high view of sin and the justice of God squares very well with Scripture's preoccupation with those elements as fundamental to salvation, and his emphasis on the centrality of the cross places his position in line with Christian tradition.

A view that comes to the defense of a *Christus Victor* framework for understanding atonement might be rightly called "dualistic," but Treat's version is a *soft* dualism at that. From the perspective of conflict, one can observe in this particular construal that God's chief opponent is not Satan *per se*, nor sin as an isolated entity. The true nemesis, it would seem, is *guilt*. Treat himself admits: "The most common way that Scripture speaks of sinning against God is by breaking his law . . . Scripture not only describes sin as being against God (breaking *God's* law) but does so primarily with judicial language (breaking God's *law*)."[97] The author is unwilling, and perhaps rightly so, for humans to be mere victims of Satan's allurements to sin; he insists that they be fully complicit in their willful disobedience. But if this is the case, then accusation does not strictly come from Satan, but from divine law (Rom 3:20, 7:7, 1 John 3:4). Treat rightly states that "while both problems of enmity and bondage are clearly found in Scripture, the right order is imperative: bondage to Satan *is a result of* enmity with God."[98] Despite being aware of this, the implications in fact are damaging to his view. If bondage to Satan is the result of expulsion from God, what is the driving force behind the accusation if not the law (1 Cor 15:56)? Now, if we corroborate this with Paul's declaration that the law is holy, just, and good (Rom 7:12), then our only conclusion, using Treat's framework of victory, would be that God's enemy is God's own law. This simply cannot be, especially not within Treat's Reformed worldview.

---

doctrines. He believes they round each other out: "So, to the *Christus Victor* proponents I would say that if you lose penal substitution, you lose the kingdom . . . And to the penal substitution advocates, I would say that the justice of God has broader application than the justification of individuals," 226.

97. Ibid., 199.
98. Ibid. Emphasis in original.

The language of victory in this case is, ironically, *self-defeating*. Treat needs to present Christ as conquering, shaming, and exalting himself over something that does not so easily implicate God.[99] Satan's force of influence and agency must be formidable and genuinely antithetical to the divine will for Christ's victory to have any weight or meaning. Short of this, the victory metaphor, which is essential to the theme of kingdom, simply ends up being a strained attempt to dress up and dramatize penal substitution.[100] Herein lies the problem with establishing atonement merely on the abstract notion of justice (which the Reformed tradition has tended to do) and why a revenge framework better elucidates the *personal nature* of conflict and more clearly identifies the combatants involved.

If we set up the antagonism between God and whatever his nemesis might be (sin, Satan, death, etc.) as a victory that is circumstantial in nature, one runs into the problem that many struggle to answer: How can we account for the horrifying death that Jesus suffered? In order to grant adequate weight to the gruesome reality of the cross, the battle must a worthy one; we must be able to invoke some ground of necessity for what he endured.

Narrative Christus Victor and nonviolent atonement: J. Denny Weaver

In the thought of Anabaptist theologian, J. Denny Weaver, we find much less sympathy for atonement as satisfaction, which he believes is the main breeding ground for violence in general. For Weaver, what is at stake is whether violence is divinely willed and whether God's *modus operandi* depends upon violence.[101] He notes that in the transition between the devil's ransom theory and Anselmic satisfaction, the prevailing question addressed the objects of Jesus death. Where *Christus Victor* visualized the devil as the object to whom ransom was paid, Anselm "deleted the devil from the salva-

---

99. Granted, Treat's Reformed commitment holds to God's comprehensive sovereignty over creation. Yet, God's authorship of evil is thoroughly negated by all Christian standards.

100. As per Darrin Belousek, who notes that in Treat's thesis, "penal substitution and *Christus Victor* do not forge an equal partnership—penal substitution does all the heavy lifting." He concludes: "In effect, [Treat] does not consider how the kingdom might reorient our view of the cross because, I think, he does not expect Jesus' enactment of the kingdom to reveal anything about how God achieves victory," Darrin W. Snyder Belousek, "The Crucified King: Atonement and Kingdom in Biblical and Systematic Theology," *The Conrad Grebel Review* 33, no. 1 (2015): 97.

101. J. Denny Weaver, "Narrative *Christus Victor*: The Answer to Anselmian Atonement Violence," in *Atonement and Violence: A Theological Conversation*, ed. John Sanders (Nashville: Abingdon, 2006), 1.

tion equation."[102] From this, two questions marked the trajectory of atonement logic, namely, *who or what needs the death of Jesus?* Additionally, the more provocative correlate is: *Who arranges or is ultimately responsible for Jesus death?*

Weaver discusses three implications that emerge from this history. First, by deleting the devil, Anselm's advocates have no recourse but to admit God's responsibility in the death of Jesus. He is the only actor, who orchestrates the crucifixion needed to satisfy God's honor or humanity's penal debt.[103] Second, all versions of satisfaction atonement assume a "God-induced and God-directed" violent retribution.[104] Third, theories characterized by satisfaction "structures the relationship between humankind and God in terms of a historical, abstract legal formula."[105] Such a view absolutizes Jesus' death at the expense of his life, teaching, and resurrection and does little to address ethics and the injustices of the social order. Weaver finds that all contemporary attempts to defend satisfaction ultimately either neglect ethics or mask the imagery of abuse inherent in the system. He correlates such models with the Constantinian church, and his own nonviolent view with the pacifist, early church.[106]

The heart of Weaver's solution to the atonement problem is to reintroduce the devil into the equation. In what he terms "narrative *Christus Victor*," the story of Christ's victory over the devil is told in terms of narratives from the Gospels and Revelation in a way that distinguishes itself from the classical theory while being explicitly nonviolent. The framework relies on Rev 12, in which the battle between the baby "snatched up to heaven" and the "dragon" (Satan) represents a "confrontation in history between the Roman Empire and Jesus and his church."[107] This is hammered out more concretely in applying the same interpretation to the seven seals of Rev 6 and 7, which, in his reading, correspond to historical events during the imperial reigns of Tiberius (14–37 CE) and Domitian (81–96 CE). Scenes of mayhem and devastation become juxtaposed with the glorified Lamb in the midst of the throne (v. 10), thereby revealing the triumph of God through the death and, especially, the resurrection of Jesus. "With eyes on the resurrected Jesus as the living and the bodied representative of God, those who have come through the 'great ordeal' of Rome, including the mayhem

102. Ibid., 4.
103. Ibid., 5.
104. Ibid., 9.
105. Ibid.
106. Ibid., 23.
107. Ibid., 17.

and destruction of Jerusalem, can celebrate life in the reign of God, where salvation is found."[108]

Weaver takes pains to argue for the nonviolent nature of this cosmic victory. Even the military motifs of Rev 12 and 19 are distilled of their violent content. For example, he notes that the robe of the "Rider on the white horse" is dipped in blood *before*, not after, any supposed battle (19:13). That the name of the Rider is the "Word of God" and the sword proceeding from his mouth, when viewed in conjunction with Eph 6:17 and Heb 4:12, is likewise identified as the "Word of God," suggests that no actual battle is in view. Rather, by sheer virtue of his resurrection, Jesus procures victory over evil without violence.[109]

With the narratives from John's Apocalypse representing God's victory and final rule from the perspective of heaven, Weaver believes this same narrative is the essence of the Gospels' telling of Jesus' confrontation with evil from an earthly vantage point.[110] Concurring with Walter Wink, he reads Jesus' ethical instructions in the Sermon on the Mount as "nonviolent resistance strategies" of activism.[111] In a similar vein, through moves such as interacting with the Samaritan woman (John 4:4–26) and healing on the Sabbath (Luke 6:6–11), Jesus steps outside conventional expectations, thereby defying the accepted order and making visible the reign of God by defeating sexism, racism, physical ailments, and various oppressive ills.[112]

Jesus' activism that confronted social and physical evil is what leads to his death: "When Jesus made present the reign of God, he was killed by an array of forces that represent the rule of evil."[113] Because this model has no basis in retribution, Jesus' death "pays God nothing and is not Godward directed."[114] Therefore, it does not satisfy a legal requirement nor serve as a substitutionary sacrifice. For Weaver, the death of Jesus "is the ultimate contrast of methodology between the reign of God and the reign of evil."[115] It was necessary only in the sense that Jesus' faithfulness to his mission required him to be steadfast even unto death. Because his life and minis-

---

108. Ibid., 19.

109. Ibid., 20.

110. Ibid.

111. Ibid., citing Walter Wink, *Engaging the Powers: Discernment and Resistance in a World of Domination* (Minneapolis: Fortress, 1992), 175–84.

112. Weaver, "Narrative *Christus Victor*," 20–22.

113. Ibid., 22. For Weaver, this "array" ultimately implicates Rome but also includes the "religious authorities in Jerusalem" (note, Weaver does not call them "Jewish" authorities), Judas, Peter, other disciples who fled, and the mob.

114. Ibid., 25.

115. Ibid.

try was a "visible witness against oppression," his death reveals humanity's complicity in systems of oppression and beckons repentance. God invites sinners by grace, but more importantly, by ceasing their collaboration with evil forces of oppression, and sharing in the struggle against oppression, "former oppressors join together in witnessing to the reign of God."[116]

Evaluation

Weaver's thesis has two objectives:

1. remove the divine will from any complicity in the violent death of Christ; and

2. re-envision salvation nonviolently in terms of participation in the reign of Christ inaugurated by his resurrection.

In attempting to achieve these ends, he constructs a theory that uses the Gospel accounts of Jesus' earthly life and the symbolic imagery in Revelation to construe the atonement as a narrative retelling of Christ's victory over oppressive powers. Although his emphases concerning the role of these regimes (which finds its focus in imperial systems whether Roman or Constantinian) and the cause of liberation has much in common with the "solidarity" view explored below, I have placed him in the "dualist" camp because his overall thrust rests on God's reign *in opposition to* that of oppressive powers; the ongoing reign of God is marked by this oppositional "witness." Ironically, for all the effort that is made "to restore the devil to the equation," the devil, as such, does not fare much in his constructive theological proposal. What seems to be the case is that the devil embodies those systemic ills that befall God's people in the analogous way Jesus "embodies" the reign of God through his person, life and ministry.[117] Thus, Weaver is able to use the language of "struggle," "resistance," and "confrontation" in nonviolent ways, that is, in ways that do not imply bodily harm or damage. In fact, Weaver's emphasis on God's nonviolent dealings with the cosmos precludes even the possibility that God confronts satanic powers with violence. Insofar as the devil is still one of God's creatures, Weaver seems unwilling to allow violence to factor into his demise. This view, if correct, has profound implications for the feasibility of a *Christus Victor* model in general.

---

116. Ibid., 23.
117. Ibid., 22.

While understanding Christ's "victory" as a defeat of the devil embodied in abstract concepts like oppression, racism, and militarism is convincingly nonviolent, Weaver is unfortunately at a loss to put any positive spin on Jesus' horrific death in history. He writes:

> The outcome of Jesus' arrest and trial was that brute force killed him in what appeared to be a triumph for the powers of the evil. Yet that triumph was limited and momentary . . . In the living Jesus the reign of God displayed its power over the ultimate enemy—death—and thus over the worst that evil could do, namely, deny Jesus his existence.[118]

The crucifixion, then, is the devil's victory; resurrection is God's victory. It seems that the reign of God is inaugurated by virtue of Jesus withstanding evil's most powerful weapon (death), but this victory is unrelated to the cross. For narrative *Christus Victor* to function it is imperative that the forces of evil plot Jesus' death. As Weaver writes, "the closest thing to a need for Jesus' death is that the powers of evil need his death in order to remove his challenge to their power." Assuming that this "power" is that which Jesus resisted through his ministry of activism, and which led to his execution, then the mode by which Jesus died has *everything* to do with the triumph of his resurrection. If Jesus died by accident, like slipping and falling off a cliff, rising from death would fail to sustain Weaver's emphasis on resurrection as a victory over evil. Weaver understands this well in that while atonement rests *primarily* on resurrection, he rightly never discards the crucifixion: "Both the Gospels and Revelation locate the victory of the reign of God on earth and in history—narrative *Christus Victor*—and make quite clear that the triumph occurred not through the sword and military might, but nonviolently through *death and resurrection*."[119]

This reveals that Weaver is inherently "traditional" on the inextricability of Jesus' violent death for understanding the reign of God. The victory of the resurrection requires the violence of the cross. Either we accept that the violence of the cross is a necessary component to Christ's reign over oppressive and unjust evil, or we admit that Jesus' victory is an accident, an arbitrary label applied to the fact that he happens to now live again. Weaver's attempt to dislodge violence from any sort of divine orchestration, therefore, only serves to separate the resurrection from the crucifixion, and by extension, Jesus' entire life and ministry—the very elements that are central to his theory.

---

118. J. Denny Weaver, *The Nonviolent Atonement*, 2nd ed. (Grand Rapids: Eerdmans, 2011), 42.

119. Weaver, "Narrative *Christus Victor*," 21. Emphasis added.

While Weaver fails to bring logical coherence to his theory, I applaud his move to wrap atonement theology in a narrative framework, especially one where Scripture forms the content and structure. This allows several elements of doctrine as well as biblical and ecclesiastical history to be stitched together to form some sort of "plot" and avoids the rational compartmentalizing and abstraction that is common to dogmatics. In heavily relying on John's Apocalypse, however, the stylized, symbolic images juxtaposed with one another are not at all obvious as elements of a single narrative, not to mention being subject to a host of interpretative problems due to the complex hermeneutics and wide range of alternative views of the book as a whole. The classic *Christus Victor* model, though theologically questionable at points, is at least richer in narrative form and therefore offers more explanatory potential as a narrative theology.

A warfare worldview: Gregory A. Boyd

Gregory Boyd's theology constitutes what I regard as a "strong dualism" and thus vitally contributes to any idea that presents Christ's salvific work as a victory over the forces of evil. In what he calls a "warfare worldview," Boyd champions a "perspective on reality which centers on the conviction that the good and evil, fortunate or unfortunate, aspects of life are to be interpreted largely as the result of good and evil, friendly or hostile, spirits warring against each other and against us."[120] Through a systematic analysis of Old and New Testament texts, in corroboration with Ancient Near Eastern creation accounts (especially *Enuma Elish*), he argues that the biblical world presupposes the existence of evil spirits that operate freely and independently of any overarching divine motive or control. His goal is ultimately to present a theodicy that completely removes divine involvement in sin and calamity in opposition to a "providential blueprint worldview," which follows Augustinian tradition. In fairness, Boyd wishes to avoid the conclusion that Satan, angels, and humans are "metaphysically ultimate alongside God," admitting that the construal of evil forces as coeternal and coequal competitors with God is a "dualistic heresy."[121] For Boyd, the created order is inherently chaotic and in need of combative restoration.[122] While he concedes

---

120. Gregory A. Boyd, *God at War: The Bible & Spiritual Conflict* (Downers Grove: IVP, 1997), 11.

121. Ibid., 56.

122. This leads Boyd to take some issue with the "normative status" that Gen 1 has over other creation accounts that include conflict motifs. He argues that the supposed threat that mythological accounts pose to a "pure monotheism" is arbitrary and does

that Scripture and church tradition affirmed God as the ultimate creator of all beings, his thesis pushes for the reality of human and angelic freewill to eliminate further suppositions of a higher divine will for particular evil in the world.[123] In short, evil forces operate in *rebellion* to divine intention.

Boyd takes pains to counter the "Hellenistic philosophical tradition" that portrays a timeless, purely actual deity devoid of contingency and promotes a dynamic theism derived from a more literal reading of Scripture, one that takes more seriously the anthropomorphic descriptions of divine risk, responsiveness, and inter-relationality. Believing to side with "the conservative, evangelical faith perspective" on this point, his approach is to take conflict passages literally even if their particular portrayals do contain cultural or mythological elements.[124] Boyd sketches out the portraits of three "cosmic beasts," Leviathan, Rahab, and Behemoth, arguing that their identities as mythological monsters square with creation accounts thereby prompting the tentative speculation that God warred with them to bring the universe into being. The resultant earth, though good, has been birth in an "infected incubator" in which hostility remains normative.[125]

Boyd designates Satan as the personal focal point of comic evil whose kingdom is in direct conflict with the kingdom of God ushered in at the advent of Christ. Through his healings and exorcisms, Jesus "binds the strong man." However, the fact that the victories are not always complete landslides, as in the case of the demon-possessed boy (Mark 9:14–30; Matt 17:14–21; Luke 9:37–45), demonstrates the potency of the demonic realm and helps explains the sense of unfairness felt within a creation where spiritual and physical realities are continuations of one another.[126] Jesus' entire ministry, then, is marked with a deep pity for enslaved and harassed individuals as well a profound antagonism toward satanic forces. He provocatively asserts:

> There is no suggestion in the Gospels that Jesus believed that demons or evil angels were carrying out a secret providential plan of God, despite themselves. Rather, Jesus treated each case of demonization as an instance of spiritual rape: an alien force had illegitimately and cruelly invaded a person's being.[127]

---

not square with biblical data or early church belief. Furthermore, Gen 1 itself contains mythological elements and is, therefore, "hardly a modern, scientific, literal documentary of creation, ibid., 102.

123. Ibid., 57.
124. Ibid., 328 n 46.
125. Boyd, *God at War*, 107.
126. Ibid., 200.
127. Ibid., 201.

Moving to the specific theme of the atonement, Boyd criticizes post-Anselmic theology for prioritizing the "anthropological dimension" (Christ's satisfaction of divine justice *for us*) to the neglect of what he believes to be the NT's focus on the "cosmic dimension" (the defeat of demonic forces and the establishment of Christ as the ruler with human beings as his "viceroys" on earth).[128] Boyd calls for a broader perspective that appreciates the greater sway that cosmic free agents wield over creation relative to the exercise of human free will, which forms but a small part of the overall picture. Therefore, the cross—and resurrection—is fundamentally about "dethroning a cruel, illegitimate ruler and reinstating a loving, legitimate one: Jesus Christ."[129] As for how the cross accomplishes this victory, Boyd naturally favors the "divine deception" mechanism put forward in the classical "fishhook" analogy. Central to his argument here is that the "rulers" (*archontōn*) of 1 Cor 2:6-8 be understood as demonic personalities, who, in crucifying Jesus "sealed their own doom."[130] Correlated with this is the "harrowing of hell" image that favors the interpretation of the "spirits in prison" in 1 Pet 3:19-20 as vanquished demonic captors. Short of embracing a literal "buying off" of Satan through a ransom price, Boyd construes the jist of the metaphor as simply communicating that "Christ was willing to do whatever it took—to pay whatever 'price' was necessary—in order to defeat the tyrant who had enslaved us and thereby to set us free. What it took, the New Testament teaches, was nothing less than the Son of God becoming a man and dying a hellish death upon the cross."[131] Freedom from bondage to Satan becomes equated with forgiveness of sin as a natural by-product of Christ's cosmic victory.

Evaluation

There is much to appreciate in Boyd's near-exhaustive biblical theology of Yahweh as warrior, a lot of which is the product of sensible exegesis.[132] Over and against the so-called "Western tradition" that has tended to downplay the influence of spiritual entities operating in cosmic realms, Boyd rightly discerns the combative thread that runs throughout Scripture in describing God's work with and for creation. The "organic" mode by which a warfare

128. Ibid., 240.
129. Ibid., 246.
130. Ibid., 259.
131. Ibid., 266.
132. For a fine hermeneutical and exegetical critique, see Donald A Carson, "God, the Bible and Spiritual Warfare: A Review Article," *JETS* 42, no. 2 (June 1999): 258–69.

framework fleshes out the atonement, Boyd believes, is capable of subsuming the substitutionary aspect of Protestant orthodoxy while avoiding its problematic legal language.[133] Rather than unleashing judgment upon the incarnate Son as a vicarious sacrifice, God wars with and defeats creaturely, spiritual entities. Thomas Schreiner, however, questions whether Boyd correctly identifies the fundamental problem of sin that elicits the need for atonement. In emphasizing our willful participation in sin, Schreiner makes the case: "The devil and demons rule over us because we are sinners, not because we are in some mysterious way at the mercy of outside powers."[134] That said, while it is true that sin usually involves voluntary participation, we will later see that Scripture reasonably attests to multifaceted and objective views of sin.

Boyd's suggestion of a dualism between God and demonic powers, however, is overstated. By affirming that these powers often succeed in wreaking real havoc on creation, he is in the precarious position of implying that at least *some* malevolent forces are coequal in strength with God. If Yahweh is superior to his cosmic opponents, there should be no point at which he "loses" *any* battle to an evil force. The only conceivable reason why a superior combatant could lose to an inferior one is that there is a higher, secret motive at work. But this form of meticulous providence Boyd expressly rejects. Therefore, if at any time God were to lose to an opponent, resulting in a particular manifestation of real evil, it is necessarily because the opposing force is, at least in that instance, *superior*. If Boyd is to stake his claim upon a combat metaphor, the mode of describing the process of waging war must be consistent with what combat actually entails. The irony is that the attempt to galvanize this view into a theodicy that purports to offer comfort and reduce confusion actually *establishes* a God who sometimes loses battles against evil forces and has neither a reason nor redemptive plan for why it happened, nor a guarantee of victory in any subsequent encounter.

Solidarity: the Cross as Divine Partnership with Human Pain

We move now to trends in atonement thinking that are similar enough in spirit to be viewed collectively. The second category I label "solidarity" focuses on what the death of Jesus means for the oppressed and victimized. It is thought that traditional expressions of salvation through Christ are largely products of dominant groups in power, be it in terms of politics,

133. Beilby and Eddy, *The Nature of the Atonement: Four Views*, 43.
134. Ibid., 52–53.

status, race, or gender. The relevance and significance of the cross, therefore, do not reflect the felt needs of those who are not only outside these spheres of power, but are especially abused under them. Theologians of this stripe seek to view the cross afresh through the eyes of those who suffer and conclude that Jesus' solidarity with the oppressed best expresses the significance of his sufferings and the hope for change.

Prolegomena: historic subjugation and abuse

Theologies of atonement within this framework have the distinctive of working from within the unique perspective of the oppressed minority and addressing their specific concerns. Jürgen Moltmann famously remarked that within Christianity there have been two crosses: a "murderous gallows of terror and oppression" on which a victim of injustice was hung, and a "dream-cross of an emperor," which has become a symbol of violent world domination.[135] Reflecting over his three years in a prisoner-of-war camp after WWII, he writes:

> During my imprisonment, I found Christ the crucified as my brother in need and my liberator. This was a very different image of the cross than the one presented by the sacrifice religion within wartime Germany. The Son of Man came "to seek and save the lost" (Luke 19:10), and he found me in my godforsakenness and took me with himself on the way to the "broad place where there is no oppression anymore" (paraphrased from Job 36:16). Christ crucified liberated me from affirming the terrors produced by those who utilize the cross as military symbol.[136]

Identifying historic injustice is a crucial first step in solidarist theologizing. Theodore W. Jennings, Jr. similarly takes as his starting point the aftermath of the Holocaust and the role that anti-Semitic Christian theology (especially, Luther's infamous 1543 text, "The Jews and their Lies"[137]) played in legitimizing the atrocities of the Nazi regime. Central to Jennings' thesis is that the "real culprits" surrounding Jesus' execution is the Roman Empire and the values they inculcate in subsequent structures of power. Jennings warns that failure to understand the cross from its historical reality is poten-

---

135. Jürgen Moltmann, "The Cross as Military Symbol for Sacrifice," in *Cross Examinations: Readings on the Meaning of the Cross Today*, ed. Marit Trelstad (Minneapolis, MN: Augsburg Fortress, 2006), 259.

136. Ibid., 263.

137. See, Martin Luther, *Luther's Works, Volume 47: Christian in Society IV*, ed. Franklin Sherman and Helmut T. Lehmann (Philadelphia: Fortress, 1971), 137–306.

tially devastating. In a similar vein as Denny Weaver, Jennings writes: "This means that we will have to anchor reflections on its meaning or significance in the historical reality that it evokes: the execution of the enemies of Rome, and hence the enemies of empire and of military rule."[138]

Diverging only slightly from the military-political perspective are feminist/womanist theologians who question the language of violence and abuse inherent in traditional, patriarchal descriptions of Christ's passion. The identification of the cross with divine child abuse is also widely attested among these writers leading to the lamentable conclusion that Christian theology glorifies suffering.[139] Delores S. Williams, for example, notes the problematic association of substitutionary suffering with black women's coerced and voluntary surrogacy during the era of slavery in America. For her, the cross is "an image of defilement, a gross manifestation of collective human sin."[140] The agenda of many feminist theologians like Williams is to dispel the "sacred aura" that surrounds theological reflections of the cross by critiquing the forces that caused it in the first place.

Because liberation from acts of inhumanity press urgently upon these theologians' agenda, a full recognition of the historic processes that cause and perpetuate these injustices is the starting place for their reflections. According to Jennings, only when we anchor theological reflection on the cross in its historical and public reality can we avoid getting lost in speculation and "mythopoiesis" and can the message of the cross have the effect of transforming the public and political reality in which our lives are situated.[141]

The crucified Messiah as victim

The prevailing image of Christ on the cross for solidarist interpretations is that of a victim. Jesus is the quintessence of unjust suffering. Jennings surmises that early Christians deflected blame for Christ's death unto the

---

138. Theodore W. Jennings, *Transforming Atonement: A Political Theology of the Cross* (Minneapolis: Fortress, 2009), 12.

139. See Rita Nakashima Brock's discussion on the dynamics of parent-child relationships in traditional patriarchal atonement theories in *Journeys by Heart: a Christology of Erotic Power* (New York: Crossroad, 1988), 55–57. She writes: "The emphasis in on the goodness and power of the father and the unworthiness and powerlessness of his children, so that the father's punishment is just, and children are to blame," 56.

140. Delores S. Williams, "Black Women's Surrogacy Experience and the Christian Notion of Redemption," in *After Patriarchy: Feminist Transformations of the World Religions*, ed. Paula M. Cooey, William R. Eakin, and Jay B. McDaniel (Maryknoll, NY: Orbis Books, 1991), 12.

141. Jennings, *Transforming Atonement*, 18–19.

Jews for fear of political repercussions, but he is forcefully certain that the Romans executed Jesus with the cross as the imperial tool of domination.[142] He argues that many references to the crucified Messiah in the New Testament are coded indictments against the Roman establishment strategically employed by early Christians to survive the scrutiny of the state.[143] Militaristic antagonists, envisioned in the patristic era, therefore, are allegories that "transpose" the visible expressions of imperial force "onto the wider canvas of cosmic reality."[144] These images highlight the brutality of the political order and function to model the anticipated fate of persecution and martyrdom on the part of Jesus' disciples.

Why was Jesus crucified? From the perspective of solidarity, the key to Jesus victimization lies in his earthly ministry. Jennings traces Jesus' ministry and movement toward Jerusalem as a restorative mission of justice and mercy. The announcement of his "empire" was in such conflict with that of Roman rule that it was perceived to be a threat to the military establishment.[145] Delores Williams concurs that Jesus' ministerial vision emphasized the promoting of human life, which finds its full flourishing in resurrection.

That Jesus' death is ultimately a tragedy is a common feature of solidarist conceptions of the cross. Williams asserts strongly, "There is nothing of God in the blood of the cross,"[146] and Elizabeth A. Johnson describes it as a "disaster."[147] In efforts to distance the cross from any implication in God's will, Jennings, referencing the Roman centurion who recognized Jesus as "Son of God" at the crucifixion and the change of heart of Joseph of Arimathea, suggests that those belonging to the structures of domination might have been persuaded to follow another course besides violence. "It is only if the logic of violence does not renounce its own force that the cross becomes the inevitable outcome of the way of justice and mercy."[148]

The recognition of Jesus as a victim embroiled in abusive structures of domination seems to be a universal feature of solidarist thought, so theologians tend to emphasize this point. Elizabeth Schüssler Fiorenza writes:

---

142. Ibid., 12.

143. Especially Paul, e.g. "the rulers of this age" (1 Cor. 2:8), "those who by their injustice imprison the truth" (Rom 1:8, Jenning's translation), and those "filled with every kind of injustice" (1 Cor. 1:29–30), ibid., 41–42.

144. Ibid., 53.

145. Ibid., 34.

146. Ibid., 12.

147. Elizabeth A. Johnson, *She Who Is: The Mystery of God in Feminist Theological Discourse*, 10th ed. (New York: The Crossroad Publishing Company, 2002), 159.

148. Jennings, *Transforming Atonement*, 58–59.

> A theology that is silent about the sociopolitical causes of Jesus' execution and stylizes him as the paradigmatic sacrificial victim whose death was either willed by God or was necessary to propitiate God continues the kyriarchical cycle of violence and victimization instead of empowering believers to resist and transform it.[149]

One of the most powerful and meaningful aspects of Jesus' passion is his representative solidarity with victims, but it is simply not enough that Jesus is merely another example, albeit the finest example, of suffering unjustly at the hands of abusive power. Before exploring how Jesus' passion is thought to have redemptive value, it behooves us to understand what exactly is meant by "solidarity."

The meaning of solidarity

In the solidarist framework, terms like "injustice," "oppression," and "exploitation" operate as keywords around which the present theological reaction is conceived. Andrew Sung Park contextualizes the various modes and expressions of this wounded state in the single Korean term, *han*: a victim's deep, inner grief "generated by political oppression, economic exploitation, social alienation, cultural contempt, injustice, poverty, or war."[150] *Han* can manifest itself as "frustrated hope," bitterness, resignation, a cry of abandonment, and is felt at the individual, collective, and structural levels.[151] Left unattended, *han* can self-propagate or result in sinful, evil acts.[152] Jesus' ministry was one of standing in solidarity with the "*han*-ridden", in which "a common goal, communal identity, commiseration, and liberative work" are included.[153] It is imperative that Jesus himself experiences and participates in humanity's *han*; by bearing their *han*, he not only understands but *identifies* with those who suffer. This wound is far-reaching and extensive. In stressing the triune involvement in the atonement, Park suggests: "The intensity of Jesus' unfair execution developed *han* in the Holy Spirit. The Holy Spirit that underwent suffering with the crucified Jesus is called the

---

149. Elizabeth Schüssler Fiorenza, *Jesus: Miriam's Child, Sophia's Prophet: Critical Issues in Feminist Christology* (New York: Continuum, 1994), 106.

150. Andrew Sung Park, *Triune Atonement: Christ's Healing for Sinners, Victims, and the Whole Creation* (Louisville: Westminster John Knox Press, 2009), 39.

151. Ibid., 39–41.

152. Ibid., 41.

153. Ibid., 42.

Paraclete."[154] Having been wounded together with Christ, the Paraclete understands human suffering, advocates for victims' rights, and works to daily comfort and heal the wounds of injustice.[155] As shall be seen below, the emphasis on the Paraclete is important for understanding how Jesus continues to stand with the oppressed.

An important feature of Jesus' identification with humanity is the distinct and preferred group with whom solidarity is forged. Jesus specifically identifies with those *on the receiving end* of injustice, those who are objects of victimization. Jennings unabashedly declares: "[Jesus] wants to be clear that God sides with the accused and against the accusers. In this, God is not 'evenhanded' or neutral. God resolutely takes sides—for this one and against that one; for the oppressed and against the oppressor; for the poor and against the rich; for the accused sinner and against the accusing righteous."[156] His term "accused sinner" is very revealing. It does not refer to an absolute state of guilt in which the divine law identifies every human being as a transgressor (e.g. Rom 3:23). Rather, the stress is on the fact that the political and religious establishment *identifies* one as a sinner. He writes:

> Attention to the mission and ministry of Jesus shows that he is remembered as one who was in solidarity with those who were identified as sinners. This identification includes those who are branded as outlaws by the political order and as outsiders by the structure of religious privilege . . . By living in solidarity with sinners, Jesus' ministry anticipates the fate by which, as crucified, he is made out to be sin, sin itself, separated and abandoned by God, the very form of the accursed.

Likewise, Park does not place victims in the category of "sinner." "[Jesus'] life proved that he withstood Pharisees' attacks on so-called sinners. These 'sinners' were shepherds, tanners, the sick, and the poor. In fact, they were the sinned-against."[157] Jennings and Park seem to lay the largest brunt of the term "sinner" unto oppressors, not victims.

---

154. Ibid., 61.

155. Ibid., 67–68.

156. Jennings, *Transforming Atonement*, 95. So strong is Jennings on this point, it is reflected in his theological considerations of other points of doctrine. In excursus on Israel's election, he writes: "As a Christian theologian in the aftermath of the Holocaust or Shoah, however, I am reluctant to adopt the view that Israel is no longer the elect people of God, even when I wish to deny that election to Christians also . . . Nothing so clearly marks Israel as God's elect as does the history of Christian anti-Semitism and anti-Judaism," 83.

157. Park, *Triune Atonement*, 44.

One might pause to ponder the logical conclusion that Jesus does not stand with (and therefore does not save) oppressors as well. By and large, Park maintains that Jesus' challenges were against the abstract and systemic principles of injustice, legalism, tyranny, and exploitation, but where "oppressor" is mentioned with respect to the cross, the word is virtually synonymous with "sinner" and linked to some confrontational posture and conditions that need to be met prior to being "saved": "The cross is the concrete historical emblem of God's suffering because of the sins of oppressors or sinners . . . It urges the oppressors to turn away from these and to come back to God's rule."[158] The seeming prejudice that governs who qualifies for solidarity with Christ becomes even clearer with Park's suggestion that the natural, created order of earthly things and animals also share in *han* and will be finally restored.[159] It is safe to conclude that the only ones who do not experience *han* (and thus are not in solidarity with Jesus) are the oppressors who cause it.

How solidarity "saves"

Because the solidarist scheme exists within a theology-from-below framework that is concerned with historic and bodily realities, the ways in which redemption is understood is multifaceted and organic; they depend on the nature of the perceived problem and the agents involved. Theologians in this vein understandably avoid speaking of the cross as the sole site of redemptive activity. Rather, the ministry and mission of Jesus as a whole is the paradigm for thinking about God's liberative work. As Park writes: "Any atonement theory that excludes Jesus' work through his proclaiming, healing, teaching, and liberating is incomplete."[160] Fundamentally, Jesus works to end oppression, set captives free, and proclaim the Lord's favor to the poor, as per his own self-understanding in Luke 4:18–19.

There are several aspects to this work. First, redemption involves abolishing the walls of division and privilege that create categories of superior and inferior. In the cross, the barriers of division are broken down. Jennings

---

158. Park, *Triune Atonement*, 52. He also writes: "Jesus did not shed his blood *for* his afflicters, torturers, and wrongdoers, but he shed his blood *because* of them. They afflicted, tortured, and executed him." The only sense in which it is *for* them is that "Jesus resisted and challenged his persecutors and oppressors unto death so that they might come to their senses and be saved," 88–89.

159. Ibid., 105–106. Park draws on Romans 8:19–23 and the motif of Abel's blood "crying out from the ground" (Gen 4:1–16) to argue that *han* resides in animals and nature and must also be redeemed by Christ's ongoing atoning work.

160. Ibid., 73.

argues that exclusionary ideologies modeled upon Israel's election as the privileged people of God are undercut by Gospel narratives and culminate at the cross. Jesus himself is "handed over" to the Gentiles and cast out by his own people. This brings the principle of exclusion and religious privilege to an end. "Jesus now 'belongs' to the nations, to those who were on the outside of the divine covenant, to those who are decidedly pagan, secular, the outsider and the excluded."[161] This undermining of division extends well beyond the religious sphere and includes the abolition of distinctions between slave and free, male and female. It envisions "a radical restructuring of our social reality."[162]

Second, redemption involves the healing and restoration of that which has been harmed. For Park, this is to be located primarily in the post-resurrection, ongoing atoning work of Christ through the Paraclete.[163] Rita Nakashima Brock balks at the idea of a one-sided formulation of atonement in which redemption is procured through a cosmic transaction between an omnipotent God and humanity without any possibility of interdependence and mutuality.[164] She proposes the conception of Christa/Community, an integrated and revelatory witness of God's work in history,[165] which redeems by generating "erotic power" that destroys power hierarchies and promotes connectedness through "creative synthesis."[166] On a similar front, Mary J. Streufert proposes that the "life-for-life" paradigm involved in motherhood is a hermeneutical alternative to an overemphasis on the heroic that fosters passivity. Through the maternal body and the maternal life, the courage to endure the physical demands of childbirth and childrearing emphasizes the active, life-giving nature of sacrifice as restorative rather than "necrophilic."[167]

For Jennings, this healing includes restoring the broken relationship between God and humans more generally. Contra the Western tradition

---

161. Jennings, *Transforming Atonement*, 70.

162. Ibid., 19.

163. Park, *Triune Atonement*, 71. In fact, for Park, the cross is merely the necessary gateway to one's "new life in God," namely, the resurrection and the arrival of the Paraclete, 73.

164. Rita Nakashima Brock, *Journeys by Heart: A Christology of Erotic Power* (Eugene, OR: Wipf & Stock, 2008), 56. Intrinsic to this scheme is how it perpetuates heroism, dualism, and dominance.

165. Ibid., 69.

166. Ibid., 39.

167. Mary J. Streufert, "Maternal Sacrifice as a Hermeneutics of the Cross," in *Cross Examinations: Readings on the Meaning of the Cross Today*, ed. Marit Trelstad (Minneapolis, MN: Augsburg Fortress, 2006).

following Anselm, Jennings insists that it is not God who is reconciled through the cross of Christ; it is humanity's enmity against God that has been overcome. "God has done something dramatic in the Messiah, and this comes to a head in the fate of the Messiah. This act/event has the effect of removing any cause of complaint we might have against God."[168] He argues that the solidarity of the cross is meant to undo the damages perceived on the part of the oppressed, un-chosen, condemned, afflicted, and abandoned. Where the vast majority of history has used "God-talk" to legitimize and sanction oppression and domination, the cross says that God is on side of the victims of state-sponsored violence. Where religious privilege has formed a distinction between elect and non-elect, the cross abolishes this wall of hostility. Where the law accuses people as sinners, the cross disables its condemnatory power by featuring an executed Messiah who was innocent. Where the message of a God who is indifferent to human plight afflicts people with a sense of abandonment, the cross shows forth the abandonment of the beloved Son of God.

Third, redemption involves dealing with sin, but in a different way than traditionally understood. Sin, in the strong sense of the term, tends to be reserved for oppressors and their systems of domination. Feminist theologian, Cynthia Crysdale, regards sin not as disobedience to a divine command, but a disjuncture between who we are and who we can become.[169] Normally, this manifests in the form of hubris, which sabotages and rejects the Self. For "non-persons," whose lives have been marked by constant capitulation to others, "the Self has to be issued before it can be rejected."[170] Transformation, therefore, is the strengthening of the *ego* through identification with the crucified Jesus as one's "true Self," and resurrection is "God's raising of one's belief in Self in the face of powerful messages to the contrary."[171]

Another strategy for softening the gravity of sin, as applied to victims, is by redefining what is meant for Jesus to be "without sin." As Jennings suggests:

> It is critical that we notice that Jesus is *not* said to be 'without sin' because he complied with each and every commandment and prohibition in the various legal codes of Israel. These legal codes are not a sort of checklist that can be used to determine whether Jesus was or was not without sin. What makes him 'without sin'

---

168. Jennings, *Transforming Atonement*, 130–31.

169. Cynthia S. W. Crysdale, *Embracing Travail: Retrieving the Cross Today* (New York: Continuum, 1999), 9.

170. Ibid., 10.

171. Ibid.

is that he fully and radically enacted God's mercy and justice, the mercy and justice that include or welcome "sinners."[172]

By envisioning Jesus' relation to sin in this way, Jennings narrows the ontological distinction between Jesus and sinful humanity and makes way for a new understanding of salvation: humanity, especially victims, are not saved from sin but from *accusation*. Within this theological framework, the divine will does not involve accusation and exclusion, but affirmation and inclusion. Jesus' solidarity with the accused is the grace that "reaches out to the excluded and the condemned in order to claim them as God's own children and heirs, and therefore as the designated recipients of divine favor."[173] The outline of the logic is as follows:

1. Jesus represents the divine will;
2. The law condemns Jesus, the one "without sin"; therefore,
3. The law as accusatory and condemnatory is "rendered obsolete."[174]

With condemnation thus disarmed, humanity is emboldened to turn to God in confidence and trust.[175]

Fourth, redemption involves unmasking and exposing the systems of oppressive domination. Feminist theologians, in particular, are eager to point out the way in which Christ's suffering works to protest through contrast. Korean feminist theologian, Choi Man Ja, writes: "Suffering exposes patriarchal evil. Jesus endures the yoke of the cross against the evil powers of this patriarchal world. This obedience is different from simple submission to the worldly authority."[176] Likewise, Elizabeth Johnson also stresses how Christ "manifests the truth that divine justice and renewing power leavens the world in a way different from the techniques of dominating violence."[177] The tendency is to blame abstract principles and "techniques" rather than individuals, as when Park declares, "The cross does not condemn the oppressors but rebukes the falsehood, manipulation, and dark side of their power."[178]

172. Jennings, *Transforming Atonement*, 99. Jennings alludes also to Jesus' physical contact with "contaminated" persons, whereby "[o]bjectively, Jesus is made a sinner," e.g. the bleeding woman (Mark 5:25ff), lepers (Matt. 8:3, Luke 5:13), and a Jairus' dead daughter (Mark 5:41), 90–91.

173. Ibid., 100.

174. Ibid.

175. Ibid., 20–21.

176. Choi Man Ja, "Feminist Christology," in *Consultation on Asian Women's Theology*, 1987, 6.

177. Johnson, *She Who Is*, 159.

178. Park, *Triune Atonement*, 52.

When it comes to detailing the mechanism of deliverance, the natural link between oppression and oppressors becomes unavoidable. Jennings reasons that the intention of martyrs aims to liberate both victims and oppressors. However, there is a bifurcation in how this is achieved. The deliverance of the victim is direct—to end suffering; the deliverance of the oppressor is indirect—to convict them of injustice and thereby renounce their support of such systems.[179] Solidarists strive to make clear that "Jesus did not shed his blood *for* his afflicters, torturers, and wrongdoers, but he shed his blood *because* of them."[180] The only sense in which it is *for* them is that "Jesus resisted and challenged his persecutors and oppressors unto death so that they might come to their senses and be saved."[181] This repentance on the part of oppressors is demanded as a condition for their salvation and is praised in the examples of Joseph of Arimathea and Justin Martyr, converts who were awakened to their belonging to the "wrong side" and subsequently bound themselves to the persecuted minority.

Evaluation

Exponents who interpret the cross in terms of Christ's solidarity with the oppressed make several points worth considering for developing an holistic atonement theology. Many of these reflect convictions found within traditional understandings but in a repackaged form that prioritizes the perspective of the marginalized. In the first place, they unreservedly identify the enemy: oppression, domination, and injustice are, for them, the definitive pariahs with which God has no part, and for which atonement becomes necessary. As a theology-from-below, historic, systemic, and/or personal experiences with victimization are the indispensable foundations for understanding Jesus' own sufferings, and without the elimination of this problem, no idea of atonement is conceivable. The solidarist scheme rightly recognizes that while these evils are abstract in nature, they necessarily manifest themselves historically in human agency. This fact notwithstanding, the antagonism against these evils is yet so strong as to imagine a polarization in God's attitude toward the two groups in question: God is *for* the oppressed and *against* the oppressor. Establishment of this stark, prejudicial treatment at the human level is ironic, especially within a theology that supposedly promotes God's love and a vision of creaturely and cosmic wholeness. A possible way around the dilemma

---

179. Jennings, *Transforming Atonement*, 107.
180. Park, *Triune Atonement*, 88–89.
181. Ibid., 89.

confronting solidarity proponents, as I will argue, is to maintain a clear antagonism between God and the proper object, sin.

A second helpful feature of solidarist thought is the emphasis on the despair of victimhood. Once again, we see the positive effect of grounding theology not on speculation, but real, lived experiences. Theologians are convinced that unjust suffering is the worst imaginable harm, out of which a cry bursts forth. It is this cry of suffering, as in the case of Abel's blood that cries from the ground (Gen 4:10) and the Israelites under slavery (Exod 3:7, 9), that "provokes or summons the divine into action" thereby "inaugurating the redemptive activity of God."[182] This is a powerful image that is often not given enough exposure in other, more "stoic" models of the atonement. Because of its rootedness in historic abuse, this motif gives dramatic appeal to the story of redemption while being neither fictitious in its presentation nor manipulative in its intentions. I will argue that this image can be incorporated into a doctrine of the atonement that deals with victimhood at a more fundamental, cosmic level that transcends the dichotomy of earthly oppressors and the oppressed. Instead of God responding merely to *instances* of victimization, God responds to ultimate and absolute victimization—the enslavement of humanity under sin.

Third, solidarist theologies reveal the deep angst that resides on the part of the offended. Park's deployment of *han* to express the festering wound that demands justice captures the sense of long-enduring pain, which includes a hopeful desire for change, frustrated though it may be in the meantime. Within a dramatic rendering of salvation, this serves as a reminder of "unfinished business" and highlights the expectation of a climactic reversal. The danger, perhaps, lies in the possibility (or tendency?) for *han* to give birth to sin and violence. At least, such would be the case if sinful humans were the ones who primarily bear it. While Park suggests that Jesus' bears the *han* of victims to enact his solidarity with them, it is also conceivable that God bears this *han* in a much deeper and far-reaching sense. People bear *han* as a result of abuse by earthly powers, but God bears it at the absolute, cosmic level in God's struggle against evil and the powers of sin. That God is the one who bears it means that this deep-seated grudge is "satisfied" with perfect justice and equity. In the end, however, *han* is an untranslatable concept native to a particular culture and history. It may be that the notion of offense or grudge as understood within a revenge framework more ably expresses this idea on a popular level.

Fourth, solidarity envisions the cross as an expression of defiant resistance. Jennings is quick to point out that the passive suffering of victims

---

182. Jennings, *Transforming Atonement*, 109.

should not be regarded as "redemptive" *per se*. The difference between suffering as a result of confronting oppressive power and that of merely being a victim of that power has everything to do with "agency."[183] Only when suffering is seen as an active rebuke of oppression is it redemptive. The horrors of Christ's execution by tyrannical oppressors, for example, serve to reveal how unjust they are. In theory, the idea is tenable, but it faces some challenges. First, it demands that reality be construed in very black and white terms. Those who oppress must clearly belong to the dominant class, often described in terms of empire, capitalism, patriarchy, etc. Even among postcolonial critics, this has been shown to be too simplistic.[184] Second, a victim's suffering is only at best a signifier of unjust abuse, not an outright protest. As a mild form of resistance, its agency rests on perception and its success lies in persuasion. Oppressors must come to their senses of their own accord. In reality, suffering does very little to actually voice a complaint. The proposal of dualists might serve as a positive supplement to this feigned form of agency in its vision of the cross as a site of actual battle.

The single greatest weakness of atonement via solidarity is, once again, its view of sin. Because it regards oppression as the quintessential sin that necessitates redemption, there is the need to amplify the notion of sin with respect to the dominators and play down the sins committed *by* victims. Sin thus becomes relativized as something people do to one another, rather than as something done against God. The cross rebukes and pleads with oppressors, but there is no unconditional forgiveness available. Only upon repentance and "welcoming" is acceptance into the "community of the Crucified" possible. While liberation is graciously granted to victims, oppressors are saved through repentance and good works. A Pelagian soteriology is close at hand. Furthermore, it is argued that the cross renders the law obsolete and ends accusation; however, accusation against oppressors remains intact. It seems that a hermeneutic of privilege is at work here with the only difference being the inversion of the participants involved. A double standard that favors the oppressed is still a double standard nonetheless and should evoke some reservation. Within this scheme, the oppressed seem to be elevated to an exalted status as the ones "truly" allied with God, and those of the dominating class are stripped of dignity and excluded. A valid atonement theology needs to demonstrate God's loving preference and his bitter indignation in ways that absolutizes, not relativizes, sin and sinners.

183. Ibid., 106.

184. See, for example, Sung Uk Lim, "Biopolitics in the Trial of Jesus (John 18:28–19:16a)," *The Expository Times* February 2016, no. 127 (2015): 209–16, doi:10.1177/0014524615574665. He argues that Jewish and Roman influences were responsible for Jesus' trial and execution, contrary to Jennings' insistence that the Jews cannot be blamed.

Invalidation: the Cross as Deconstruction of Scapegoating Sacrifice

In this last category of contemporary critiques and reformulations of traditional atonement, theologians speak most specifically—and forcefully—against divinely sanctioned violence.[185] This position seeks to invalidate once and for all any notion that violence, sacred or otherwise, possesses any spiritual or redemptive value. In fact, it is from violence itself that we must be saved. Fueling this movement is the work of French literary critic, René Girard, whose theory of violence rooted in "mimetic rivalry" and the mechanism of the "surrogate victim" or "scapegoat" has had profound influence on contemporary soteriology.[186] His basic argument is that in societies composed of differences, one's desire for what their model has and is can turn into rivalry that threatens violence. In order to regulate the escalating threat of violence and avert total chaos, communities unconsciously impute their ills unto a scapegoat, who bears the violence that would otherwise have been unleashed between rivals. This scapegoat is subsequently "deified" and religion is formed in which myths conceal the mechanism so successful at establishing peace. Old Testament religion inherited and repeated this ritual, with some glimmers of light issuing from the prophetic and poetic voices that denounced it. In the Christian gospel's announcement of God's own innocent Victim, the structure of persecution and sacrifice is demystified and exposed for what it is. Along the way, however, Christianity has lost this message and rehashed the image of suffering as propitiating divine anger. Theologians who view the cross in light of Girard's theory naturally wish to deconstruct and invalidate the ancient myth of redemptive scapegoating once for all and call for universal harmony through the abandonment of all violence.

185. From a sampling of the major works along these lines, the titles are suggestive: Raymund Schwager, *Must There Be Scapegoats?: Violence and Redemption in the Bible* (San Francisco: Harper & Row, 1987); James G. Williams, *Bible, Violence, and the Sacred: Liberation from the Myth of Sanctioned Violence* (San Francisco: HarperCollins, 1991); Robert G. Hamerton-Kelly, *Sacred Violence: Paul's Hermeneutic of the Cross* (Minneapolis: Fortress, 1991); Gil Bailie, *Violence Unveiled: Humanity at the Crossroads* (New York: The Crossroad Publishing Company, 1996); Willard M. Swartley, ed., *Violence Renounced* (Telford, PA: Pandora Press U. S., 2000); T. Scott Daniels, "Passing the Peace: Worship That Shapes Nonsubstitutionary Convictions," in *Atonement and Violence: A Theological Conversation*, ed. John Sanders (Nashville: Abingdon, 2006); Mark S. Heim, *Saved from Sacrifice: A Theology of the Cross* (Grand Rapids: Eerdmans, 2006).

186. Most notably, René Girard, *Deceit, Desire, and the Novel* (Baltimore: Johns Hopkins University Press, 1965); *Violence and the Sacred* (Baltimore: Johns Hopkins University Press, 1977); *The Scapegoat* (Baltimore: Johns Hopkins University Press, 1986); *I See Satan Fall Like Lightning* (Maryknoll, NY: Orbis Books, 2001). These refer to the English titles and their corresponding publication dates.

This view, although having some (or many) elements in common with the solidarity view and Weaver's narrative *Christus Victor*, differs in its appraisal of Jesus' passion. Whereas the previous views have either little to say about Jesus' death or maintain some form of positive assessment of Jesus' identification with victims in their suffering and the spiritual effects thereof, Girardian invalidation denounces all glorifying in the cross, labeling it as the heart of the problem from which we need to be saved. As with the previous category above, I will survey the main lines of argument according to relevant topics within the theory.

Humanity's problem: myth

According to Girard, religion finds its roots in society's tendency to want to avoid chaos of which violence is the main expression. Biblical religion, like every other religion, has been caught up in repeated cycles of ritual scapegoating to achieve this end. Violence is what necessitates religion, but the end of violence cannot be completed as long as the mechanism of scapegoating continues, for it has the effect of legitimizing violence as sacred. It can be said that violence is not the problem per se; *the myth of sacred violence* is. The illusion of redemptive violence through scapegoating masks and perpetuates more violence. As Girard states:

> It was not the discovery of some authentic criminal, as claimed by myths, that reconciled these archaic communities; it was the illusion of such a discovery. The communities mimetically transferred all their hostilities to the single victim and became reconciled on the basis of the resulting illusion.[187]

Leading pluralist theologian, S. Mark Heim, hails mimetic theory as describing events whose "origins date from a crucial transitional moment when life in the earliest social groups was just in the process, literally, of making us human." He continues, "What distinguished emergent humans from other primates was an increased mental plasticity coupled with susceptibility to cultural formation, a combination that spurred an explosion beyond simple genetic selection."[188] An evolutionary anthropology undergirds the theory

---

187. René Girard, "Violence and Religion: Cause or Effect," in *The Hedgehog Review*, vol. 6 no. 1 (Spring 2004): 9, quoted in Daniels, "Passing the Peace," 131.

188. Mark S. Heim, *Saved from Sacrifice: A Theology of the Cross* (Grand Rapids: Eerdmans, 2006), 41. See also Heim's "A Cross-Section of Sin: The Mimetic Character of Human Nature in Biological and Theological Perspective," in *Evolution and Ethics: Human Morality in Biological and Religious Perspective*, ed. Philip Clayton and Jeffrey Scholss (Grand Rapids: Eerdmans, 2004).

culminating in a reading of primeval history where "the central plot of much myth is a very real and recurrent historical event. Myth itself is a lie humanity has been telling itself about that event."[189] Girard finds the story of Cain's killing of Abel serving nicely as a primitive mythic tale of the "founding murder" that elicits the spiral of violence. However, Adam and Eve's "fall" into sin is thought to set up what would be the story of societal breakdown by describing envy and rivalry as the chief precipitating forces.

For Heim, the Hebrew Scriptures in particular and the God it describes are heavily embroiled in the dynamics of mythical sacrifice and must be viewed from the outset as "very bad myth." He goes on to compare classic myth with the Bible's concrete, "down-to-earth" character and concludes, "Rather than the universal abstraction of myth, it gives us the tales of a tangled tribal family, an ancient petty state and its jealous deity."[190] Thus, a large part of the invalidationist project lies in deconstructing the mythic dimension of scapegoating. Only then is there the hope of ending violence.

The uniqueness of Jesus' victimization

In *Saved from Sacrifice*, Heim scours the biblical text interrogating instances of divinely-sanctioned violence, of which he finds many, including the slaying of Cain, the sacrifice of Isaac, and priestly atonement rituals. He argues that the Hebrew Bible testifies to an increased disavowal of divine support for sacrificial practices, especially seen in the prophets' denunciations of sacrifice in the face of Israel's disobedience and injustice (i.e. neglecting the victimized).[191] The book of Job serves as something of a "hermeneutical gavel" that pronounces the verdict of whether God is the sacrificial deity of myth or the biblical God who sides with victims."[192]

The disavowal of sacred violence comes to a climax in Heim's reading of the famous Servant Song of Isaiah 52:13—53:12. Thought to many as the

---

189. Heim, *Saved from Sacrifice*, 60.

190. Ibid., 67. For example, Heim is convinced that "[t]here is no foundational violence in God or God's creation of the world. But the biblical God is quickly implicated in killing. In fact, the story of Cain and Abel begins a short, vivid portion of scripture in which God is caught up in the intensive spiral of violence at the end of which God destroys the entire world (save Noah and his ark) by flood," 73.

191. Ibid., 93–95.

192. Ibid., 91. He concludes: "Job has seemed to talk of two different Gods—an adversary God for whom he is only a sacrificial target, and a divine vindicator, the God who sides with victims. And we may say that Job has spoken what is right about both of them . . . [I]t may reflect not merely a literary but historical struggle between two religious realities, a sacrificial divinity and the God of victims."

key proof text in favor of penal substitutionary atonement, Heim reads just the opposite: in the death of the Suffering Servant, God is invalidating their killing and their reasons for doing it. "He was wounded for our transgressions" means that a sacrifice is required because of our inability to maintain peaceful relations;[193] "Upon him was the punishment that made us whole" means that we are reconciled and freed from violence by this act of scapegoating; "All we like sheep have gone astray" means that we are all involved and implicated; and "By a perversion of justice he was taken away" means that while the killing seems to have a moral basis, it is unjust to the core.[194] Finally, "the Lord has laid on him the iniquity of us all," and "we esteemed him stricken by God" should be understood as "the victim was allowed to be struck down by a God who counted his sufferings as an atonement for the faults of the very mob that inflicted them on him."[195] Heim admits a transaction is occurring but of another type, one in which "Christ died for us to stop us from having people die for us."[196]

The willingness of Jesus to enter into and participate in scapegoating sacrifice is key to understanding how his death differs from others' within the same cycle. In allowing himself to fall under the judgment of his killers, "Jesus frees humanity from the need to continually participate in patterns of rivalrous mimesis that lead to death."[197] As an innocent and willing victim, he exposes the will of the people to kill and the injustice of their method. On pondering what import there must have been that Christ was crucified as opposed to dying of old age or a fall, Heim reasons that God uses the occasion of this type of execution "because we desperately need deliverance from the particular sin this death exemplifies."[198] The active intention of revealing and reversing the scapegoat mechanism dissociates Christ from random, passive victimhood.[199] For Raymund Schwager, humanity's "grudge" against God and subsequent rejection (Ps 118:22) is central to his logic of the cross: "Jesus *had* to die because only in that way could human beings transfer their

---

193. Ibid., 98.

194. This is Heim's own preferred translation of verse 8, rendered in the ESV as: "By oppression and judgment he was taken away . . . ," ibid., 99.

195. Ibid., 100, quoting Gil Bailie, *Violence Unveiled: Humanity at the Crossroads* (New York: The Crossroad Publishing Company, 1996), 45.

196. Heim, *Saved from Sacrifice*, 307. Heim does, in fact, admit that these are variations of traditional language, the problem of such language being that they "balance on a knife's edge of interpretation," 306.

197. Daniels, "Passing the Peace," 132.

198. Heim, *Saved from Sacrifice*, 193–94.

199. Daniels, "Passing the Peace," 133.

hatred of God to the Son of God."²⁰⁰ It is in the rejection of Christ that God's self-giving, non-satisfaction requiring forgiveness of God is highlighted and the scapegoat mechanism exposed and rendered powerless.²⁰¹ As a Girardian Pauline scholar, Robert Hamerton-Kelly understands the Mosaic law, with its in-built principle of retribution, as "inverted" by Jesus' willing submission to this temporal legal demand.²⁰² The main point in all Girardian readings is that it is humanity's vengeance—not God's—that is operative in Jesus' death.

"Salvation" within a Girardian framework

Atonement that invalidates scapegoating sacrifice has no place for any violent action made on account of sin. The very point of Jesus' death is to abolish the idea that God requires retribution by revealing the myth that perpetuates it. It is not that God needs to be appeased but that humans must be delivered from their hatred.²⁰³ At the heart of invalidationist theology, sinners are already welcomed through God's freely offered love. It is loyalty and spiritual progress that God expects, not sacrificial death.²⁰⁴ Similar to solidarity proponents, therefore, the life, teaching, and resurrection are the main positive contributors for understanding how inner and communal transformation occurs in those who have renounced sacred violence. Jesus' life establishes his innocence, and his resurrection vindicates it. "Human scapegoats," writes Heim, "have no way of proving their innocence against the inflated charges against them, but Jesus, in his resurrection, is vindicated so as to expose the process that killed him."²⁰⁵

Becoming enlightened to the truth is not enough, however. Once disciples of Jesus become aware of their complicity in mimetic rivalry and scapegoating can they transcend the process by practicing its inverse: "'sacrifice' is redefined to be an offering of praise, and rivalry is transformed into

---

200. Schwager, *Must There Be Scapegoats?*, 242.

201. Ibid., 213, 233.

202. Hamerton-Kelly, *Sacred Violence*, 76–77.

203. Schwager, *Must There Be Scapegoats?*, 209.

204. Stephen Finlan, *Problems With Atonement: The Origins Of, and Controversy About, the Atonement Doctrine* (Collegeville, MN: Liturgical Press, 2005), 109.

205. Heim, *Saved from Sacrifice*, 327. Drawing from Markus Barth's *Acquittal by Resurrection*, Heim contends that the resurrection not only acquits Jesus of the charges against him, but also his killers, by virtue of the fact that he is not dead. Though he might seek retribution, he declines his right to because the new covenant speaks a better word that that of Abel (whose blood cried out for vengeance). See Markus Barth and Verne H. Fletcher, *Acquittal by Resurrection* (New York: Holt, Rinehart and Winston, 1964).

outdoing each other in love."[206] The mark of the converted life is community that no longer engages in mimetic rivalry nor imputes guilt on scapegoats to establish harmony. T. Scott Daniel proposes reconceiving Christian worship practices in ways that reflect an invalidationist framework. He links the waters of baptism to the primeval chaos of Gen 1:2 and reinterprets the sacrament as our identification with Christ-as-victim, one who is plunged into the *tohu vabohu* of mimetic rivalry and violence and is resurrected to new life.[207] Similarly, the Eucharist serves as the constant reminder of our communal culpability in Christ's death, and with Paul's warning in 1 Cor 11:29 to "discern the body," a call to remember that the unity of the body has not been achieved through scapegoating sacrifice but by collective identification with the one who ended it and joins us by grace.[208] In liturgical worship and daily living, cross-bearing within an invalidationist framework seeks to expose and end violence for the sake of universal reconciliation.

Evaluation

As this reformulation of atonement theory has much in common with the solidarity position, as well as employs the stress on nonviolence evident in J. Denny Weaver's narrative *Christus Victor*, it shares many of the same strengths and weaknesses seen in those perspectives with special emphasis on Jesus' death as carried out with the full agency of persecuting powers and not divine intention. The breadth of territory that the theory covers and its applicability to many facets of exegetical and theological inquiry makes it all the more compelling. Like the theories of helio-centrism or evolution, it potentially changes everything by explaining practically everything. The implication of mimetic scapegoating upon atonement theory gives substantial theoretical substance to what might be lacking in the general and vague notion of "empire" employed by solidarists (and Weaver, to some degree). It allows what is regarded as humanity's root problem to run deeper and in a more complex way than the power politics of strong regimes. Invalidationists argue that mimetic scapegoating is fundamental to human culture, especially as reflected in religion. The narrative construal of this theory and the way it is used a lens to read and tie together the Bible is impressive and very much in line with my own aspiration for this study.

A detailed critique of Girard's theory is not within my scope here, and, in fact, such a comprehensive theory that runs the entire length of human

---

206. Ibid., 245.
207. Daniels, "Passing the Peace," 139.
208. Ibid., 140.

history and is hidden behind every human motive is very difficult to prove or disprove.[209] The most significant issue that this theory touches in light of the present study asks how God is involved in the death of Christ. In greater measure than most of the other options already surveyed, Girardian invalidation most strongly insists on the impossibility of divine involvement in Christ's death by asserting the opposite: scapegoating sacrifice is the *devil's lie*, which divine intention and the entire outworking of biblical religion works to radically oppose. Stephen Finlan understands this well: "We cannot say that sacrificial violence is illegitimate and also have God taking part in a sacrificial murder."[210] In the end, however, Jesus does fall prey to the system and is killed by it. While it is argued repeatedly that his particular death exposes and dismantles the mechanism and that resurrection is the key redemptive element, this does not negate the idea of redemptive death; very ironically, it establishes it. Jesus by willingly participating in this evil system changes human history at a fundamental level and ushers in a new reality. The fact that cannot be denied is that Jesus' violent death is *essential* to achieving this result. All proposals of this theory as applied to the atonement recognize the *benefit* that the crucifixion brings. It is inconceivable that Jesus' death, therefore, can be labeled as anything other than "redemptive."

If Scripture supposedly moves in a trajectory that foresees the abandonment of redemptive sacrifice, as invalidationist theologians are wont to prove, then what, if not the divine will, is moving this redemptive intention along? Girardians, like Heim and Schwager, affirm that God uses the occasion of Jesus' death to expose the myth of scapegoating while simultaneously attempting to pit the blame solely on mythic systems etched in human culture. One cannot have it both ways. Either the disavowal is foreseen in Scripture and finally executed in the cross by way of divine intention, or the event is an accidental fluke for which God can claim no credit and offer no hope of ultimate success.

Conclusion

In this chapter, I have attempted to articulate the traditional Protestant doctrine of the atonement along with recent critiques by theologians opposed to any model that views the violent death of Christ as something initiated by or satisfying to God. In an effort to avoid the problem of divine and human complicity in violence and/or redemptive sacrifice, alternative models have

---

209. See also Stephen Finlan's critique that the theory is too simplistic and reductionistic. Finlan, *Problems With Atonement*, 91–92.

210. Ibid., 95.

been proposed that modify, challenge, or abandon notions of divine satisfaction *via* the violent death of Christ. In categorizing the options in terms their view of the cross I have employed the taxonomical domains of duality, solidarity, and invalidation. Dualists seek to recover the idea of God's struggle against evil forces; solidarists emphasize Jesus' identification with victims; and invalidationists renounce the myth of redemptive sacrifice. Seen from a broader, historico-theological perspective, it could be said that the burden to discard violence-dependent models have compelled theologians to retreat in the direction of one of the other historic models—devil's ransom and moral influence. Indeed, even Heim from an invalidationist perspective concludes: "An exemplarist view of the cross is the correct one: the effect of Jesus' death is the response it has inspired in Christians . . . it is only what people make of it, and has no intrinsic impact of its own."[211]

The flurry of recent activity in atonement theology points to an urgency to reformulate our understanding of the cross. Among the insights that can be drawn from these options for an adequate atonement model are the following: First, theologians of atonement find value in a narrative approach to understanding redemption that remains rooted in Scripture, in contrast to speculative and overly rationalistic philosophical categories that seem to be drifting out of vogue in contemporary theology. Second, in light of the push to absolve the violence of the cross as an act of divine abuse, there is a need to identify a clear and objective "enemy" for which Jesus' engagement in conflict is required. Third, recent theological emphases wish to highlight the reality and nature of victimization, both in the case of Jesus and victims in general. Fourth, there is a need to continue developing a robust theodicy that can accommodate the reality of violence, its limits, and the degree of acceptable divine involvement. Lastly, an effective atonement theology must establish an integrative path that relates Jesus' life, death, and resurrection with the believer's discipleship without falling into Pelagianism.[212]

The difficulty with reworking atonement theology is its close relation to most—if not all—other doctrines within a given tradition.[213] As much as

---

211. Heim, *Saved from Sacrifice*, 261.

212. This charge is in fact anticipated by those who tend toward a subjective view. For example, Stephen Finlan writes: "It is false humility to condemn the notion of immediate access to God as being insufficiently dependent upon the grace of God. On the contrary, those who use 'Pelagian' as a bludgeon against the pure in heart have obscured and blocked the grace of God by hedging salvation about with doctrinal complexities and clerical authority," Finlan, *Problems With Atonement*, 111.

213. In the case of Anselmic models adopted by confessional Protestants and evangelicals, revulsion to the alleged violence inherent in those systems are often believed to be the result of caricaturing the tradition, as in Hans Boersma, "Response to J. Denny Weaver," in *Atonement and Violence: A Theological Conversation*, ed. John Sanders

possible, the center of the debate needs to be the degree to which a theology or theological tradition is able to respond adequately to the question of redemptive violence while maintaining the integrity and coherence of its thesis. The centuries-long debates concerning issues like evil, predestination, and final judgment (while important and will be addressed where relevant to this study) need not distract us too much from tackling the problem in question. Total doctrinal unity is unlikely. However, as it stands, I believe atonement theologians on all sides of the debate can submit to a minimal standard of shared conviction, namely, the violence Jesus experienced on the cross was an historic reality, which has redemptive value, and which involves God *to some degree*. With this level of common ground secured, we can better clarify our understanding of the cross.

(Nashville: Abingdon, 2006), 35, or failing to plumb the depths of the traditions to see how they have responded to criticisms in ways they believe is satisfactory. See Steve Jeffery, Michael Ovey, and Andrew Sach, *Pierced for Our Transgressions: Rediscovering the Glory of Penal Substitution* (Wheaton: Crossway, 2007); Charles E. Hill and Frank A. James III, eds., *The Glory of the Atonement: Biblical, Theological & Practical Perspectives* (Downers Grove: IVP, 2004).

3.

Film as Theological Resource

Survey of Theological Approaches to Film

Introduction

IF THEOLOGY IS IN need of new vocabularies for dealing with violence, cinema may have something to offer. History attests to some level of religious interaction with film. With film's rise as a new technology in the early twentieth century, the church's responses were that of excitement for the evangelistic and instructive potential of the new medium, as well as ethical concerns over the quickly expanding subject matter to which people were exposed.[1] It is not until the late 1960s and 1970s that serious theological engagement with the cinema ensued with what Cooper and Skrade (in their 1970 work, *Celluloid and Symbols*) considered as a basis for "a fruitful dialogue between the church and the world."[2] Publishing that same year, Neil Hurley argued that "film as much as theology can lead to 'transcredal' affirmations of religious truth."[3]

Contemporary leading scholars in the field have suggested frameworks for sorting out Christianity's response to film largely based on the cultural typologies of H. Richard Niebuhr and Paul Tillich. Chris Deacy adopts Niebuhr's classic five-fold typology[4] to categorize various theologians of film and the movies that tend to garner the most attention within

---

1. For a detailed historical account of development along these lines, see John Lyden, ed., *The Routledge Companion to Religion and Film* (London ; New York: Routledge, 2009), 11–86.

2. John C. Cooper and Carl Skrade, eds., *Celluloid and Symbols* (Philadelphia: Fortress, 1970), 17–20. Quoted in Brant, 18.

3. Neil Hurley, *Theology Through Film* (London: Harper & Row, 1970), ix, 8, and 13. Quoted in Brant, 18.

4. H. Richard Niebuhr, *Christ and Culture* (San Francisco: Harper & Row, 1975).

the respective approaches.⁵ Clive Marsh views the extreme ends of "Christ Against Culture" (deliberate opposition) and "Christ of Culture" (reducing theology to culture) as largely unprofitable for the theological enterprise. Rather, he favors a third option—theology and film "in dialog: existing in a critical, dialectical relationship"⁶ with theology maintaining a normative upper hand. Robert K. Johnston, acknowledging his parallel with Niebuhr, casts new categories of "Avoidance," "Caution," "Dialogue," "Appropriation," and "Divine Encounter" with theology's specific engagement with film in mind. Drawing on Tillich's discussion of "heteronomy," "autonomy," and "theonomy,"⁷ Roman Catholic scholar, John May, likewise develops a five-fold typology that almost exactly approximates Johnston's categories.⁸ While all of five domains are acknowledged as relevant to the larger field of film criticism in the humanities, most theological approaches hover within the vicinity of "Dialogue," "Appropriation," and "Divine Encounter."

Dialogue

For Johnston, the idea of "dialogue" stands at the nexus on a continuum between the ethical and the aesthetic on one axis, and film and theology on another. At this intersection, the narrative shape of theology intersects and interacts with our stories and God is heard.⁹ While he advises viewing films on their own terms and allowing them to set the agenda for meaning, "religious faith demands that film viewing be completed from a theological

5. Christopher Deacy and Gaye Williams Ortiz, *Theology and Film: Challenging the Sacred/Secular Divide* (Malden, MA ; Oxford: Wiley-Blackwell, 2008), 26–65. Deacy acknowledges that the differences can be subtle, resulting in much overlap among the approaches. This is partially due to Niebuhr's own definitions of terms as well as the fact that approaches may vary depending on the films chosen and the audiences addressed (p. 65–6).

6. Clive Marsh and Gaye Ortiz, eds., *Explorations in Theology and Film: An Introduction* (Malden, Mass: Wiley-Blackwell, 1997), 27. Marsh also gives criticisms of Tillich and finds his method of correlation not adequately conversant with the arts, too univocal in its reading of culture, and too focused on "high art." He amends "correlation" with a theology of "negotiation" instead.

7. Paul Tillich, *What Is Religion?*, trans. James Luther Adams (New York: Harper & Row, 1969).

8. John R. May, ed., *New Image of Religious Film* (Kansas City, MO: Sheed & Ward, 1997), 17–37.

9. Robert K. Johnston, *Reel Spirituality: Theology and Film in Dialogue*, 2nd edition (Grand Rapid: Baker, 2006), 82–6. Johnston also suggests that the categories can roughly be distributed according to era as well as denominational affiliation. See Robert K. Johnston, "Theological Approaches," in John Lyden, ed., *The Routledge Companion to Religion and Film* (London; New York: Routledge, 2009), 314.

perspective."[10] Rather than imposing an outside perspective on movies, the theologian recognizes the religious themes and elements within movies that invite a theological response.[11] One version of this approach involves employing films to illustrate traditional theology as enshrined in the Apostles' Creed, for example,[12] or laying them alongside the church lectionary to promote spiritual growth.[13] Giving more consideration to movies themselves, it can also take the form of noting provocative cinematic elements that prompt theological reflection or discerning the worldview that certain films promote.[14] Key to the methodology inherent in such exercises is that of comparison and contrast, which comes out most clearly in works dealing with films that feature Jesus Christ (or Christ figures more metaphorically).[15]

Some scholars have undertaken to orient the dialogue toward biblical hermeneutics and inter-textual readings of Scripture. Robert Jewett invites movies into an "interpretive arch" that helps to understand contemporary American culture,[16] while in another book, he uses them draw out deeper truths concerning the theme of shame within Paul's theology, which he believes mainstream theologians might not yet have penetrated.[17] Larry Kreitzer productively applies film insights to biblical studies in four separate volumes.[18] In what he terms "reversing the hermeneutical flow," he argues

10. Johnston, *Reel Spirituality*, 64.

11. Ibid., 65.

12. See, David S. Cunningham, *Reading Is Believing: The Christian Faith Through Literature and Film* (Grand Rapids: Brazos, 2002); John May, *Nourishing Faith Through Fiction: Reflections of the Apostles' Creed in Literature and Film* (Franklin, WI: Sheed & Ward, 2001); Bryan P. Stone, *Faith and Film: Theological Themes at the Cinema* (St. Louis: Chalice, 2000).

13. Peter Malone and Rose Pacatte, *Lights, Camera, Faith: A Movie Lectionary Guide to Scripture* (Boston, MA: Pauline Books & Media, 2003).

14. For example, Roy M. Anker, *Catching Light: Looking for God in the Movies* (Grand Rapids: Eerdmans, 2004); Brian Godawa, *Hollywood Worldviews: Watching Films with Wisdom & Discernment*, Updated and Expanded edition (Downers Grove: IVP, 2009).

15. For example, Peter Malone, *Screen Jesus: Portrayals of Christ in Television and Film* (Lanham, MD: Scarecrow, 2012); Lloyd Baugh S.J, *Imaging the Divine: Jesus and Christ–Figures in Film* (Kansas City, MO: Sheed & Ward, 1997); and Thomas Robin Riley, *Film, Faith, and Cultural Conflict: The Case of Martin Scorsese's The Last Temptation of Christ* (Westport, CT: Praeger, 2003).

16. Robert Jewett, *Saint Paul at the Movies: The Apostle's Dialogue with American Culture* (Louisville: Westminster/John Knox Press, 1993).

17. Robert Jewett, *Saint Paul Returns to the Movies: Triumph over Shame* (Grand Rapids: Eerdmans, 1998), 20.

18. Larry J. Kreitzer, *The New Testament in Fiction and Film: On Reversing the Hermeneutical Flow* (Sheffield, UK: Sheffield Academic Press, 1993); *The Old Testament*

for film's use as a lens to interpret biblical material. The same expression is employed by Craig Detweiler and Barry Taylor in *A Matrix of Meanings: Finding God in Pop Culture,*[19] but much more enthusiastically in favor of popular culture's potential to disclose (and perhaps add to?) special revelation. Johnston employs a more nuanced, bi-directional dialogue, using films like *American Beauty* (1999) and *Magnolia* (1999) to illuminate the book of Ecclesiastes and for the text to illuminate the films.[20] Leaning towards a more critical/cautious approach, Bernard Scott's *Hollywood Dreams and Biblical Stories*[21] analyzes popular films as examples of American mythology. By "unmasking" the hidden (but influential) myths within movies and placing them in "conversation" with Biblical narratives and themes, Scott attempts to reveal how Scripture might speak subversively to contemporary American culture.

Appropriation

Akin to Niebuhr's "Christ Above Culture" paradigm, this mode of theological film criticism understands human nature as incomplete and in need of greater insight into our experience and destiny, which comes through grace as synthetically mediated through culture.[22] The attraction of this program particularly among Roman Catholic scholars is noticeable, for in line with the synthetic theology of Thomas Aquinas, it does not submit a strong distinction between religious and secular. Rather, because the "universal spark of the divine"[23] pervades all of life, the narratives provided in movies move the emotions and broaden our understanding, making film watching a kind of "exercise in spirituality"[24] in which people find their true center and are

---

in Fiction and Film: On Reversing the Hermeneutical Flow (Sheffield, UK: Sheffield Academic Press, 1994); *Pauline Images in Fiction and Film: On Reversing the Hermeneutical Flow*, (Sheffield, UK: Bloomsbury T&T Clark, 1999); *Gospel Images in Fiction and Film: On Reversing the Hermeneutical Flow*, (London; New York: Bloomsbury T&T Clark, 2002).

19. Craig Detweiler and Barry Taylor, *A Matrix of Meanings: Finding God in Pop Culture* (Grand Rapids: Baker, 2003).

20. Robert K. Johnston, *Useless Beauty: Ecclesiastes through the Lens of Contemporary Film* (Eugene, OR: Wipf & Stock, 2011).

21. Bernard Brandon Scott, *Hollywood Dreams and Biblical Stories* (Minneapolis: Fortress, 2000).

22. Deacy and Ortiz, *Theology and Film*, 40–41.

23. Neil P. Hurley, *Theology Through Film*, 3.

24. Clive Marsh, *Cinema and Sentiment: Film's Challenge to Theology* (Eugene, OR: Wipf & Stock, 2014), 34.

transformed in the process.²⁵ Also included within this general domain are scholars who interpret films as embodying myths,²⁶ the manifesting of religion through stories "that provide human communities with grounding prototypes, models for life, reports of foundational realities, and dramatic presentations of fundamental values."²⁷ By enabling people to "mythologize their lives," myths provide a coherent narrative that brings meaning and purpose to their daily struggles, as religion aims to do.²⁸

Doing theology within this vein means being open to broader definitions of the "spiritual," which include introspective journeys of self-discovery, and having a high regard for the material order and its capacity to point to, and mediate, the holy. It calls on theologians to discern "religious influences in film that may lurk so far beneath the surface that they are not even detected on a conscious level by the filmmakers themselves."²⁹ Rather than read religion *into* the films, "religious interpretation fulfills and completes the secular cry of pain and suffering" evoked in films regardless of the religious affiliation of its creator(s).³⁰ The humanistic bent is worth highlighting here. Antonio D. Sison, in his *World Cinema, Theology, and the Human*, views his film reflections as theological insomuch as it is an "apophatic rather than a kataphatic quest for God."³¹ "God," he writes, "who is ineffable holy mystery, is known through the refracted light of the human who is *imago dei*. Our project then is to look for the divine presence written not on tablets of stone, but the 'tablets of human hearts' depicted on the screen."³² Sison writes, "It is indeed the human that is the royal road to God."³³

---

25. Johnston, *Reel Spirituality*, 72. Johnston, for example, reports scores of people (including his own students) seeking reconciliation with estranged family members after screenings of *Field of Dreams* (1989) and *Life as a House* (2001), the plots of which narrate near-missed opportunities to mend broken relationships (pg. 70–71).

26. For example, John C. Lyden, *Film as Religion: Myths, Morals, and Rituals* (New York: NYU Press, 2003); Joel Martin, *Screening The Sacred: Religion, Myth, And Ideology In Popular American Film*, ed. Conrad E. Ostwalt Jr. (Boulder: Westview Press, 1995).

27. Martin, *Screening The Sacred*, 6.

28. Ibid., 71.

29. Deacy and Ortiz, *Theology and Film*, 46.

30. Lyden, *Film as Religion*, 23.

31. Antonio Sison, *World Cinema, Theology, and the Human: Humanity in Deep Focus* (New York: Routledge, 2012), 6.

32. Ibid.

33. Ibid., 8.

Divine encounter

More recently, some scholars echo the approach of theological aesthetics, arguing for the possibility of the film experience as *inherently* religious in the sense of being a locus for substantive revelation.[34] John C. Lyden goes so far as to argue that film deserves a place alongside religion as a cultural expression and for religion-film dialogue to be regarded as interreligious dialogue.[35] Personal "testimonies" of "transcendent moments" while watching movies are not uncommon among film theologians of this ilk. Craig Detweiler devotes an entire book on a receptor-oriented study based on the comments of Internet Movie Database (IMDB) users, who reported divine communication taking place in and through the top 250 films of 2007.[36] Catholic writer, Andrew Greeley, interprets the phenomenon in terms of sacramental theology: "The pure, raw power of the film to capture the person who watches it, both by its vividness and by the tremendous power of the camera to concentrate and change perspectives, is a sacramental potential that is hard for other art forms to match."[37]

Though much of the writing in contemporary film-theology touches this experiential element on some level, they tend to be anecdotal in nature. Perhaps the best recent attempt to answer the *what* and *how* of cinematic transcendent moments is in Jonathan Brant's work, *Paul Tillich and the Possibility of Revelation Through Film*,[38] which insists upon and employs empirical research methodology to quantify actual audience accounts of religiously impacting film-watching experiences. Some trained practitioners have taken strides to analyze the actual cinematic elements of certain films that give rise moments of divine encounter. In *Images of the Passion: the Sacramental Mode in Film*,[39] Peter Fraser analyzes films where divine presence breaks into the physicality of the film narrative and redeems it in a fashion analogous

---

34. With some overlap with the previous approach of "appropriation," the distinctiveness of this line of theological reflection involves experiences of a more intense magnitude and/or those with a characteristically Christian slant.

35. John C. Lyden, *Film as Religion: Myths, Morals, and Rituals* (New York: NYU Press, 2003).

36. Craig Detweiler, *Into the Dark: Seeing the Sacred in the Top Films of the 21st Century* (Grand Rapids: Baker, 2008). Note, Detweiler categorizes the experiences of communication in terms of "general revelation."

37. Andrew Greeley, *God in Popular Culture* (Chicago: Thomas More, 1988), 250. Quoted in Johnston, *Spirituality*, 75.

38. Jonathan Brant, *Paul Tillich and the Possibility of Revelation through Film* (Oxford ; New York: Oxford University Press, 2012).

39. Peter Fraser, *Images of the Passion: The Sacramental Mode in Film* (Westport, CT: Praeger, 1998).

to Christian liturgy and piety. Accomplished film director and screenwriter, Paul Schrader, identifies what he calls a "transcendental style,"[40] a system of slow and drawn-out camera work and prolonged silence, together with a narrative arc that moves from banality to a climactic moment of transcendence. Implicit in his cross-cultural selection of directors to study is the idea that this "style" is common and universally recognized.

Critical issues in methodology

With the terrain roughly mapped for where theology's engagement with film generally finds itself in the contemporary scene, I will now highlight in greater detail two pertinent methodological issues that have been the subject of concern and debate.

The nature of "dialogue"

For theologians to interact with film as a potential resource, the phraseology of "dialogue" can be construed as vague, or worse, dishonest. Gerard Loughlin, rather bluntly, states that "except when discourses on theology and film are reports of actual conversations between film-makers and theologians, such dialogues are nearly always *acts of ventriloquism*, since film itself is a cultural product about which we may talk, but which is not itself a conversing partner."[41] His point is well taken. It is true that worldviews and opinions can inhere in movies such that it seems to be making a statement, but ultimately viewers, critics, and theologians are the ones who must discern it to be so through methods of interpretation. With the net spread so wide as to possible approaches and differences in terminology, along with the relative lack of training in film criticism among theologians, it is not surprising that confusion ensues over what constitutes a valuable dialogue with film. Melanie J. Wright incisively warns against film-religion dialogue becoming an isolated intellectual exercise in which the resonance between films and religious texts exist only subjectively in the interpreter's mind and bears no connection to the actual experience of the average movie-watcher.[42] The fear of "ventriloquism" is mainly that theologians may conveniently find

---

40. Paul Schrader, *Transcendental Style In Film* (New York: Da Capo Press, 1988).

41. Gerard Loughlin, "A Theological Introduction," in Eric S. Christianson, Peter Francis, and William R. Telford, eds., *Cinéma Divinité: Religion, Theology and the Bible in Film* (London: SCM, 2005), 5. Emphasis mine.

42. Melanie J. Wright, *Religion and Film: An Introduction* (London; New York: I. B. Tauris, 2006), 20.

what their already looking for, narratives or cinematic elements that confirm their religious convictions, rather than "listening" to a film on its own terms. The insistence that theologians not impose dogmatic categories into their reading of films so as to "baptize" them as Christian is so well attested that it has almost become cliché.

In order to maintain some credibility among academicians of film, theologians are desperate to find neutral ground on which to base their work. Clive Marsh, in debating with John Lyden on religious approaches to film, is pessimistic of the possibility of such neutrality and views it as a weakness in the overall endeavor. Rather than adopting a religious studies approach that tones down specific ideological agendas and posits some general sense of the "spiritual," he argues for a more explicitly theological framework wherein interpreters are more consciously aware of the "religious particularity" of the traditions from which they operate.[43] He suggests that the dialogue work "from within a single—but diverse—tradition which the interpreter knows well, in all its complex diversity," and "examined at the point at which they interact with the commended or critiqued ideologies of the films being interpreted."[44]

A truly critical and correlational dialogue, according to Gordon Lynch, is one "in which the implicit answers to contemporary struggles offered within popular culture are also treated seriously as a resource for thinking about issues of meaning and value."[45] We must be open to the possibility that film may "require us to challenge or revise ideas and practices that have been an established part of traditional religion.[46] The risk involved in such a *modus operandi* is immediately obvious: the theologian must brace herself for criticisms against her own theological position if she operates from within the framework of her religious presuppositions. But the upshot is that the potency of film as a "voice" in the conversation is bolstered if the alternative it presents to our views persuades change. Difficult though this path may be, Marsh is confident that dialogue at this level should yield "maximum theological creativity."[47]

---

43. Clive Marsh, "Religion, Theology and Film in a Postmodern Age: A Response to John C. Lyden," *Journal of Religion and Film* 2, no. 1 (1998), http://www.unomaha.edu/jrf/marshrel.htm.

44. Ibid.

45. Gordon Lynch, *Understanding Theology and Popular Culture* (Malden, MA: Wiley-Blackwell, 2005), 104.

46. Ibid.

47. Marsh, "Religion, Theology and Film in a Postmodern Age: A Response to John C. Lyden."

Film analysis

After a proliferation of film-related works by theologians and exegetes in the 1990s, critique ensued that has shifted the focus to films themselves. Jonathan Brant helpfully summarizes the criticism launched by those who call for a more serious study of film "*qua* film."[48] First, current theological discourse has become too literary and focused on the story plot of films rather than the fundamental elements of actual filmmaking; second, theological baggage is being "smuggled" in and read onto film texts; third, there is lack of responsible and engaging film selection; and fourth, the result is the lack of true interdisciplinarity and dialogue. With such being the case in current film-theology discourse, Melanie Wright wonders if film is actually being studied *at all*.[49] She chides the current practice of giving only brief lip service to the language and process of film production and the vast ignorance of most film theologians to the discipline of film studies in general.[50]

Wright proposes that religion-and-film specialists adopt an interdisciplinary cultural studies approach to study where rather than over-emphasizing films as narrative "texts," more coverage is lent to style, cultural and religious context, and audience reception.[51]

> A willingness to take on board findings and perceptions from those working in a variety of fields means that cultural studies is integrative the range of strategies used by specialist film critics. That same openness allows for conversation with the particular specialist knowledges [sic] and methodologies that practitioners of religious studies (and theology) can bring to film.[52]

The renewed interest in film *qua* film should be viewed in tandem with the trend (especially among evangelicals) to highlight the aesthetic dimension in the arts in general, and film in particular. Brant's attempt to empirically ground Tillich's theory of revelation through culture is indicative of this shift. Proponents of a multi-dimensional, multi-perspectival cultural studies methodology seek after the essence of a film's greatness as objectively as possible. They are quick to point out that some readings of a specific may give rise to varying, sometimes starkly opposing, interpretations, which are likely due to a viewer's theological hermeneutic.[53] But the concerns, valuable though they

---

48. Brant, *Tillich*, 23.
49. Wright, *Religion and Film*, 22.
50. Ibid., 23.
51. Ibid., 29.
52. Ibid., 30.
53. For example, Brant, *Paul Tillich and the Possibility of Revelation through Film*,

may be for promoting more rigorous analysis of films and their public impact, seem to have particular validity within a divine encounter type of approach. If it is assumed that a movie is mediating transcendental experiences, it is natural for a full-scale "investigation" of the production and reception of a film to ensue. The push for greater care in listening to films, however, need not stifle nor set the agenda for religious film criticism that has a uniquely theological purpose or serves a particular confessional tradition. Clive Marsh's argument concerning the role of a theologian's particular perspective and its warranted use in genuine dialogue, therefore, is a welcomed balance to the insistence on studying film *qua* film.

A methodological agenda for cinematic theology

In making a case for a cinematic approach that aims to aid systematic theology in working out dogmatic concerns with fresh perspective and vocabulary, we do well to ask: Does Scripture itself allow fiction and imagination, of which cinema operates with dominance, to supplement interpretation? On the matter of retribution that pertains to the focus of this book, I believe the answer is yes. The parable of the wicked tenants in the synoptic Gospels (Matt. 21:33–46; Mark 12:1–12; Luke 20:9–19), tells the story of a landowner, whose hired servants repeatedly abuse and evict those sent to inspect the business. Jesus closes off his description of the tenants' evil deed of killing of the landowner's son with a question: "Now when the owner of the vineyard comes, what will he do to those tenants?" (Matt 21:40). It is clear that the story is framed so as to have the hearers identify with the landowner by retaining the "who among you" formula that called for a judgment on the part of the hearers.[54] The audience is meant to assent to a natural conclusion, of which Jesus approves; but nonetheless, a "performative function" is employed wherein the hearers are invited to give their own ending to the story. R.T. France suggests that the fact of the story's symbolic quality may have even emboldened the hearers to prescribe a "high-handed," vigilante-style justice, rather than suggest recourse to the courts, as per the socioeconomic reality of that time.[55]

36, where he observes Anker and Christianson making conflicting conclusions regarding the role of violence in the Godfather films.

54. Dan O. Via, *The Parables: Their Literary and Existential Dimension* (Eugene, OR: Wipf & Stock, 2007), 53.

55. R. T. France, *The Gospel of Matthew*, New International Commentary on the New Testament (Grand Rapids: Eerdmans, 2007), 814 n 29.

Interestingly, Jesus' ending in Mark and Luke, compared with that of his listeners' in Matthew, reveals that the latter is more evocative and detailed in its description. Mark and Luke record Jesus as merely saying that the owner will "come and destroy (*apolesei*)" the tenants and "give the vineyard to others" (Mark 12:9, Luke 20:16) whereas the chief priests and elders respond, "He will put those wretches to a miserable death (*kakous kakōs apolesei*), and lease the vineyard to other tenants who will give him the produce at the harvest time" (Matt. 21:41). The colorful literary enhancements of "wretches" dying a "miserable" death[56] suggest an underlying emotional reaction that Jesus in no way dismisses. For France, "Matthew's vivid double addition of 'bad' emphasizes that the punishment fits the crime.[57] In fact, he may have deliberately attempted to elicit such a response,[58] in the same way that Nathan's parable of the stolen lamb prompted David's anger to be "greatly kindled against the man" in the story (2 Sam 12:5), leading to Nathan's justified and direct accusation and David's subsequent repentance.

Might not the opening up of a parable's narrative to the dictates of the hearer's emotion and imagination offer the possibility of mutually enhancing and understanding stories that are congruent with each other? We must be wary, however, lest enthusiasm over the possibility for cinema to play a role in hermeneutics becomes another occasion for idiosyncratic interpretation. I propose some guardrails for a methodology that I believe are found within the narratives and cinematic medium themselves.

First, analyses must be focused on the concrete, surface-level features (i.e. setting, action sequences, character depictions, etc.) and general plot of a wide selection of films so as to safely conclude that these films *intend* a message and response that are encoded in an obvious manner. When laid alongside a biblical story of revenge, the physical aspects, styles of speech, and personal motivations and methods will reveal their own functions and can be aligned with its cinematic analogue and vice versa. Furthermore, if it is true that the narrative of vengeance is universally recognized (and regularly practiced!) by human beings, whether through repeated exposure in cultural myth or the "emplotment" of our own life experiences, then the human subject becomes an invaluable interpreter of the narrative. While it does not eliminate the possibility of "variant readings," the emphasis on

---

56. Or, as Luz translates, "viciously destroy the vicious men," in Luz, *Matthew 21–28*, 34.

57. France, *The Gospel of Matthew*, 814.

58. Warren Carter, *Matthew and the Margins: A Socio-Political and Religious Reading* (London: T&T Clark, 2004), 428. He argues that the words of the priests and elders are meant to be self-condemning, in which they predict their own destruction at the hands of Rome in 70 CE.

surface-level details as they are presented in patterned sequences greatly reduces the need to make creative, metaphorical associations that are foreign to the scene in question.

Second, some of the predictability of these ideas lay in the fact that films across a genre display stable patterns of style that work to "sediment" (to borrow from Ricoeur) myths we tend to rehearse. Genre operates according to cultural conventions and functions as a "style-guide" that constrains interpretation.[59] The audience's expectation of certain outcomes produces a communally dependent means of mediating—in many ways, *dictating*—how films are read.[60] Thomas Sobchack puts it simply: "In the genre film the plot is fixed, the characters defined, the ending satisfyingly predictable."[61] Film within the revenge genre present us with a "closed world," whose plots, characters, and settings are unrealistic and do not reflect how events unfold in our real world.[62]

This lack of realism might seem alarming and counterintuitive to the theological task, but it offers the benefit of alleviating the need for the audience to make cognitive, emotional, or moral judgments; in fact, "the genre makes them for us."[63] Sobchack argues that moral problems are the result of ambiguity, placing us in a "muddle."

> We know things aren't quite right, but we are not sure if it is a conspiracy among corporations, the world situation, politicians, our neighbors down the street, our boss, our spouse; but whatever it is, we can't call it out of the saloon for a shoot-out or round up villagers and hunt it down.[64]

"Genre characters," on the other hand, "inhabit a world that is better than ours, a world in which problems can be solved directly, emotionally, in action."[65] Audiences naturally interpret and applaud the consistency and determination of such one-dimensional characters as moral virtues. In

---

59. Michael Goldberg, *Theology and Narrative: A Critical Introduction* (Philadelphia: Trinity Press International, 1991), 203.

60. Andrew Tudor, "Genre," in Barry Keith Grant, ed., *Film Genre Reader III* (Austin: University of Texas Press, 2003), 8.

61. Thomas Sobchack, "Genre Film: A Classical Experience," in Grant, *Film Genre Reader III*, 103.

62. Recall, however, that some effort has been made to affirm some level of truth-value in generic forms of art. Aristotle considered Greek drama as a *mimesis* of human action. John Lyden, in *Film as Religion*, and Martin and Oswalt, in *Screening the Sacred*, employ the idea of myth to relate films with authentic religious experience.

63. Knight, "Making Sense of Genre."

64. Sobchack, 109.

65. Ibid.

truth, when viewed alongside biblical stories of revenge, the narratives are not as far-fetched after all. Readers of the Bible can immediately bring to mind instances where characters and plots display an uncanny resemblance to those who supposedly inhabit the "utopian" worlds of genre films. At any rate, the moral judgments that recognize a villain's act as heinous and a hero's act as just are built into the film (and biblical text) in unambiguous ways[66] and provide an apologetic to the ethics of employing this particular genre for theology.

As for method in cinematic theologizing, I submit that comparing scenes with remarkable congruity offers two positive effects. First, where features are similar with each other (resonance), they tend to affirm one another's logic as generally universal. For example, if an offense elicits anger in both mediums, it becomes easier to recognize and accept that this is a reasonable and natural response. Second, and more significantly, where features in one text differ from its counterpart (dissonance), there is an intensification of the internal logic of a given medium that calls for justification. Keeping mind that the stories are "essentially" congruent, moments of dissonance becomes fertile ground for genuine dialogue and discovery as new narrative logics are revealed.

My approach to theology in this study assumes the normative role of Scripture as the authoritative source for grounding doctrine while employing cinema as a hermeneutical lens and exegetical resource that help to draw scenes into a narrative logic, fill narrative gaps, form new connections, and propose new interpretive paths. Biblical motifs of divine retribution are numerous, and on their own, may only convey one aspect, which often results in a questionable view of God. If it can be shown that cinematic portrayals of retribution/rescue accords congruently with biblical motifs of the same theme, and if those motifs are components of a narrative that runs through Scripture, then we can establish a potential for cinema to supplement and structure a re-telling of divine violence as a conceptual analogue to atonement.

While it is certainly conceivable that what a film "reveals" may be expressions of ultimate reality that can be palpably experienced in a moment of transcendence," I make no push for films as a site for revelatory encounter in the Tillichian mode; my search is for obvious resonances with human experience rather than divine presence. In this way, then, my method adopts the aims of dialogue rather than appropriation or encounter with the hope that elements found within individual movies as well as across a genre should also help to temper the possibility of a private, idiosyncratic

---

66. Knight, "Making Sense of Genre."

interpretation. Loughlin's modest proposal of a "cinematic theology" is a helpful summary of my approach, where he speaks of "that kind of looking that seeks to enter into the world of a film before speaking about it and then using film—the language of cinema—to speak theologically."[67]

---

67. Loughlin, *Cinéma Divinité*, 5.

4.

The Cinematics of Vengeance

IN THIS CHAPTER, I will begin to address specific elements within the revenge film genre that shapes a "hermeneutical lens" with which to approach Scripture and theology. For the purposes of this study, I have chosen three aspects of the cinematic process to guide our exploration of films within revenge-themed films: narrative, character, and spectatorship. Because a large part of my thesis involves demonstrating the ubiquity and stability of the story of revenge in cinema and Scripture, I will draw on a cross-section of several films that best serve as examples of the issue in question.

Narrative Elements in the Revenge Genre

The most basic, three-act framework of most popular films, constituting of the beginning, middle, and end, serves to structure the plot of most revenge films. The first act introduces the characters and establishes the bond or intimacy shared among protagonists and ends with the introduction of the problem. The second act is devoted to the hero's preparation and pursuit of the villain. The ending of the film features the final showdown and closes with a brief but meaningful epilogue.

The bond

The pairing of gritty, male gunman and sweet young girl comes up often in revenge films, and many opening sequences establish the strong bond they share. The opening credits of *Taken* (2008) feature grainy home video footage of an adorable little girl's birthday, replete with cake, hat, a gifted toy horse, a loving mother, and plenty of kisses and smiles. In the flash-forward to present day, our hero, Bryan Mills (Liam Neeson), purchases a karaoke machine to bring to his teenage daughter's birthday party. The love between Mills and his daughter, Kim (Maggie Grace), is obvious, as she runs and hugs him and takes a photo with him. The bond is further strengthened by the contrast we see in the relationship between Bryan and now-ex-wife, Lenore (Famke Jansen), with whom conversation has reduced to curt, rude remarks. He returns home and carefully places the photo in an album full of memorable moments with his daughter, including the birthday of the opening montage.

A husband's love for his wife is the feature of the American horror Western, *Bone Tomahawk* (2015), which, "flirts with horror but remains rooted in the physical frontier world and grounded in character."[1] In the small settlement town of Bright Hope, Samantha (Lili Simmons), the doctor and beloved wife of cowboy, Arthur O'Dwyer (Patrick Wilson), along with the Sherriff's deputy, are abducted at night by a group of cannibalistic cave dwellers (troglodytes), which sparks a rescue attempt by a band of gunslingers from the town. Writer/director, S. Craig Zahler, devotes much attention focusing on O'Dwyer's relationship with his wife through the care she gives him on account of his injured leg and a tenderly-written letter he wrote to her in the past. The rich development of the relationship between O'Dwyer, Sheriff Hunt (Kurt Russell), his backup deputy, Chicory (Richard Jenkins), and bounty hunter, Brooder, (Matthew Fox), though at times hostile, is one in which the audience becomes "invested" in their lives and genuinely cares for them, thus heightening the emotional element of the final showdown.[2]

In situations where the hero's beloved is not a principal cast member in the film, other elements are employed to signify the bond. The narrative time of *John Wick* (2014) takes places after the loss of hero's wife to illness, but artifacts such as a romantic video recording, jewelry given as an anniversary gift, and brief flashbacks of kisses and tender moments are sufficient to provide the backstory of John's (Keanu Reeves) love for his wife. As the introduction unfolds, we find that the wife has posthumously sent John a card and a puppy to remember her by. The puppy serves as surrogate to his absent beloved, and its death at the hand of thugs unleashes Wick's wrath. The ex-assassin's brief interaction with the helpless dog is awkward but adorable nonetheless. It humanizes him and puts the viewer "on his side." The opening of *Old Boy* (2003) employs a phone conversation between Dae-su

1. Sean Axmaker, "'Bone Tomahawk' on Amazon Prime," *Stream On Demand*, December 31, 2015, http://streamondemandathome.com/bone-tomahawk-on-amazon-prime/.

2. Brian Roan, Amanda Waltz, and Bill Graham, *Bone Tomahawk and Krampus*, The Film Stage Show, n.d., https://thefilmstage.com/features/the-film-stage-show-ep-167-bone-tomahawk-and-krampus/.

and his daughter on the eve of her birthday. Although the call is one-sided, his tenderness in talking with her is evident despite his drunken state. Also in the shot are the white angel wings he plans to give her as a gift, which become significant at the end of the film.

The bonding motif is particularly intense in protective-type revenge films where the hero's relationship with the beloved begins with indifference, or even disdain, and the bond is forged over time. In *Man on Fire* (2004), John Creasy (Denzel Washington), is a broken and tormented ex-CIA operative-turned-alcoholic, who takes up a job protecting a rich Mexican tycoon's daughter, Pita (Dakota Fanning), who is later abducted causing Creasy to go on his vengeful rampage. Initially, Creasy is cold and distant, telling her sharply that she is a job, not a friend. His misery leads him to attempt suicide only to find that his bullet is defective. He turns over a new leaf, stops drinking, reads his Bible, and starts training Pita for her upcoming swimming competition. The audience sees that Pita has affected him profoundly, as Creasy's old comrade, Rayburn (Christopher Walken) interprets it: "She showed him it was alright to live again." Of Fanning's portrayal of the nine year-old Pita, film reviewer, Todd McCarthy writes: "Fanning impresses here more than ever as a precocious but never overbearing dream child. Her readings and reactions are marvelously fresh and natural, without any child star "sell" behind her energetic enthusiasm."[3] In the 2010 Korean action thriller, *The Man from Nowhere*,[4] a young, neglected girl, So-mi (Kim Sae-ron), manages to elicit the compassion of the hero, Cha Tae-sik (Won Bin), a socially-blunted ex-intelligence operative who lost his pregnant wife in the aftermath of a recent mission.

In often uncomfortable but understandable ways, the bonding between hero and pre-pubescent damsel-in-distress sometimes touches on the romantic. We are given peeks into Pita's diary, where she writes of her love for her "Creasy Bear" and hopes he loves her too. In *Leon* (1994) a young girl from a troubled home, Mathilda (Natalie Portman), befriends her neighbor, a recluse hitman (Jean Reno), and requests him to train her to exact revenge on the corrupt detective who killed her little brother. At first, Leon rejects her completely and even aims a gun at her head while she sleeps. In time, her spunk and perseverance pays off and she becomes his beloved apprentice, who teaches him how to read while he teaches her how to "clean" (a euphemism for assassination). She becomes convinced that she loves him romantically and is not shy to confess her feelings. The

---

3. Todd McCarthy, "Review: 'Man on Fire,'" *Variety*, April 21, 2004, http://variety.com/2004/film/markets-festivals/man-on-fire-2-1200533909/.

4. Korean title, *Ajeossi*.

uncomfortable development of romantic feelings on the part of Mathilda "adds another complex layer onto what is already a strange relationship."[5] This romantic type of bond is seen in Clint Eastwood's classic 1985 western, *Pale Rider*, where the damsel, Megan Wheeler (Sydney Penny), attempts to convince "The Preacher" to make love to her on account that she is nearly fifteen years old. The Korean hit, *Old Boy* (2003) takes the idea to an extreme, where incest between Oh Dae-su and his grown-up daughter (unbeknownst to him until the end) is integral to the villain's vengeful plot against Dae-su. The image of him drying her hair after they had made love is in stark contrast to his general anti-social barbarism throughout most of the film. Although the two parties in these equations have almost nothing in common and contrast each other profoundly, they seem to need each other deeply and fulfill some void in each other's lives, even to the point that they become like one another through the course of their relationship: the killer softens up; the damsel toughens up.

The offense

The strong bond of affection having been established, the offense that incites the hero's wrath is portrayed as a clearly evil act. The most direct means is through an action sequence in real time, which usually occurs when the hero is physically absent or incapacitated. In *Taken*, Mills is on the phone with his daughter before and during her abduction by Albanian sex-traffickers. Two shaved-headed men clad in black enter and carry Kim's friend away as she looks on from a bathroom window in a panic. The brutal physicality of the abduction is accented by the use of hand-held camera work. Mills' instructions to Kim serve as a play-by-play commentary on the thugs' description, intentions, and actions. She hides under a bed, two men enter (with a point-of-view shot of their boots), and Mills tells her, "Now, the next part is very important. [Beat]. They are going to take you." She is to shout out any descriptions of the men within the few seconds it takes to subdue her. Believing that the thugs have left the room, she is momentarily relieved but is suddenly dragged out from under the bed in a rapid, Superman-style flight away from the camera with a blood-curdling scream. It cuts to Mills' face as he holds back tears, listening in focused horror at her frenzied shouts until there is nothing but silence. A similar breaking-and-entering offense takes place in *John Wick*, in which the title character is savagely ambushed

5. Jeff Beck, "Leon: The Professional: A Wonderful Character Study," *Examiner.com*, November 17, 2015, http://www.examiner.com/article/leon–the–professional–a–wonderful–character–study–blu–ray.

in his own home by hooded and masked Russian thugs and his beloved new beagle pup is clubbed to death in front of his eyes.

Perhaps one of the most protracted displays of the offense (and retribution) is depicted in the revenge horror, *I Spit on Your Grave* (2010).[6] In the story, a writer, seeking some peace and quiet to complete a novel, leases a cabin in the woods in rural America and is raped by a group of local rednecks. Nearly thirty full minutes is devoted to the taunting, assault, and vicious gang rape of the protagonist, Jennifer Hills (Sarah Butler), by four misfits and a crooked Sheriff. Each of the men add a "personal touch" to her extreme despair: Johnny (Jeff Branson) forces her to act like a horse and show him her teeth; Andy (Rodney Eastman) plunges her face into a filthy pond; Stanley (Daniel Franzese) captures her humiliation on video; and Sheriff Storch rapes her anally. A third, mentally disabled man named Matthew (Chad Lindberg) is caught in the middle and forced against his will to be the first to rape her. Throughout the entire ordeal, she is completely at their mercy, pleading for them to stop as they incessantly abuse her for sport. With the exception of Matthew, there is never any hint of remorse on the part of the villains, only juvenile laughter, unrelenting taunts, and violent brutality. The cinematography includes blurry point-of-view images capturing her dizzying torture. The actress employs a post-traumatic twitch to illustrate her character's shock as she walks away from the men naked before plunging herself into a river.

Some instances of the villain's evil deeds have less of a faced-paced, edge-of-your-seat quality, but other storytelling techniques are employed to help viewers sympathize with the hero's rage. In *13 Assassins* (2010), a small band of samurai led by Shinzaemon Shimada (Koji Yashuko) comes together to take down a cruel and murderous lord, Naritsugu (Goro Inagaki), an heir to a high political office. Here, the offense is reckoned in terms of Naritsugu's past evil exploits *and potential future ones*. The warriors' sheer love of country warrants the assassination mission. In *Old Boy*, Dae-su is imprisoned in a sealed hotel room for fifteen years for reasons unknown to him. He learns through television that his wife has been murdered and he is the prime suspect, and his captors rob the success of his many attempted suicides. Even upon release, he continues to be taunted and lured by a villain who remains anonymous through the entire first act. In the Japanese revenge film, *Sun Scarred* (2006),[7] the shot frames the villain, a young thug, Kamiki Akira (Satoshi Morimoto), walking hand in hand

---

6. This film is a remake of the 1978 film with the same name, and spawned sequels *I Spit on Your Grave 2* and *3* released in 2013 and 2015, respectively.

7. Japanese title, *Taiyo no kizu*, directed by acclaimed thriller/horror director, Takashi Miike.

toward the camera with the daughter of the protagonist, Katayama (Sho Aikawa), after luring her away from her mother with an ice cream cone. In the following mid-shot, she is lying dead in an abandoned yard, much of her body shrouded behind bushes and shrubs. In almost all films, brutal violence against children is only implied, not screened. *Lady Vengeance* (2005)[8] depicts paedocide primarily through the horrified reactions of the parents, when the title character, Geum-ja (Lee Yeong-ae), shows video footage of their child's final moments before Mr. Baek (Choi Min-sik) kills them. Through a montage of close-ups and slow-motion action, we are given a portrait of extreme emotional distress through their weeping, vomiting, and fainting from shock.

The Coen brothers employ voice-over verbal descriptions to paint the picture of the villain's deed in *True Grit* (2010), where a plucky teenage girl,"[9] Mattie Ross (Hailee Steinfeld), describes throughout the film how the villain, Tom Chaney (Josh Brolin), killed her father and stole his horse. Although we see nothing of this historic event (except for a slow mid-shot zoom on a body outside of a saloon in the opening credits), her incessant re-telling of the wrong done to her establishes her as the "controller of her own narrative,"[10] and subsequently, controller of how we should assess Chaney (whom we do not meet until the final act) and "what he done." The characteristic verbosity and narrative style of westerns as adventure films leaves more to the imagination in terms of the harm done. *Bone Tomahawk* depicts the offense on multiple levels. One involves the abduction of Arthur O'Dwyer's wife by the savage cave dwellers, which occurs off screen but nonetheless begins the protagonists' protective manhunt. Nearing the end of the film, the protagonists witness the savage murder of the Sheriff's deputy in which he is scalped and butchered in half. The Sheriff's captivity in a holding cell prevents him from doing anything but promise his deputy that the cavalry is on their way and they will have vengeance on these "godless beings."

As a result of the viewer's omnipresence, portrayals of the villain's vileness, it can be argued, is often primarily for the sake of the viewer rather than the hero. Lee Jee-woon's 2010 *I Saw the Devil*[11] is a particularly poi-

---

8. Korean title, *Chinjeolhan Geumja ssi*.

9. Roger Ebert, "True Grit Movie Review & Film Summary (2010) | Roger Ebert," accessed June 24, 2016, http://www.rogerebert.com/reviews/true-grit-2010. Ebert describes Mattie as one with the "steely resolve of a girl who has been raised in the eye-for-an eye Old West, seen some bad sights and picked up her values from the kind of old man who can go and get hisself shot."

10. Philip French, "True Grit—Review," *The Guardian*, February 13, 2011, sec. Film, https://www.theguardian.com/film/2011/feb/13/true-grit-coen-brothers-review.

11. Korean title, *Akma-reul po-at-da*

gnant example of the viewer being privy to horrific scenes that depict the vileness of the villain. While waiting for a tow-truck after getting a flat tire on a rural road, the fiancée of NIS agent, Kim Soo-hyeon (Byung-hun Lee) talks tenderly to her about their baby-on-the-way. The murderous psychopath, Kyung-chul (Choi Min-sik), in the guise of a school bus driver, offers to help, and when declined, attacks her. We see a close-up of the villain's devilish face on which blood splatters as he bludgeons her with a metal rod. The viewer is unfortunately not spared the graphic violence that follows. We soon find the fiancée's naked and bloody body on Kyung-chul's wet, concrete floor. In her quiet whimper, she pleads for him not to kill because she is pregnant. In a sequence that signifies this as a fairly routine procedure, he chooses his preferred instruments, chops up her body, places the parts into a box, and washes his floor thoroughly. From the hero's perspective, he only comes to know of the brutal murder through the forensics officers' discovery of her head in a local stream. The director, rightly I think, determined it unnecessary for Soo-hyeong to witness the gory details himself. It might be said that the viewer has already digested the full force of it and "imputes" onto him the desire for a full reckoning that certainly pays off in the end.

A key element of the offense in revenge or manhunt films that cannot be overstated is its *personal nature*. Even in instances where the main overarching premise involves the authorities seeking to apprehend a perpetrator of some institutional criminal activity that threatens civilian lives in general, the relationship between the hero and the villain is one in which the offense has touched the hero in an obviously direct way.[12] In *Enter the Dragon* (1973), British Intelligence seeks to apprehend Han, the leader of a drug and prostitution operation, but Lee (Bruce Lee) is on the hunt because Han has, in the words of Lee's master, "perverted all we hold sacred," and "brought disgrace to the Shaolin temple." Furthermore, in a flashback sequence, Lee remembers Han's henchmen harassing his sister, which leads to her suicide, thus supplying the personal motive. His final words to Han before their showdown is clear: "You have offended my family, and you have offended a Shaolin temple." In *Man on Fire*, while the authorities and media attempt to take down the Mexican crime syndicate, *La Hermandad*, it is not their criminal activity in general that gets Creasy's attention, but their abducting of his beloved Pita that mobilizes him to action. The same can be said of *Robocop* (1987), who, while himself belonging to the police department seeking to apprehend Detroit's most notorious gangster, Clarence Boddicker (Kurtwood Smith), it is Boddicker's previous gunning down of Murphy

---

12. Stephen Hoover, *Payback: The Essential Revenge Thriller Films* (San Bernardino, CA: Stephen Hoover, 2013), 12.

(Peter Weller) before he becomes "Robocop" that particularly motivates his manhunt. The short elevator scene in *Taken* when Bryan Mills finally meets St. Clair, the man who sold his daughter into prostitution, sums up this idea nicely. Bryan points a gun at his head (directly at the audience, from St. Clair's shaky point of view) after shooting him three times to find out his daughter's final location. St. Clair's last words: "Please understand. It was all business. It wasn't personal." Mills responds, "It was all personal to me," and fires the remaining five rounds of ammunition at him in rapid succession as smoke from his gun fills the elevator.

The vow

As is typical after the villain's offense and the hero's full recognition of the personal harm that has been done, the hero verbally binds himself to his mission of justice usually in some form of promise or commitment. When spoken directly to a nemesis, the vow tends to be dialogical and is a more than a threat, but a strongly worded promise of what will happen, as when Bryan (*Taken*) speaks to the abductors of his daughter on the phone:

> I don't know who you are. I don't know what you want. If you're looking for ransom, I can tell you I don't have money. But what I do have, are a very particular set of skills; skills I have acquired over a very long career; skills that make me a nightmare for people like you. [Beat] If you let my daughter go now, that'll be the end of it. I will not look for you. I will not pursue you. But if you don't, I will look for you. I *will* find you. And I will kill you.

Vows often recount the past to remind the assailant(s)—and the audience—of the avenger's reasons. While captured and bound, John Wick tells his nemesis, Viggo, a Russian mob boss and father of the thug who killed his dog and stole his car:

> When Helen died I lost everything, until that dog arrived on my doorstep—a final gift from my wife. In that moment I received some semblance of hope, [beat] an opportunity to grieve unalone. And your son took that from me. Stole that from me! Killed that from me! People keep asking if I'm back, and I haven't really had an answer. But now, yeah, I'm thinking I'm back! So you can either hand over your son, or you can die screaming alongside him!

In *Unforgiven* (1992), William Munny (Clint Eastwood) makes two sets of vows. One is made to the town's brutal Sheriff, Little Bill (Gene

Hackman), where he tells him how he's "killed just about everything that walks or crawls at one time or another. And I'm here to kill you, Little Bill, for what you did to Ned." The second vow closes the film, in which he sternly warns the entire town: "You better bury Ned right! You better not cut up nor otherwise harm no whores![13] Or I'll come back and kill every one of you sons of bitches!"

Of course, words of commitment are of another tone altogether when spoken to allies. To those most affected, the promises are words of comfort, as when John Creasy (*Man on Fire*) makes a vow to the grieving mother of Pita Ramos, who asks, "What are you going to do?" He responds, "What I do best. I'm gonna kill him. Anyone who was involved, anybody who profited from it, anybody who opens their eyes at me." In *Bone Tomahawk* the characters make their commitment to go in search of Samantha O'Dwyer and the Sheriff's deputy. Sheriff Hunt tells the group of notable townspeople, "I'm riding out with Mr. O'Dwyer, because there isn't a choice for either of us." Despite the Sheriff's attempt to dissuade him, Chicory, old man though he is, insists on joining the rescue the party citing that it is his job as the Back-up Deputy. Another compatriot, John Brooder, also commits himself, telling O'Dwyer, "I'm the one who fetched your wife and got her involved. I've got a responsibility to you both." The commitment of the team is highlighted by affirmations of the danger of the mission, as when the mayor's wife tells the group, "You'll be killed," and "This is suicide." Sheriff Hunt's wife tells her husband, "There are limits to the responsibility of a town Sheriff," but she is cut off with Hunt's insistence, "Lorna, I'm going. There isn't an option." Visiting the grave of his wife, Chicory tells her, "There are some good people in trouble. And I gotta do what I can for 'em. So, I'll see you back here, or way up high."

At times, the personal nature of vows is highlighted when the hero makes the vow to himself. This comes about as the protagonist processes his own thoughts about the wrong done. In *Sun Scarred*, Katayama speaks to his friend about daughter's death and the ineffectiveness of the justice system. He says of the young thug who murdered her: "I want him to be executed rather than going to juvie. I want to kill him with my own hands." We later find this to be a prophetic statement fulfilled during his final retribution upon the villain. In one film in particular, *Manhunter* (1986), this theme of the protagonist's self-speech is featured prominently. FBI profiler, Will Graham (William Petersen), attempts to track down an elusive serial killer, but when his family becomes threatened, he obsession focuses into

---

13. The original reason William comes to the town is to kill a cowboy that cut up the face of a saloon prostitute, Delilah (Anna Levine), an act for which the saloon prostitutes pool money to pay to any bounty hunter who help them get justice.

an all-out pursuit of the bandit. One of his most powerful tactics involves speaking to himself and "to" his enemy while reconstructing his vicious crimes. In so doing, he gets into the killer's mind, in effect, *becoming* him. This is confirmed when he seeks the counsel of insane, criminal mastermind, Hannibal Lecktor, whom he had previously caught and brought to justice. Lecktor tells him, "You know why you caught me, Will? The reason you caught me, Will, is you're just alike." He proceeds to re-enact the killer's actions by climbing the tree he used to voyeuristically stalk his victims before killing them. He speaks out loud:

> You used a cutting tool on the branch so that you could see. Then you passed the time whittling and dreaming. When night came, you saw them pass by their bright windows. You watched the shades go down, then you saw the lights go out one by one. And after a while, you climbed down and went into 'em, didn't cha? Didn't cha, you son of a bitch! You watched them all goddamn day long!

After he sends his wife and son away temporarily for safety, telling his wife that he must continue alone, Graham looks out into the dark rainfall and says, "It's just you and me now, Sport. I'm gonna find you, goddammit!" Interestingly, as his obsession deepens and he draws closer to his target, he begins reconstructing the murder scenes in the first person, "I," rather than "you."

The skills

Before embarking to pursue the target culprit, the avenger often demonstrates some measure of skill. In an effort to put the audience on the side of the protagonist and "root" for his victory, many films elevate this confidence by providing some light displays of the hero's past experience as well as physical and mental capabilities. The classic image is that of the intelligence/military operative or assassin, whose minor skirmishes with low-level goons demonstrate a nearly invincible mastery of hand-to-hand combat, weapons, explosives, high-tech gear, and tradecraft. Such is the case with Robert (*The Equalizer*), Creasy (*Man on Fire*), Leon (*Leon*), John Wick (*John Wick*), Tae-sik (*Man from Nowhere*), Su-hyeon (*I Saw the Devil*), and, of course, Bryan (*Taken*), who himself claims to have "a particular set of skills" when vowing death to his daughter's assailants. The films often include a montage depicting the hero's gathering and survey of his weapons and tactical equipment.

In period-oriented films, the skills match that of the main storyline. The opening scene of *Gladiator* (2000) demonstrates that Maximus is not only a brilliant military strategist, but also a formidable warrior in his own right. Heroes in westerns are (or become) expert gunslingers, such as Django (Jamie Foxx) in *Django Unchained* (2012). Perhaps one minor exception is William Munny (*Unforgiven*), whose skills with the gun only appear at the end when he learns of Ned's death (displayed on the saloon's front porch), drinks whiskey (which he "ain't had a drop of in over ten years"), and once again becomes the brutal killer of his past. In *Hara-Kiri: Death of a Samurai* (2011), Hanshiro (Ichikawa Ebizō XI), is an impoverished ronin, whose son-in-law attempts to garner some charity from a feudal lord by feigning *seppuku* (honorable samurai suicide) on their grounds. When the lord learns of his ruse, he forces him to kill himself anyway. The enraged Hanshiro seeks vengeance on the cold, unsympathizing samurai house, and although an unemployed ronin, he is a more highly skilled swordsman than the inexperienced so-called warriors who have never fought in actual combat before.

The skills needed to exact revenge are not always physical in nature, but they are always particular to the plot in question. In *Manhunter*, Will Graham's his unique ability lies in his investigative process in which he fully absorbs himself in his villain's mental world to the point that, in his obsession, he "becomes" his enemy and thinks like him. For Geum-ja, the title character of Park Chan-wook's *Lady Vengeance*, her skill set includes an uncanny aptitude for deception, play-acting, and manipulation. This is demonstrated when she "befriends" the prison's meanest bully and gradually poisons her by feeding her bleach. The literal translation of the Korean title for the film ("Kindhearted Geumja") thus speaks to her twisted ability.

In cases where the avenger is just an average citizen, with no prior training or experience with violence, there is still some display of ability requisite for the completion of a mission. Arthur O'Dwyer (*Bone Tomahawk*), Katayama (*Sun Scarred*), and Dae-su (*Old Boy*), are all average men who fall prey to circumstance. When everything important to them is taken away, they are left with nothing but a sheer, tenacious resolve to make things right. Arthur hobbles a few days' journey over open country with a gangrenous leg to find his wife and kill her abductors. Katayama is crushed by a justice system working against him, yet hunts down young thugs half his age with nothing but grit and patience. Dae-su is locked in a hotel room for fifteen years but trains himself to become a "monster," even accidentally breaking his own hand against the wall he uses for punching practice. During an encounter with some street punks upon his release, he wonders to himself (voice over) if all his years of make-believe combat can translate into actual victory. His brutal thrashing of the hoodlums confirms a resounding "yes." In each of these cases, the audience is made to feel confident in the hero's ability to accomplish his plan despite his weakness relative to his opponents. Even if all he has are courage and determination, they are enough.

The pursuit

Tracking down and making contact with the villain is the necessary process that forms the main bulk of all revenge films. The hero must first face challenges and obstacles that strengthen him and demonstrate his resolve. Because the villain is formidable, and often with many resources that keep him hidden and/or protected, the obstacles represent the difficult but manageable "tests" that the hero must successfully surmount before obtaining his prize of a one-on-one confrontation. A few aspects of the pursuit are typical of the genre. First, the hero must find the villain. In most cases of abduction, the assumption (usually correct) is that the beloved is held captive in the villain's keep. The hero's investigative prowess comes into play here. Professionals trained in war make use of comrades in the intelligence field to gain information, while laymen use instinct, memory, and raw aggression. For example, Dae-su (*Old Boy*) uses his memory of a fifteen-year diet of fried dumplings to scour the city in search of the exact restaurant his captor uses. Katayama (*Sun Scarred*) can do little else than retrace his steps, look for clues, and aggressively force his will on those with information regarding his daughter's killer. When he finally comes close, he wraps himself in a tarp and sits in the teen gang's lair for two days waiting for someone to show up. The camera's extreme close-up on his eyes shows his reluctance to blink as he fights off sleep in the pouring rain.

The process of finding the villain(s) varies according to plot. The characters Creasy (*Man on Fire*), Tae-sik (*Man from Nowhere*), and Bryan (*Taken*) must infiltrate several layers of a criminal syndicate to get to their final targets. In the case of Hanshiro (*Hara-Kiri*), he is already fully aware of the location and identity of his enemies, but must work craftily to gain audience with the lord. Much of his strategy for vengeance involves re-telling the story of his son-in-law and his family's impoverishment in the presence of all his samurai enemies. Similarly, in *Django Unchained*, the heroes are granted access to the villain, who does not yet know the true identities or intentions of his guests. As tensions rise and the villain, Calvin J. Candie (Leonardo DiCaprio) forcefully manhandles Django's wife, Broomhilda (Kerry Washington), Django is tempted to draw his gun but cannot for fear of prematurely blowing his cover. Because the villain is surrounded by loyal subordinates, timing on the part of the protagonists becomes critical to their success. They must act at precisely the right time and not a moment sooner.

This idea of having a fabricated or concealed identity to get within close proximity with the villain is prominent in *Lady Vengeance* and *Gladiator*.

The second aspect of the pursuit involves the hero fighting his way past lower level goons that obstruct the path to the arch villain. *Taken* (and its sequels), *The Equalizer*, and *Man from Nowhere* feature kill counts in the dozens as the highly trained hero rampages his way through to his objective. True to the clear moral lines that these films exhibit, these "expendable" opponents are always hired thugs, never innocent civilians. In *Unforgiven*, William Munny explicitly tells bystanders to "stand clear" of the men he intends to kill. He shoots the owner of the saloon, to our initial surprise. Little Bill calls him a "cowardly son of a bitch" for shooting an unarmed man, setting up a momentary ethical quandary. However, Munny provides the rationale: "He should've armed himself, if he's gonna decorate his saloon with my friend." The threat posed to heroes by low-level goons is challenging but not insurmountable. *Oldboy* illustrates this by featuring a single-take fight sequence in which Dae-su fights through approximately twenty thugs in a narrow hallway. The viewer observes how the thugs (with their makeshift weapons) frantically sprawl all over the frame, while Dae-su (fighting mostly unarmed) occupies the dominant center.

Thirdly, when the hero has the upper hand, it is common for the act of vengeance to be drawn out. *I Spit on Your Grave* depicts this idea well, for the protagonist is a female, up against four men, each physically stronger than her. To exact her revenge on her assailants, she must knock them out (with a tire iron or baseball bat) and bind them one by one. The ethic of payback in many of these films involves making the villain suffer instead of ending his life immediately. In *I Saw the Devil* and *Out of the Furnace*, two films where the protagonist seeks retribution for the killing of a loved one, the avenger "toys" with his enemy by inflicting non-fatal wounds before killing him. Su-hyeon (*I Saw the Devil*) captures the evil Kyung-chul, wounds him, and lets him go. A tracking device allows him to repeat his capture-and-torture procedure. One interpretation regards the avenger's rage as having to be quelled in successive stages or degrees before being finally satisfied. Another point of view posits that the villain must be made to feel the full extent of the harm done. A quick death is "painless" and therefore, in some sense, too merciful for what the villain deserves. In *Out of the Furnace*, Russell shoots DeGroat once in the leg and allows him to attempt to hobble away before shooting him in the abdomen. As he lies on the ground spitting blood, Russell crouches down and tells him calmly, "I'm Rodney Baze's brother." Only after DeGroat makes a final slow walk across a field does Russell put him down with a rifle shot to the back of the head.

The showdown

The final confrontation and demise of the villain is the climax and most important part of any true revenge film. Having witnessed the horrific offense and followed the hero through the arduous pursuit, the audience's ultimate "payoff" moment is when the protagonist finally ends the villain's life. For this reason, the showdown is highly stylized and dramatic, and often occurs in a dark or dimly lit setting. Brief dialogues between the hero and villain are very common as preambles to the final battle. They can be thought as conclusions to the vows made at earlier points in the film, a moment to tie off any remaining loose ends. Often, the hero once again reminds his opponent (and the audience) of the offense and why his death is necessary. Not surprisingly, the villain remains defiant and never apologetic. Their responses include laughter, scorning the memory of the beloved, and deflecting blame. When the villain's defeat is imminent, he often curses the hero and goads him to finish him off.

Within the action genre, the villain is of comparable caliber with the hero, so a lengthy hand-to-hand combat sequence typically ensues, with the villain often one-upping the hero with a concealed blade of some sort, further demonstrating his lack of honor relative to his opponent (e.g. *Taken*, *John Wick*, *Gladiator*, *Enter the Dragon*). These exhibitions of speed, strength, and endurance are at least a few minutes long and almost always involve the hero suffering physical trauma in the process. Viewers are made to remember that these heroes are still human, arriving at their confrontation with the arch villain only after numerous prior battles and a difficult pursuit. In the end, the hero's victory is achieved through skill and never by fluke. In *Oldboy*, Dae-su does not face his nemesis, U-jin (Yoo Ji-tae) directly, but his bodyguard, Mr. Han (Kim Byeong-ok). Dae-su's frantic running attacks are met with Mr. Han's calm but calculated physical responses that send Dae-su flying into glass display cases. The sound cuts to soft, ambient music as we witness Dae-su thrown around like a rag doll repeatedly. However, we come to know that Dae-su has managed to fatally stab Mr. Han in the ear with a pair of scissors at some unseen point during his last pummeling. The use of repetition is also employed in *Sun Scarred*, where Katayama, keeping with his vow to kill his daughter's murderer "with my own hands," unleashes his wrath by slamming Kamiki's head into the concrete floor several times until dead.

Revenge films outside the broad action or modern crime genres typically employ a display of the hero's wits rather than physical prowess. This is especially true of *I Spit on Your Grave*, where Jennifer uses sadistic, but creative, torture methods on her rapists, each appropriate to their prior infliction upon her. Johnny wakes up bound and naked, with a horse's bit in his mouth, and Jennifer proceeds to yank out his teeth with pliers before castrating him with gardening shears; Stanley is taught a lesson for his voyeuristic videography by having his eyelids stretched open with fish hooks for the crows to peck out his eyes; Andy is bound and his upper body is laid over a tub of lye, his fatigue forcing him to lower his head into the corrosive liquid; and Sheriff Storch wakes up to a shotgun inserted deep into his anus. Although horrifyingly twisted in each of her modes of afflicting suffering, she does not deal any final deathblows, as such, to her captives; she merely creates the situation in which her villains ultimately kill themselves in a slow and painful way. A very similar concept marks Su-hyeon's retribution upon Kyung-chul in *I Saw the Devil*. As the final scene opens, we find Kyung-chul bound, bleeding, and kneeling over a guillotine. After the two exchange some words, Su-hyeon walks away from the warehouse as Kyung-chul's son and parents arrive. The guillotine is held suspended by two ropes, one in the villain's mouth, the other tied to the door that his family members are about to open. Releasing either one results in his decapitation, which the film unflinchingly portrays in its totality, to the obvious horror of Kyung-chul's parents.

More common, however, are times when the hero delivers a decisive deathblow, usually called for in films where the hero's loved one already is dead or presumed dead. This finishing move serves as the visual focus of the hero's determination and resolve, a deep hate developed and demonstrated throughout the film and culminating in a focused strike. This is nicely illustrated in the climax of *Man from Nowhere*, in which Tae-sik finally hunts down the crime boss, Man-seok (Kim Hee-won), who holds himself up in a bulletproof car waiting for the cops to arrive. Tae-sik climbs on the hood the car, presses his pistol against the windshield, and fires fourteen successive rounds at a single spot. The final round pierces a hole in the glass. He then fires once into Man-seok's shoulder before we see an extreme close-up shot of Tae-sik's lips: "There's one round left." We view the cathartic headshot from behind Man-seok as he whips back from the blast with Tae-sik's blurred image pointing the gun toward the camera. The blood blackening the camera lens gives the feeling that the audience has been shot as well. A similar, carefully-aimed headshot also puts down DeGroat from Russell's hunting rifle (*Out of the Furnace*), and one-shot takedowns are featured in many films, including *Unforgiven*, *Django Unchained*, *The Equalizer*, and *Se7en* (1995).[14] Both *Out of the Furnace* and *Se7en* share strikingly similar

14. Technically, *Se7en* is a crime thriller and not generally regarded as a revenge film, but the theme of revenge brings the film to its final climax. In a dramatic reveal, Detective Mills (Brad Pitt) and his partner, Somerset (Morgan Freeman), learn that the suspect, John Doe (Kevin Spacey), has decapitated Mills' wife and placed it in a box

scenes: they take place in an open field; the co-star (a cop) pleads for the avenger to stop. The avenger ignores his ally completely, and fires a decisive headshot at a subdued, unarmed villain. Thus a major rule of the revenge genre is reinforced: the harm done is so great that the protagonist has the right—or, at least, the resolve—to transcend the rule of law.

Arguably, the most dramatic showdowns are those that involve the hero's deliberate self-infliction. Here, the protagonist secures victory through a wound or a glorious suicide. In *John Wick*, John and Viggo struggle hand-to-hand in the final showdown until Viggo brandishes his concealed switchblade. After a grappling stalemate, John thrusts Viggo's knife-bearing hand toward his own abdomen, causing a near-fatal wound. Viggo's surprise allows John to break his elbow and counter-attack, stabbing Viggo in the neck with the same knife. In *Leon*, the villain, Detective Stansfield, shoots Leon from behind as he attempts to walk out of a building. As Stansfield crouches gloatingly over his gasping victim, they dialogue briefly:

Leon: Stansfield.

Stansfield: (*smiling*) At your service.

Leon (placing an unseen object into Stansfield's hand): This is from [long pause] Mathilda.

Stansfield slowly opens his hand and finds a grenade pin. He opens Leon's vest, sees several grenades strapped to his chest, and says, "Shit." The camera cuts to an exterior shot as a massive explosion rocks the corridor, sending flames out into the street. Equally dramatic, but surprisingly less cathartic is the climax of *Man on Fire*. Creasy makes a deal with "The Voice" (the boss of the crime syndicate): Pita's life for that of Creasy and The Voice's brother (whom Creasy had located and held hostage). Pita and Creasy reunite at the rendezvous point in a tender moment of exchanging "I love yous," but she is sent back to rejoin her mother while Creasy continues walking unarmed toward his enemies. We next find him in the villain's car staring out the window as it drives off. Montage and film text reveals that "The Voice" is killed by law enforcement at a later time. As disappointing as this showdown is in terms of visual and emotional payoff, the ending can be described in no better way than as a *substitution*, in which Creasy willingly surrenders himself to his enemies in exchange for Pita.

---

that he delivered to them. Against Somerset's plea to stop, Mills shoots John Doe in the head.

The denouement

The post-climax narrative descent of most revenge-themed films is fairly consistent and visually ordinary, at least on the surface. The films usually close with a shot of the hero, but one in which the hero's emotions remain deeply internal and unexposed. They are wearing "poker faces"—ambiguous expressions, which communicate neither relief nor happiness. They often gaze off into the distance or stare contemplatingly at memorabilia of their past relationship with their loved one. It is not that the characters are in shock, for they are fully cognizant of their actions and the skills that made it possible. In *Taken*, Bryan exhibits some signs of relief and offers consolation to his weeping daughter after he kills the sheik that purchased her. The ensuing scenes of reunion at the airport and her introduction to a famous singer for voice lessons end the film on a warm, positive note.

The other end of the emotional spectrum is explored in the final scene of *I Saw the Devil*, where Su-hyeon walks away from the warehouse where he has left Kyung-chul to his death. Initially, we see the typical expressionless face of a hardened hero. After a few cuts showing Kyung-chul's struggle with the ropes, his family's arrival, and his decapitation, we return to a midshot of Su-hyeon, who eventually breaks down into weeping as he walks. The reason for his heartbreak is unclear. Has he, like U-jin (*Oldboy*) come to realize the nihilism of life now that his mission is complete? Is he suddenly remembering his deceased fiancée? Many reviewers of this film concur that part of the message of the film involves asking the question of whether Su-hyeon has, through his sadistic cat-and-mouse game of torture, become the very murderer that he hunted.[15] Su-hyeon's weeping, I would offer, is a demonstration of his authentic humanity, over and against Kyung-chul's devilish inhumanity. His emotional display in the final scene, therefore, proves he is still a better man, one who still deserves our approval.

Where revenge films follow the general pattern of the expressionless gaze, Stephen Hoover suggests that such endings are tied to the viewers' sense of morality. After the cathartic payoff of the villain's violent demise, the only way to leave a film without feeling like bloodthirsty "monsters" is to end on a morally ambiguous note.[16] Thus, the film protagonists, for whom we have been cheering all along, anticipate and mirror this moral ambiguity through their blunted expression. Another possibility is that the character is left with a sense of meaninglessness after he has satisfied his vengeance. Unleashing his fury is the protagonist's full "emptying" of himself. We see in

---

15. Roger Moore, "Movie Review: 'I Saw the Devil,'" *Movie Nation*, January 13, 2013, https: //rogersmovie-nation.com/2013/01/13/movie-review-i-saw-the-devil/.

16. Hoover, *Payback*, 32.

Oldboy how the antagonist, who himself was out to get revenge on Dae-su for spreading the gossip that led to his sister's death decades ago, shoots himself in the head after the climax of his vengeful act is complete. After fifteen years of fantasizing, meticulous planning, and execution, there is nothing left to live for once it is over. Upon killing his foe, Tae-sik (*Man from Nowhere*) attempts to shoot himself in the head until his beloved So-mi emerges and is revealed as unharmed after all. Although each film has its own way of narrating its end, there is a strong sense in which the heroes have, in some sense, died as a result of bringing about the villain's death. Things are never the same for them again.

Character Profiles in the Revenge Genre

The beloved

As previously alluded to in the discussion regarding the narrative element of the "bond," revenge films that portray the protection/rescue of, or retaliation on behalf of, a protagonist's loved one often features the beloved as a young girl. Taking Su-hyeon's rampage as a prime example (*I Saw the Devil*), in which he hunts down the killer of both his fiancée and unborn baby girl, it is safe to generalize that the younger and more innocent the beloved is, the more sadism and mayhem is expected from the hero. In the opening scene, his fiancée, Joo-yeon (Oh San-ha), talks with Su-hyeon about visiting an orphanage once a month and hoping to raise her future daughter in the countryside. When featured in the film as a lead character (e.g. *Leon, Man on Fire, Man from Nowhere, True Grit, Oldboy*), the young girl tends to be chatty and courageous, often having endured some measure of suffering. In *Leon* and *True Grit*, it is the girl herself who has suffered the loss for which she recruits an avenger. This gives them the means and willingness to befriend the (initially) antisocial protagonist, and renders her capable of disarming and humanizing his cold, stoic personality. It is toward her alone that the protagonist's propensity for violence vanishes. A scene in *Man on Fire* brings this out nicely, in which Pita points out that she has made Creasy smile for the first time since they met.

An alternative to the typical trope of cute, young girl is that of a victim, who has made foolish choices in life. External forces beyond their control strip them of agency and determine their painful destinies. In *Out of the Furnace*, Russell's younger brother, Rodney (Casey Affleck), is portrayed as a struggling Iraq war veteran, who gets involved in a street fighting circuit and winds up offending the wrong people and is killed. An uncle describes him as "troubled" since his youth, especially since their mother died. Rodney tells Russell of the horrors he experienced in war that caused a change in him, making it impossible for him to lead a normal life. In *Hara-Kiri*, Hanshiro's son-in-law, Motome (Eita), ends up dying in an attempt to receive charity for his ill wife and newborn son by deceiving a local feudal lord and his samurai. Teri (Chlöe Grace Moretz), in *The Equalizer*, is a call girl hired by the Russian mob, who is constantly abused by them and their clients, unable to free herself from their grip. While not entirely exonerated as "innocent" in the strict sense, these characters are depicted as having suffered from circumstances that highlight their fragility and diminish their morally questionable behavior.

The avenger

The image of a specialist in the arts of combat and investigation is prominent in revenge films. A common device used to establish the legend of the lead protagonist is through the testimony of secondary characters. Of John Creasy (*Man on Fire*), a long time associate, Rayburn (Christopher Walken), says of him, "Creasy's art is death. He's about to paint his masterpiece." In *John Wick*, a conversation between Viggo and his son is an excellent example of legend-crafting:

> Viggo: He once was an associate of ours. We called him *Baba Yaga*.
>
> Iosef: Boogeyman?
>
> Viggo: Well John wasn't exactly the Boogeyman. He was the one you send to *kill* the fucking Boogeyman.
>
> Iosef: Oh.
>
> Viggo: John is a man of focus, commitment, sheer will . . . I once saw him kill three men in a bar—[beat]—with a pencil. [Beat]. A fuckin' [beat] pencil.

Spliced between lines and beats of this conversation are shots of John Wick unearthing his massive arsenal and preparing for action. When seeking to recruit William Munny (*Unforgiven*) for a lucrative bounty killing, the "Schofield Kid" (Jaimz Woolvett) relays to William what has been said of him, that he's the "meanest, goddamn son of a bitch alive. And if I ever wanted a partner for a killing, you were the worst one—meaning the best.

On account as you're as cold as the snow. You don't have no weak nerve, nor fear." Similarly, when Mattie Ross (*True Grit*) asks a local sheriff to recommend a U.S. Marshall who can bring her father's killer to justice, he responds, "the meanest is Rooster Cogburn. He's a pitless man, double tough, and fear don't enter into his thinking." The image that emerges from the legend of the lead protagonist is that he is (or used to be) a brutal and nasty person. A close association with the very evil they are combating is a discernable theme. In the classic Clint Eastwood western, *Pale Rider*, the title is a reference to Rev 6:8 (the rider on a pale horse, whose name is Death), a text that Megan Wheeler reads while their hero, "The Preacher," rides into town. In the beginning of *Lady Vengeance*, Geum-ja emerges from prison after having gained the reputation as a truly "kind-hearted" convert to the cause of goodness. She soon dumps that act and applies blood red eye shadow to symbolize a dark descent into vengeance.

The reversal of the hero's morally compromised identity, however, occurs quite early in revenge films. One interesting pattern that emerges is the tendency for the hero, at the time that we are first introduced to him, to be inactive in the very profession by which he learned and practiced his "particular set of skills." By and large, the lead protagonists in such films are retired or have quit their jobs as agents, operators, assassins, etc. in pursuit of a new and better life. The screen text at the opening of *Unforgiven* describes the old William Munny as "a known thief and murderer, a man of notoriously vicious and intemperate disposition," but as the film begins, we are introduced to a William who is father of two children, and raises hogs (rather ineffectively) on a dilapidated farm. Throughout the film, he insists, "I ain't like that no more," on account of the moral reforms enforced by his late wife. Likewise, John Wick's marriage to his wife motivates him to leave his life as a hired killer, and we find Tae-sik (*Man from Nowhere*) living as an antisocial pawnshop clerk because his former profession resulted in the death of his pregnant wife. A more extreme version is the backstory of Robert McCall (*The Equalizer*), whose passion to remove himself from his life of killing involved staging his own death and starting a new life as an employee at a home supplies depot.

As the film plot typically goes, the hero's attempted "new life" is cut short by circumstances in which he has no choice but to act. We see that his propensity for ruthless brutality is still ever present, but now exercised for a good cause and often driven with deep affection and concern for a beloved one. The idea communicated in both indirect and explicit ways is that the hero cannot escape his true self and that returning to his core identity is essential to complete his mission. When asked by an old colleague, Susan (Melissa Leo), why he chose to defend the Russian call girl, Robert (*The Equalizer*) responds:

Robert: I couldn't tell you why it mattered. Why what they did to her, why it mattered to me so much. One day somebody does something unspeakable to someone else, someone you hardly knew, and you [beat] do something about it because you can.

Susan: Because it's who you are? Who you've always been? Sometimes we make the wrong choices to get to the right place. I know a part of you died when [your wife] Vivian did, but not the part you loved the most. Go be him.

In cases where heroes have no prior combat experience, and therefore no excess talent to help people "because they can," they rise to the occasion *because they must*, because of the sheer horror of the offense done to them. Due to their lack of training, resources, and personnel, they often go through much more hardship than "professionals." For example, Katayama (*Sun Scarred*) endures the constant frustration of a legal system rigged in favor of his daughter's killer, an unrepentant juvenile. The film's cinematography communicates this by having Katayama frequently blocked by pillars and walls while other minor characters (e.g. office workers, police personnel, lawyers) are given full constitution. This illustrates Katayama's frustrated lack of agency, a sense of being "sidelined" by his environment and circumstances. This same frustration torments Russell (*Out of the Furnace*), in which the non-action of the police leads him to undertake vigilante justice. For characters like these, it is by force of will alone (or, "true grit") that carries them above the law and through their fight for *true* justice.

The villain

Villains occupy less screen time but have very important roles. In the typical revenge film, it is incumbent upon filmmakers to rally audiences around the hero and give them the most satisfying cathartic payoff as possible. In order to establish the sheer wickedness of villains they are portrayed according to very consistent patterns. Broadly speaking, villains are absolute characters, exhibiting no character arc or improvement in moral disposition throughout a film. The only difference in attitude may come when they are finally pleading for the hero to have mercy, but this is rare. By and large, villains remain abusive and defiant to the very end. Their moral depravity is usually established early in the film. In the opening sequence in *Out of a Furnace*, Harlon DeGroat is on a date with a woman at a drive-in movie. The door opens and he spits out his food. The woman asks if he is okay and hands him a napkin. "Are you gonna be able to drive?" Harlon sipping vodka out a bottle answers, "This fucker drives itself." The woman's chuckle in response sets off a series of unfortunate events. He shoves a hotdog into her mouth and slams her face against the dashboard. When a man in the neighboring car offers to intervene, DeGroat gets out, beats the man nearly to death, yanks his sobbing date of the car, threatens other onlookers, and drives off.

DeGroat's unshaven and dirty physical appearance is representative of one mode of portraying villains as grizzly and unkempt. This is true of the Albanian captors in *Taken*, Tom Chaney in *True Grit*, and Kyung-chul in *I Saw the Devil*. In *Bone Tomahawk* the image is brought to an extreme, in which the abductors of the doctor and the deputy are uncivilized troglodytes, who paint themselves in white clay, wear loin cloths, and possess no language other than to produce high pitched screams through modified vocal chords. Their pregnant women are blinded and crippled as a result of their cultural practice. The town's "Professor," a Native American man, refuses to identify them as "Indian," and as the rescue party learns about them, they regard them as non-human, "godless beings."

Another mode of physical portrayal occurs in many modern crime thrillers, where villains are clean cut and well dressed. Some of this relates to their stereotype as rich and powerful, presumably obtaining their inordinate wealth through long spans of unhindered criminal activity. These villains, like St. Clair (*Taken*), U-jin (*Oldboy*), Commodus (*Gladiator*), and Kamiki (*Sun Scarred*) frequently have styled hair and pale, unblemished skin. Kamiki's character is especially chilling in the way that his face is often hooded, with the camera catching close-up shots of his tongue sucking on a lollipop as he watches approvingly his subordinates inflicting harm on innocent civilians.

In their interactions with victims, and especially the hero, villains often like to be entertained and have a nonchalant attitude. In a scene in *13 Assassins*, we are introduced to a woman with no limbs and drooling painfully from the mouth. Shinzaemon is told that the evil lord, Naritsugu, had cut off her limbs and tongue and used her as a "plaything" until he got bored and cast her away. In another scene, we see Naritsugu casually killing off a family with arrows as target practice. Speaking in soothing, (and in the case of Kamiki, effeminate) tones and laughing at inappropriate times gives villains an air of power as well as reinforces their sociopathic personalities. They are evil because they *enjoy* suffering. Perhaps the best example is in one of the final scenes in *Oldboy*, where U-jin has Dae-su on his knees acting like a dog and pleading not to reveal to Mi-do (with whom he had had intercourse) that he is her father. As Dae-su licks U-jin's shoes to garner pity, the camera pans up to a ¾ shot of the back of U-jin's head as he holds a handkerchief to his mouth. We interpret him as weeping until the camera wraps around to

¾ shot of the front of his face, where it is revealed that he is actually trying to control his laughter at Dae-su's pathetic display.

The ally

The final notable character type in most revenge films is that of the hero's allies. For ex-professionals, these confederates are friends who often share an occupational history with the hero and are thus recruited to assist in obtaining critical intelligence, weapons, and strategic advice. As former comrades-in-arms of the protagonist, they also function to provide audiences with anecdotal backstories that illuminate the hero's past accolades, family life, and personality traits. Although they are minor characters, they are indispensable resources in completing the mission. Bryan (*Taken*) has Sam (Leland Orser), Robert (*The Equalizer*) has Susan, Creasy (*Man on Fire*) has Rayburn, William Munny (*Unforgiven*) has Ned Logan (Morgan Freeman), and even the virtually indestructible Robocop has his former partner, Lewis (Nancy Allen). John Wick's old friend, Marcus (Willem Dafoe), a former Navy Seal, even plays a critical role in saving John's life but is later killed.

The camaraderie and devotion that these figures offer to one another is a powerful device that humanizes the heroes and distinguishes them from the villain and his henchmen. *13 Assassins* brings this out nicely, in which the warriors face Lord Naritsugu's army of over 200 men in a small, abandoned village. Amazingly, they manage to kill all of their opponents through ingenious booby traps and coordinated fighting. What begins as a band of dispossessed samurai, many of whom do not know each other well, becomes the story of the strong bonds of friendship that only war can forge. Eventually, all but two of them are struck down in glorious deaths. *Bone Tomahawk* explores the theme of the rescue party risking their lives for one another as the odds against them widen. When ambushed outside the troglodyte camp, Brooder, mortally wounded, makes a last stand so that the team can storm the cave. When inside the cave, Sheriff Hunt is likewise mortally wounded and decides to fend off the remaining savages so that his deputy, Arthur, and his wife can make an escape. In a final, tender moment with his deputy, Chicory, the Sheriff warmly tells him, "Say goodbye to my wife. I'll say hello to yours." These characters and their relationship with the hero add to the positive moral quality of revenge films. They help the audience "come on board" with the mission and are reminders that although the hero is highly skilled and passionate, the villain and his networks are powerful and well resourced enough to pose a challenge that requires a team effort.

Violence and the Ethics of Spectatorship

In the previous section, I outlined the main elements of plot and character in specific films come together to produce what is recognizably typical and generic across films of the revenge theme. This section will extend the analysis to discuss the broader aims of this genre in relation to the viewer as ethical spectators. As this discussion potentially overlaps with protracted debates concerning the boundaries and criteria of cinema censorship and the role of media violence in juvenile behavior, it is important to limit the scope of this discussion to the films themselves and what message and purpose they intend to convey.[17] Are these films *merely* gratuitous exhibitions of blood and gore, or do they have a moral center that invites affirmation from both Christian audiences and the wider culture?

The conflation of worlds and the need for caution

That revenge films are often sensational displays of gratuitous violence is undeniable. Furthermore, as has been demonstrated, one of the hallmarks of the pursuit and showdown aspects of the revenge narrative is that the protagonist operates outside the rule of common law—and in many cases, common sense. The critical question is not whether plots and characters are moral exemplars of how to live in the world. Rather, the question is whether the films frame plots and characters in such a way that its own world makes moral sense. Many ethical and theological critiques of violence in film proceed from the conviction that cinematic forms of violence would be condemned, *were they to occur in our world*. In other words, they equate filmic worlds with the real world. For example, Robert Jewett denounces *Unforgiven* as a "dangerous film" that "invites the public to solve its problems by shooting down its sheriff and placing truck bombs in front of its federal buildings."[18] Elsewhere, he says the film "tolerates the mutilation of women and the torturing and shaming of prisoners."[19] His failure to comprehend the movie's point about the "serious hellishness of killing"[20] aside, Jewett exemplifies the temptation

---

17. For an excellent historical survey of the cinematic medium's relationship with the issue of violence, see J. David Slocum, "Film Violence and the Institutionalization of the Cinema," *Social Research* 67, no. 3 (2000): 649–81.

18. Jewett, *Saint Paul Returns to the Movies*, 149.

19. John Shelton Lawrence and Robert Jewett, *The Myth of the American Superhero* (Eerdmans, 2003), 151.

20. Peter Francis, "Clint Eastwood Westerns: Promised Land and Real Men," in *Cinéma Divinité: Religion, Theology and the Bible in Film*, ed. Eric S. Christianson, Peter Francis, and William R. Telford (London: SCM, 2005), 197. Francis suggests, further,

to confuse the descriptive and prescriptive aspects of films and to hold film characters to a traditional standard of morality. Were this to be the case, we ought to dismiss as "dangerous" every cultural artifact (including the Bible!) that portrays unkind words, violence, and death.

Cinematic violence and moral formation

While the means and ends of the hero's pursuit and destruction of the villain as individual acts set against reality's standards of morality cannot be entirely justified, it is worth asking, Do revenge films stem from an ethical core and, if so, why? As we have seen above, the narrative structure and character profiling of the typical film suggests a strong ethic at work. It is widely accepted that cinema mediates societal values and meanings. Going further, J. David Slocum suggests that displays of violence "invoke some of society's most central and guiding values, those which justify the use of force, illuminate the parameters of social order, and demarcate legitimate from illegitimate action."[21] He observes that Hollywood has tended to surge in showcasing violent images and narratives during times of war or national crisis in efforts to reinforce dominant myths of social order.[22] For example, self-sacrificial modes of death serve as "an underlying modality or logic through which violence on the battlefront and homefront alike occur" and helps to frame the redemptive narrative in terms of the values of larger society.[23] As such, violence is produced not by a need for aggressive catharsis but (with a nod to Girard) by "a social imperative to overcome competition, discover kinship by confirming otherness, and affirm hierarchies of central versus marginal."[24]

On a less national stage, James Twitchell has argued that much of the "preposterous violence"[25] consumed by adolescents in post-WWII America served to socialize them and prepare them for the anxieties of their life stage. Rather than incite violent tendencies, these exhibitions—too preposterous to be taken seriously—were cautionary fables that provided transitioning

---

that the film promotes the "debunking of the ideal of the promised land, the demythologizing of the mythic west and flawed masculinity." While some critique of the image of the unfazed, macho vigilante is certainly in view, the narrative and character aspects of the film are typical enough to situate it within the revenge subgenre.

21. Slocum, "Film Violence and the Institutionalization of the Cinema," 651.
22. Ibid., 674.
23. Ibid., 666.
24. Ibid.
25. James B. Twitchell, *Preposterous Violence: Fables of Aggression in Modern Culture* (New York: Oxford University Press, 1989).

teenagers with a sense of moral boundaries. The ethical grounding of media violence is emphasized further if one considers, following Twitchell, that "the rise of entertainment violence in popular culture has co-opted much of the force of religion and jurisprudence" by carrying the same kind of "ritualized content."[26] Cinematic violence, then, rather than a mere indication of the state of society, can be thought of as providing a positive ethical contribution by reflecting and heightening society's core moral values, especially in the face of distress.

A number of theories have been put forward to explain the mechanism at work that makes screen violence not only appealing, but also morally beneficial. Perhaps the most popular theory posits that viewers of violence experience *catharsis*, by which they are purged of negative emotions such as fear, rage, and disgust. Horror films, it is suggested, helps "to render the mind more healthy and to protect the social order by providing a safe outlet for 'unsafe' emotions,"[27] or as acclaimed horror novelist, Stephen King, says, "we make up horrors to help us cope with the real ones."[28] Another theory suggests that cinematic gore appeals to our curiosity and sense of fascination; they command our attention insofar as they present us with societal norms that are challenged but later reconstituted once the film is over.[29] Some theorists believe that horror and violent depiction simply appeal to those who rate high on a sensation or thrill-seeking scale and are easily bored, while others believe that these films are occasions for men and women reinforce traditional gender roles: women viewers express their sensitivity and need for protection, while male viewers are given the opportunity to demonstrate fearlessness in the face of cinematic gore. Some have suggested the choice to view horror films is contextual in nature, depending upon the viewers' mood, which they would like to alter or cure. Finally, the "relief hypothesis" suggests that horror films are appealing for the calming effect of the resolution at the film's close.

---

26. Ibid., 46.

27. Clark McCauley, "When Screen Violence Is Not Attractive," in *Why We Watch: The Attractions of Violent Entertainment*, ed. Jeffrey Goldstein (New York: Oxford University Press, 1998), 147.

28. Stephen King, *Danse Macabre* (New York: Berkley, 1981), 13, quoted in ibid.

29. See Noel Carroll, *The Philosophy of Horror: Or, Paradoxes of the Heart* (New York: Routledge, 1990), 195, 201 quoted in McCauley, "When Screen Violence Is Not Attractive," 149–50.

The beauty of violence?

By way of a series of psychological studies on visual disgust, Clark McCauley et. al. find the above hypotheses lacking in terms of a comprehensive explanation for why horror films are attractive. The main study involved undergraduate students exposed to documentary footage of shocking, but real, images (a monkey killed and its brains served to epicure diners, a cattle slaughter, and open-head surgery involving a face being peeled off a skull). A vast majority of viewers opted to stop watching the film partway through and only ten percent of participants watched the reels to the end.[30] Not surprisingly, this form of disgust is not present in viewers of commercial horror films. McCauley posits "the emotions experienced in drama are qualitatively different from everyday experience of the same emotions."[31] In other words, the fact that cinematic horror is fiction has everything to do with its appeal. Furthermore, in observing that viewers most enjoy Hollywood horror films during, and not after, it is shown, and that empathetic involvement with characters—even those who experience tragedy—correlates with their enjoyment of the film, McCauley concludes that the dramatically induced emotion operates on a different plane and may, in some sense, be deeper and more transcendent.[32] The distance created by fiction allows the viewer to attend more sensitively and engage more transformatively with what are regarded as "negative emotions," thus removing their preoccupation with themselves and developing an increased capacity to cope with real-life discomfort.[33] In this sense, the cathartic effect of film becomes one of "purifying" rather than "purging" emotion. McCauley writes: "The experience of fear and pity in response to dramatic tragedy can be attractive because the emotions are purified of self-interest and of the necessity to act—and to pay the costs of acting—in a complex and ambiguous world."[34]

While suspicion may remain as to whether violence can be viewed positively in an aesthetic sense, there seems to be sufficient warrant to regard cinematic violence as belonging to another category than actual bodily harm. An obvious move in this direction would involve being reminded of

---

30. McCauley, "When Screen Violence Is Not Attractive," 144–45.

31. Ibid., 160.

32. McCauley's argument leans on a precedent he finds in an ancient Sanskrit treatise on drama, *The Nayatsastra* (200–300 C.E.), which states, "The spectator can go further, and in a sense deeper. For when 'love' is awakened in him, it is not like the love that the original character felt . . . the [state of mind] is transformed into an extra-worldly state," quoted in ibid., 160.

33. McCauley, "When Screen Violence Is Not Attractive," 161.

34. Ibid.

what movies are: *stories*. They are fictitious and fundamentally, therefore, not real. For William Rothman, "Violence in live action movies is generally no more consequential than the violence in cartoons, such as the violence Wile E. Coyote suffers from the machinations of Road Runner."[35] Events in the film world are ontologically different from the real world. This separation manifests—quite literally—in the form of the movie screen, which shields us from the film world and the film world from us.[36] Moreover, cinematic conventions themselves, such as camera angles, lighting, music, and editing, create an emotional distance that elicits pleasure rather than disgust by providing a "normative aesthetic frame" through which to understand graphic violence.[37] Stephen Prince details how especially "harrowing" scenes of violence, as in the opening of *Saving Private Ryan* (1998), are crafted to produce both vividness and realism as well as provide emotional and cognitive distance from the violence portrayed.[38] The resultant effect was that "the violence was not raw, that is, it was not 'real.'"[39] Staging and effects add an "aesthetic dimension," to depictions of gory violence which, when absent, are expectedly unpleasant to behold. It is this aesthetic framing that simultaneously allows for detachment from violence as experienced in the real world as well as an opportunity to engage it on an imaginative level.

Admittedly, the reactions of viewers may vary considerably, and even the finest filmmakers cannot control the types of emotions or potential actions that may be elicited against their best intentions.[40] Postmodern critics

35. William Rothman, "Violence and Film," in *Violence and American Cinema*, ed. J. David Slocum (New York: Routledge, 2001), 40.

36. Ibid., 42.

37. Stephen Prince, ed., *Screening Violence* (New Brunswick, NJ: Rutgers University Press, 2000), 28.

38. He writes: "For some shots, they employed a shutter set at 45 and 90 degrees, instead of the more usual 180-degree configuration, in order to pixelate the action. They stripped the coating off the lenses to flatten contrast and get a foggy but sharp look. They shot with the camera shutter out of sync to produce a streaking effect from the top to bottom of the image. They used a Clairmont Camera Image Shaker to produce horizontal and vertical shaking of the camera, and they flashed the film to desaturate the color and used ENR [named for its inventor, Ernesto Novelli Rimo] to add contrast, Ibid., 29.

39. Ibid.

40. For example, sources indicated to Sam Peckinpah, director of the western *The Wild Bunch* (1969) that Nigerian soldiers had screened his film to fire themselves up before going out to battle. He responded, "I heard that story and I vomited, to think that I had made that film, ibid., 27. More recently, during a scene in *Schindler's List* (1993) of Nazis executing prisoners, a group of some seventy students in Oakland, California broke out in laughter, causing complaints, their expulsion from the theater, and some media frenzy, 30–31.

argue that screen violence has lost its depth and referentiality, becoming just as any image, "homogenized and emptied of meaning or seeming originality."[41] Rather than as social processes, they are becoming commodities for consumption. Popular blockbusters that exhibit this may well belong to a category that employs what film theorist Devin McKinney labels "weak violence." Distinguished from "strong violence," where violent depictions make a lasting, internal impact upon both the film's narrative and the viewer, are necessarily multidimensional, conjure complex emotions, and ask ultimate questions, weak violence is typical of the "Schwarzenegger school" of violent depictions, devoid of feeling and meaning, and which "reduces bloodshed to its barest components, then inflates them with hot, stylized air."[42] As McKinney quips, the "violence is used only as a device: something the crowd pays for when it goes in, but not when it comes out."[43] In films that employ "weak violence," such as Quentin Tarantino's 1992 film *Reservoir Dogs* for instance, there is no exploration of human depths but rather an effort to trivialize them. "The picture's savagery is so assiduously appointed that it demands analysis as a thing in itself, a component of the work overarching all others—which is say that the story usually serves the violence rather than the reverse."[44]

Such an assessment may well be leveled against revenge films like *John Wick* and *The Equalizer*, in which the hero's lethal rampages have been considered by some as artistic and dancelike, acts to be appreciated in themselves but bear little psychological content. But this is not to say that "weak" portrayals of violence as can be found in revenge films are *necessarily* devoid of moral substance as is claimed for strong violence, which supposedly challenges one's "moral positioning" by "engendering an immediate and very subjective confrontation with the material."[45] If McKinney is right in implying that strong violence enjoys the moral high ground because "the audience is both acted upon and made to act by acknowledging its role in the fulfillment of a wish it barely knew it had" (in other words, as "victimizer and victim"), a "strong" case can be made that the hero's justified assault upon villains is a form of violence that does not merely revel in bloodshed for its own sake, but one which takes seriously the entire narrative and fully engages the viewer at the level of identification and participation in acts that

---

41. Slocum, "Film Violence and the Institutionalization of the Cinema," 672.
42. Devin McKinney, "Violence: The Strong and the Weak," in *Screening Violence*, ed. Stephen Prince (New Brunswick, NJ: Rutgers University Press, 2000), 101–2.
43. Ibid., 102.
44. Ibid., 105.
45. Ibid., 106–07.

are morally freighted. The revenge trilogy of Park Chan-wook in particular, with their ambivalent attitude toward both the justification and inevitable unpleasantness of vindictive retaliation and their portrayal of the hero's sense of loss at exacting his/her vengeance, reveals a profound capacity for revenge films to be morally self-critical. Of the trilogy, Alison Hoffman-Han writes: "These films, when taken together, exemplify Park's signature combination of restrained form with 'extreme', violent content, an aesthetic fusion that engages, first, spectatorial shock, but then allows enough time and room for critical contemplation of that mediated violence."[46]

A genre-informed assessment of morality in violent films

For all that can be said of revenge films' ability to dabble in the type of ambiguity that destabilizes our moral positioning and cause self-reflection, the ultimate ethical payoff lies in its establishment of moral absolutes. Evil is clearly evil and must be put down with extreme and violent prejudice. As the above survey of narrative and character depictions makes clear, the offenses are unquestionably wicked, performed by villains who not only show no remorse, but who view their crimes as part of mundane—even *enjoyable*—activity. The acts are regarded as so extreme that measures of "supernatural" proportions are required on the part of the larger-than-life protagonists. Counterintuitive though it might seem on the surface, the hero's typical disdain for established law enforcement, either through his attitude toward its ineptitude, corruption, or failure to do enough, or the way he ignores the rule and consequence of law to achieve his ends, actually elevates him to a higher moral ground from which he judges ordinary justice by his personal standard.[47]

Some writers frame this in terms of American cultural myth enshrined in the classic Western, whose genre, it is argued, forms the essential story of most action, war, and crime films. Set against the backdrop of American colonization of Native Americans (Manifest Destiny) and the idea of an untamed, unexplored frontier fraught with constant threat of death from the elements, disease, and outlaws, the Western, according to John Nachbar is "the single most important story form of the twentieth century" and, for

---

46. Alison Hoffman-Han, "'You Can't Help But Feel Uncomfortable, Even Though You're Smiling': An Interview with Park Chan-Wook," *Journal of Japanese and Korean Cinema* 4, no. 2 (January 1, 2012): 186, doi:10.1386/jjkc.4.2.185_7.

47. Eric S. Christianson, "A Fistful of Shekels: Ehud the Judge (Judges 3:12–30) and the Spaghetti Western," in *Cinéma Divinité: Religion, Theology and the Bible in Film*, ed. Eric S. Christianson, Peter Francis, and William R. Telford (London: SCM, 2005), 206.

Americans, a repository of "their traditional ethics, values and sources of national pride."[48] A 1959 *Time* magazine article regarded the genre as "the American Morality Play," in which good and evil battle it out and "evil always loses."[49] Taking into account a wider of spectrum of genres within film and television, Jewett and Lawrence summarize the myth as follows:

> A community in a harmonious paradise is threatened by evil; normal institutions fail to contend with this threat; a selfless superhero emerges to renounce temptations and carry out the redemptive task; aided by fate, his decisive victory restores the community to its paradisiacal condition; the superhero then recedes into obscurity.[50]

The authors criticize this American "monomyth" for its potential to erode democracy, promote anarchy, and escalate societal violence, a position in line with postmodern attempts to deconstruction the "myth of redemptive violence."

That popular culture is often a reflection of cultural values is generally undisputed, but whether the myth has its roots in American culture and values alone is questionable. In his work, *Our Faith in Evil: Melodrama and the Effects of Entertainment Violence*, Gregory Desilet surveys melodrama throughout the history of literature and modern popular culture and concludes that a society's particular view of the dualism between good and evil is the cultural core which deserves critical attention when confronting the question of the effects of violent entertainment. He argues that media violence is surrounded by multiple layers including psychological, social, historical, religious, moral, as well as mythical, and are necessarily complex and interwoven.[51] The idea that the superhero myth (for our purposes, the revenge narrative) is somehow isolated within American history and culture is challenged by the fact that the narrative exhibits itself consistently, and glowingly, in world cinema, not least in the productions from South Korea and Japan discussed in this chapter. Although Desilet does little to interact with the fundamental difference between fictional and societal violence, pointing to understandings of conflict at a metaphysical level is more productive than assessing violence in terms of context-situated myth.

---

48. John G. Nachbar, *Focus on the Western* (Englewood Cliffs, NJ.: Prentice-Hall, 1974), 2.

49. Gregory Desilet, *Our Faith in Evil: Melodrama and the Effects of Entertainment Violence* (Jefferson, NC: McFarland & Company, 2006), 214.

50. Lawrence and Jewett, *The Myth of the American Superhero*, 6.

51. Desilet, *Our Faith in Evil*, 26.

The sharp distinction between good and evil, then, seems fundamental to the wide popularity of films that put vindictive violence on display. Psychologist of aggression and spectatorship, Dolf Zillman, argues for a strong link between audiences' emotional involvement with characters and the moral appraisal they give them. Even toward persons to whom audience are initially indifferent, the conduct of persons is judged in binary terms (e.g. virtuous/selfish, acceptable/intolerable, good/evil, right/wrong).[52] These attributions result in pleasure or displeasure when the moral sanctions or condemnations of a character's actions are confirmed or disconfirmed, and these are translated into "hopes for benefaction and fears of aversive outcomes."[53] While it has been suggested that empathy plays a large role in this relationship between viewer and screen character, Zillman finds that "for empathy to have occurred, affect in character and observer must be concordant."[54] Simply put, the screen character and the viewer share the same emotion. More importantly, "negative affective dispositions" like hatred possess a high moral potency and tend to override empathetic inclinations such that viewers "uninhibitedly enjoy the punitive action when it materializes."[55] This tendency, which Zillman terms "counterempathy" "hinges on a system of moral judgment" and explains how a character's joy can result in a viewers pain and vice versa. As for the content of this moral system that sanctions punitive violence, it is recognized that humans have the desire to live in a safe world and that violence is deemed acceptable for procuring public safety. However, Zillman rightly points out that standards vary culturally and shift over time. And yet, the concept of "fair retaliation" or "righteous violence" still remains fairly universal and is sustained by clear depictions of wrongful transgression. He writes:

> Any gruesome retributive killing has to appear just, and this appearance has to be prepared by witnessing the party to be punished perform increasingly despicable heinous crimes. This is to say that escalations in the portrayal of righteous, enjoyable violence necessitate escalations in the portrayal of morally enraging, evil, and distressing violence. The specification of

---

52. Dolf Zillman, "The Psychology of the Appeal of Portrayals of Violence," in *Why We Watch: The Attractions of Violent Entertainment*, ed. Jeffrey Goldstein (New York: Oxford University Press, 1998), 201.

53. Ibid.

54. Ibid., 202. Zillman cites Berger, S.M. (1962). Conditioning through vicarious instigation. *Psychological Review,* 29, 450–66.

55. Ibid.

depictions of enjoyable retributive violence, then, appears to a function of the depiction of deplorable violence.[56]

Recalling the protracted scenes of violent rape in *I Spit on Your Grave* and the protagonist's sadistic payback upon her assailants, for example, one can see how Zillman's theory underscores the central role that morality plays in the relationship between severe violent depictions and the audience's gleeful sanction of retribution. Insofar as films portray an obvious case of righteous violence, the average viewer's sense of justice is absolutized and solidified. Rather than the notion that morality must be "checked at the door" when watching and enjoying revenge films, the opposite is in fact true; the films *depend* on a high functioning moral standard in order to work. Thus, in the revenge film, villains are as despicable as possible, and vengeance is as decisive as possible.

Conclusion

In this chapter, I have outlined the main elements and strategies that filmmakers employ to portray what is reasonably recognized within the revenge film genre. A heinous act, or series of acts, on the part of some reprehensible figure(s) elicits the response of the lead protagonist(s), with the help of allies, to a mission of extermination for whom the offense strikes some personal cord, either directly or through a beloved third party. The films set up offenses and offenders as unambiguously vile and the hero's victory as decisive and just, yet often with a lingering sense that the payback was necessary but not necessarily enjoyable. In order to summon the will and ability to suppress so evil an opponent, the hero typically draws upon the darkest of resources within him/herself and effectively becomes like his opponent, all the while maintaining a high—even extreme—standard of morality that is likewise reinforced throughout the film.

This morality naturally spills over to the audience for whom the premise of the film and the characters must resonate in order to evoke pleasure and satisfaction. Because the nature of these films are unflinchingly violent and at times horrifyingly brutal, much effort is taken to successfully portray screen violence in ways that uphold the average viewer's sense of morality, and in turn, their enjoyment of the film. Central to these ends is the effort to maximize the fictional quality of the narrative and images. Audiences are made to remember that cinematic worlds are ontologically distinct from reality, yet, at the same time, the films are part of a moral universe that

---

56. Ibid., 206.

makes sense and is satisfying when understood in light of its own unfolding narrative and character depictions.

In terms of the appropriateness of drawing on cinematic violence to stimulate theological imagination, it is worth reiterating that this procedure in no way makes any claim that these images are morally neutral or positive in themselves and therefore can and should be used. It could very well be that these images, and their creators, have succeeded in beautifying and concealing something inescapably gruesome. The use of cinematic revenge narratives to model Christian atonement (from an evangelical perspective) is not justified on the basis that it is beautiful, but that it is *biblical*, which the next chapter will seek to demonstrate.

5.

Scripture and Cinematic Vengeance in Dialogue

WE NOW ARRIVE AT a juncture where a constructive proposal concerning Christian atonement may begin. The essential claim of my thesis deserves repetition: God deals with sin in a consistent, retaliatory manner. It follows, therefore, that instances of divine, retributive action in localized biblical narratives will reflect and inform how sin is judged in its superlative mode, i.e. in the atonement. Having surveyed the various elements of cinema featuring the theme of vengeful retribution, the contours of a hermeneutical lens is formed with which to view biblical narratives. The aim is to note the resonances and dissonances that emerge in order to establish what relationship, if any, might exist between the world of the revenge film and that of biblical narratives of divine judgment. The promise of this procedure is twofold:

1. to expand our idea of retribution in the direction of a positive appreciation of its various components; and

2. to draw the seemingly discordant images into a narrative whole that contributes to a general notion of biblical atonement.

The hopeful product of this theology-film dialogue is an answer to the question: Can a new atonement story be told in which violence has a positive place?

As with the film medium, my concern is on the concrete, surface-level details that form the biblical narratives as entire scenes of action, rather than engage exegetical minutiae and text critical debates or accommodate the wide spectrum of contextual interpretations. The sequences themselves, whether narrated by the biblical authors or produced by the filmmaker, contain the material that is most valuable to this study. I will show how the surprising congruence between Scripture and cinema, even at awkward junctures, solidifies the extent to which the two can meaningfully track with one another.

Bonds with the Beloved

Scripture is obviously replete with divine overtures of love toward covenant members. The category I have designated as the "beloved" comprises individuals that are beneficiaries of God's direct interaction as well as entire people groups with whom God engages corporately. We begin by surveying the dominant themes concerning the identity of these beneficiaries and how they relate with the cinematic paradigms previously discussed.

First, we may note God's preferential disposition toward youthfulness that repeatedly spans the narratives of biblical, and especially Old Testament, history. In his book, *When Brothers Dwell Together: The Preeminence of Younger Siblings in the Hebrew Bible*,[1] Frederick E. Greenspahn explores the younger sibling motif in Scripture and Near Eastern sources, challenging the argument that ultimogeniture has precedent in ancient legal practice or as a protest against cultural custom. Rather, the election of the younger sibling demonstrates "some sort of superhuman force, and the heroes' youth suggests their innocence and vulnerability."[2] In other words, the lack of relative agency in the status of the non-firstborn child highlights divine potency. The dominant motif of the youthful beloved in typical revenge cinema plays on this juxtaposition rather fittingly. In the films *Man on Fire*, *Leon*, and *Man from Nowhere*, the lethal male protagonist enters into a bond with a helpless, young girl. Even the undertones of a bond turned almost perversely romantic, explored especially in *Leon*, finds a biblical correlate in Deuteronomy 7:7, where it is explained why God has "set his heart" upon Israel, a verb which typically denotes "sexual craving."[3]

We should observe, however, that "innocence," as might be said of Abel, Isaac, and young David, for instance, is not always the prevailing characteristic of God's preferred ones. The most paradigmatic instance of election is Jacob, who is portrayed as a thief and swindler. Similarly, Joseph is depicted as arrogantly fueling his brothers' angry jealousy by imprudently telling them his dreams of grandeur. In considering films, we see that *True Grit*'s Mattie Ross is a feisty and shrewd dealmaker, and *Leon*'s Mathilda survives by deceit.

---

1. Frederick E. Greenspahn, *When Brothers Dwell Together: The Preeminence of Younger Siblings in the Hebrew Bible* (New York: Oxford University Press, 1994).

2. Ibid., 6.

3. Richard D. Nelson, *Deuteronomy* (Louisville: Westminster John Knox Press, 2002), 101.

In *Unforgiven*, the victims are saloon prostitutes, and in *Hara-Kiri*, Motome attempts to con a feudal lord into giving him charity. However, the characters still seem to demonstrate a strong inner resolve to do what they set out to accomplish, despite the dubious morality of their means. The congruent pattern that emerges is that while the characters are driven as well as crafty, they are in dire need of help that transcends their abilities. As Mathilda says to Leon, "If you don't help me, I'll die tonight. I can feel it."

Not only are the many chosen individuals of questionable virtue, they are often portrayed as afflicted by circumstances outside their control. In a brief exchange outside their respective apartments, Mathilda, nursing a bloody nose from one of her many daily conflicts, asks Leon, "Is life always this hard, or is just when you're a kid?" A couple scenes later, her family is gunned down and she left with no recourse but to cling to Leon. Likewise is the portrayal of Rodney (*Out of the Furnace*) whose troubled youth and traumatic Iraq war experience intensifies his difficulty to readjust to small town life with his brother. It is the harsh circumstances of these characters that often activates the sympathy of the hero to action in much the same way that Exodus narrates the distress of the Israelites in Exod 2:23–25:

> After a long time the king of Egypt died. The Israelites groaned under their slavery, and cried out. Out of the slavery their cry for help rose up to God. God heard their groaning, and God remembered his covenant with Abraham, Isaac, and Jacob. God looked upon the Israelites, and God took notice of them.

In light of this, accounts of God's preferential treatment for the younger becomes, as Greenspahn puts it, "a literature of consolation designed to assure those whose oppression contradicted their belief in God's concern."[4]

Second, it is notable that at times, the nature of God's revealed affection for his preferred people is set against a distinct indifference—or even antagonism—for others. In Deuteronomy 7:6–8 we hear of God loving and electing Israel "out of all the peoples on earth" to be his treasured possession. Their identity as the "fewest of all peoples" is contrasted to nations that were "more numerous." This preferential comparison can be said to come to a climax in the context of exilic redemption, as when Isaiah 43:3 calls on Israel not to fear "[f]or I am the Lord your God, the Holy One of Israel, your Savior. I give Egypt as your ransom, Ethiopia and Seba in exchange for you." It is because Israel is particularly precious, honored, and loved that God vows to give peoples and nations "in exchange for [her] life" (v. 4). Read within our cinematic hermeneutic, the image of ransom is

---

4. Greenspahn, *When Brothers Dwell Together*, 109.

especially relevant. Noting the obvious "crassness" of the rhetoric that might otherwise be directed against "the others," Brueggemann states: "It is clear that we are not intended to follow the metaphor to its extreme and logical conclusion, but to take it only for the single feature of *treasuring Israel* in an extreme way."[5]

In the revenge film, the hero's mode of establishing a favored status through contrast with others is typically done through dialogue. Bryan Mills' opening interaction with his daughter, Kim, in *Taken* contrasts with the disdain shared between him and his ex-wife, Lenore. In the context of redemptive vengeance, the "extreme" nature of the hero's love is demonstrated by his determination. Sheriff Hunt and O'Dwyer (*Bone Tomahawk*) embark on their dangerous rescue mission because there "isn't a choice"; and John Creasy (*Man on Fire*) vows to eliminate anyone who was involved in, or profited from, Pita's abduction. In both biblical and cinematic worlds, the motif of a strong—and extreme—bond of love provides the necessary impetus for the pursuit of the offender. As Greenspahn sums up: "God works with these figures because He can and He must. He created them, and He chose them. As things turn out, neither God nor Israel is as perfect as they should be. Perhaps that is why they make such good partners."[6]

Within the Gospels, we find the theme of the beloved manifested most directly in Jesus' choice of, and concern for, his disciples. It is said of them that he "loved to the uttermost" and that the Father loved them. The Gospel writers, understood traditionally as disciples or close associates themselves, are not shy about describing their questionable occupations (e.g. Levi the tax collector, Simon the zealot) or weakness of character (e.g. Peter's temperament, Thomas' doubt, and the general one-up-man-ship of the twelve in general), yet Jesus lovingly chooses, instructs, and protects them. He demonstrates a preference for them in divulging the "secrets of the kingdom of heaven" to them but not others (Matt 13:11), in warning them against the yeast of the Pharisees (Mark 8:15), and contrasting them to the "kings of the gentiles" (Luke 22:25–26). Even more explicitly, in his High Priestly Prayer, Jesus says, "I am praying for them, *I am not praying for the world*." As a corollary, this love was reciprocated toward Jesus through their devotion, albeit often overstated (e.g. Peter's vow to never deny him, Mark 14:31) and even physical affection (the disciple who laid his head upon his breast, John 13:23).

---

5. Walter Brueggemann, *Isaiah 40–66* (Louisville: Westminster John Knox Press, 1998), 54. Italics mine.

6. Greenspahn, *When Brothers Dwell Together*, 160.

Offenders and Offenses

Villains and their heinous deeds are colorfully depicted and narrated in cinematic and biblical worlds. In both cases, they are portrayed, presumably, from the perspective of the "good guys," so that one's assessment of them is unambiguous as to their morality and the role they play in the redemptive narrative. A broad, cursory look at paradigmatic villains in biblical history might first reveal their general status as people of power who fear usurpation. Political heads of state that have dealings with the people of God are often named, described, and narrated in the text. In the opening of Exodus, Pharaoh gives his rationale for subjugating the Israelites, arguing that they have become "more numerous and more powerful than we" (1:9) and issues orders to "deal shrewdly" with them (1:10). The narrator wastes no time mincing words and immediately describes how the Egyptians proceed to "oppress" them (1:11), become "ruthless" (1:13), and make their lives "bitter with hard service" (1:14). In his paranoia, Pharaoh launches a preemptive attack upon the Hebrew infant boys, an act that has its New Testament counterpart in Herod, who decrees the same after being "infuriated" at the Magi's trickery (Matt 2:16). The actions on the part of these powerful political villains display a veneer of logical reasoning; however, the brutality of their solutions renders them as nothing short of sociopathic. In this way, it is not difficult to identify their cinematic correlate in such characters as Emperor Commodus (*Gladiator*), who, in his utter insecurity about the approval of his people and the love of his sister and lover, Lucilla, orders the execution of Maximus for refusing to kiss his hand and stages 150 days of gladiatorial fights to honor his dead father.

In terms of physical appearance, we noted a trend in revenge films to portray some villains as clean-cut and well dressed. The clear, pale skin of Asian villains, such as Kamiki (*Sun Scarred*), Naritsugu (*13 Assassins*), and U-jin (*Oldboy*) is an obvious tactic to make the characters appear attractive. This corresponds with biblical injunctions against the deceitful allurement of beauty, as in the devil's guise as an "angel of light" (2 Cor 11:14), or Proverbial warnings against the adulteress: "Do not desire her beauty in your heart, and do not let her capture you with her eyelashes" (Prov 6:25). While cinematic villains are usually male, the medium of film has a unique way of bridging the gender disparity and allowing men to exhibit what is most often linked to feminine qualities. One of the first screen appearances of U-jin in *Oldboy* demonstrates this, in which he emerges from his shower and walks in the nude toward his wardrobe with his back facing the audience. Kelly Jeong thoughtfully analyzes: "This sequence makes an ironic reference to the typically sexualized—and in most classic examples—male-identified camera gaze of the film noir that fetishizes the female body by visually framing/cutting it in discrete parts."[7] We have in this example the possibility for a male to disclose the feminine form of sinister beauty.

From another angle, the tone of speech of many cinematic antagonists is smooth and effeminate, sometimes peppered with cryptic questions and sayings that give a sense of the villain's sinister yet intelligent designs, such as U-jin's first words with Dae-su on the phone: "Do you like your clothes? . . . Who do you think I am?" followed by his quip: "Whether it be a grain of sand or a rock, in water they both sink alike." The biblical reader might naturally relate this with the Eden scene in which the serpent, "more crafty than any other wild animal that the Lord God had made" (Gen 3:1), tempts Eve into eating the fruit by asking a question, "Did God say, 'You shall not eat from any tree in the garden'?" followed by a mystifying statement, ". . . for God knows that when you eat of it your eyes will be opened, and you will be like God, knowing good and evil" (3:5). Like the serpent, a large part of U-jin's sense of success is in the display of his cunning. He warmly and seductively approaches his opponent in order to toy with him and enjoys seeing his enemy wander the maze of his masterful plan. A similar pattern resurfaces in Jesus' temptation in the wilderness (Matt 4:1–11; Luke 4:1–15), where Satan, in an indirectly antagonistic fashion, puts him through a battery of tests designed, as classically argued, to prefigure the hardships of his future ministry.[8]

While both cinema and Scripture attest to villainy in physically attractive terms, the prevailing tendency is to portray them as wholly *other*. Biblical "bad guys" often possess distinguishing features that are abnormal, even subhuman. For example, King Eglon of Moab, who allied with the Ammonites and Amalekites and enslaved Israel for eighteen years, is described as "very fat" (Judg 3:17)—so much so, that it swallows Ehud's sword, hilt and all (3:22). Commentator, Deryn Guest, suggests that the mocking satirization of Eglon's gross obesity operates as a "cipher" for other qualities that play out in the narrative, such as gullibility and extreme greed.[9] Eglon, though a Moabite king, is mocked as nothing less than a beast. The fact that his name bears phonetic similarity with the Hebrew word for "calf" further

---

7. Kelly Y. Jeong, "Towards Humanity and Redemption: The World of Park Chan-Wook's Revenge Film Trilogy," *Journal of Japanese and Korean Cinema* 4, no. 2 (January 1, 2012): 171, doi:10.1386/jjkc.4.2.169_1.

8. For example, Hugh Farmer, *An Inquiry Into the Nature and Design of Christ's Temptation in the Wilderness: To which is Added, an Appendix* (London: J. Buckland, and J. Waugh), 1765.

9. P. Deryn Guest, "Judges," in *Eerdmans Commentary on the Bible*, ed. James D. G. Dunn (Grand Rapids: Eerdmans, 2003), 191.

underscores this intention, and results in the interesting notion that Ehud slaughters the "fattened calf," further exemplifying the idea explored in this study of a close juxtaposition between villain and sacrificial victim. In reference to the Canaanite conquests, T. M. Lemos suggests:

> Israelite authors constructed elaborate and persuasive justifications for violence that at once created an insider identity and called for the destruction of outsiders described as wholly other and as wholly dangerous, so much so that even the things associated with them must be eliminated.[10]

In the revenge film, Lemos' remarks find fullest visual expression. The image of the villain as an "animal" is common in such uncouth characters as Harlon DeGroat (*Out of the Furnace*) and Tom Chaney (*True Grit*), who display wild savagery and a lack of control. Ever clearer is the example of the cave-dwelling cannibals in *Bone Tomahawk*, who lack human language and merely burst out in loud roars through intentionally-mutilated vocal chords. The chief of this savage tribe is depicted sporting an impressive set of boar tusks protruding from his jaw reminiscent of images of the dragon and first beast in Revelation 12–13, whose horns signify kingly powers (Rev 17:12).

Of the offenses that motivate divine retaliatory violence, the terrain is broad and the data abounds. On this theme, as Scripture might well be considered a veritable anthology of crime and punishment, so only a sampling of narratives need be surveyed here. We may begin with those acts that can be said to issue from the very "hand of God" for some direct infraction. Narratives concerning violations of cultic procedure exemplify a dramatic unfolding of a vengeful type of violence. Leviticus 10:1–3 tells of God's quick and decisive retaliation upon Aaron's sons, Nadab and Abihu, who offered "strange fire" to God "such as he had not commanded them." The next verse is straightforward: "And fire came out from the presence of the Lord and consumed them, and they died before the Lord" (10:2). A similar fate befalls Uzzah, who reached out his hand to steady the cart-borne Ark of the Covenant on its way to Jerusalem (2 Sam 6:6–7). As a result, "the anger of the Lord was kindled against Uzzah; and God struck him there because he reached out his hand to the ark; and he died there beside the ark of God." In the NT, we see lethal divine interventions in two episodes in Acts. In their fraudulent financial dealings with the apostolic church, Ananias and Sapphira "lie to the Holy Spirit" (5:3) and "put the Spirit of the Lord to the test" (5:9). This leads to their immediate deaths. The author of Acts also provides

---

10. T. M. Lemos, "Dispossessing Nations: Population Growth, Scarcity, and Genocide in Ancient Israel and Twentieth-Century Rwanda," in Saul M. Olyan, ed. *Ritual Violence in the Hebrew Bible* (New York: Oxford University Press, 2015), 48.

a brief comment into the death of Herod Agrippa I in Acts 12:21–23: "On an appointed day Herod put on his royal robes, took his seat on the platform, and delivered a public address to them. The people kept shouting, 'The voice of a god, and not of a mortal!' And immediately, because he had not given the glory to God, an angel of the Lord struck him down, and he was eaten by worms and died." In each of these cases, the offenses are linked to presumption and pride on the offenders' part. It seems these actions (or in Herod's case, non-action) are perceived as direct attacks upon God's character and holiness and are worthy of direct and immediate capital punishment.

The devastating "overkill" of these scenes shock the witnesses: Aaron is speechless (Lev 10:3), David is angry (2 Sa 6:8–9), and the early church community is "seized" with fear (Acts 5:11). When compared with typical revenge films, we find that this type of reaction is virtually unprecedented. The actions of Iosef and his thugs in killing John Wick's dog and stealing his car, and John's subsequent rampage, perhaps comes closest to the revenge narrative of "biblical proportions" above. Film reviewer, Sophie Gilbert, sarcastically remarks that the tagline of *John Wick* should be changed from "Don't set him off" to "This idiot killed my puppy and now everyone must die."[11] It would seem that this is a scenario in which Scripture transcends and challenges the simpler, easier to stomach, discourse and moral vision afforded by typical revenge films.

While the instances of direct divine intervention for attacks upon God's holiness are present in Scripture, the bulk of the narrative material that reveals God's motivation toward vengeful retribution exhibits a broader social dimension. God acts when a beloved is harmed. We see this clearly in Exod 17:8–16, where the Amalekites attack the wandering Israelites at Rephidim, and God instructs Moses: "Write this as a reminder in a book and recite it in the hearing of Joshua: I will utterly blot out the remembrance of Amalek from under heaven" (v. 14). The fulfillment of this oath is taken up centuries later when God commands Saul through Samuel: "I will punish the Amalekites for what they did in opposing the Israelites when they came up out of Egypt. Now go and attack Amalek, and utterly destroy all that they have; do not spare them, but kill both man and woman, child and infant, ox and sheep, camel and donkey" (1 Sam 15:2–3). John's Apocalypse takes up this similar theme when the angel pours the third bowl of God's wrath upon the waters "... because they shed the blood of saints and prophets, you have given them blood to drink. It is what they deserve!" (Rev 16:6). The

---

11. Sophie Gilbert, "John Wick: An Idiot Killed His Puppy and Now Everyone Must Die," *The Atlantic*, October 24, 2014, http://www.theatlantic.com/entertainment/archive/2014/10/john-wick-an-idiot-killed-his-puppy-and-now-everyone-must-die/381921/?single_page=true.

lex talionis code of justice that functions in revenge films is clearly at work, but one in which the retaliation is disproportionate—yet still fitting—to the crime. This is reminiscent of John Creasy's (*Man on Fire*) approach of annihilating anyone and everyone remotely involved in Pita's death (as he believes it at the time), or the massive kill count of almost 80 in *John Wick*.

Along with physical attacks upon Israel, God takes offense at spiritual seducers, who lead his people away from his covenant commands. This is played out in the divine attitude against the Midianites in which vengeance is carried out on two levels. At the individual level, Phinehas son of Eleazar zealously spears an Israelite man and his Midinianite consort (Num 25:8), and in so doing, halts a plague that claims 24,000 Israelite lives. At the national level, God later commands Israel to "execute the Lord's vengeance on Midian" (Num 31:3) for causing Israel to "act treacherously against the LORD" at Peor (v. 16). Thus, in a sense, God makes war on foreign ideologies contrary to his expressed standard in the similar way that Hanshiro (*Hara-Kiri*) becomes enraged at the feudal lord for insisting that his son-in-law carry out *seppuku* according to a compassionless notion of honor, or when Bryan Mills (*Taken*) unleashes his vengeance on the sex trafficking network that drugged and sold his daughter into prostitution.

While divine retribution is mostly directed against enemy forces, Scripture yet again destabilizes the typical pattern of cinematic vengeance in that divine wrath is often poured out *upon* his covenant people. Not only does God put to death "wicked" individuals, like Er and Onan (Gen 38:7, 10), Nadab and Abihu (Lev 10:1–8), Korah, Dathan, and Abiram (Num 16), but serious judgments fall upon those regarded as biblical "heroes of faith," like Miriam (Num 12), Moses (Num 20:1–12), David (2 Sam 12, 24:10–17), and Uzziah (2 Sam 6:6–7; 1 Chr 13:6–10). Corporately, divine judgment upon Israel yields staggeringly high numbers of in-house fatalities: the Korah incident (Num 16:49), 14,700; the Peor incident (Num 25:9), 24,000; David's census (2 Sam 24:13), 70,000. Rhetorically, some divine pronouncements upon his people are exceedingly harsh. Asaph relates how Israel's idolatry caused God to be "full of wrath" and to "utterly reject" and "abandon" Israel and his dwelling place (Ps 78:59–60). The prophets often speak of Israel as a "harlot" (e.g. Ezek 23:3–19, 43:7, 9; Hos 4:15, 9:1; Jer 2:20, 3:6, 8). Psalm 95 describes how God "loathed" the generation that came out of Egypt and in his anger "swore" that "They shall not enter my rest" (v. 10–11). Lest we be tempted to relegate this stern language to the Old Testament alone, Hebrews cites this psalm as a warning for those who have become "partners in Christ" not to fall away in unbelief (Heb 3:12–19), and Paul uses the illustration of the church's having been "grafted" into Israel to warn believers against spiritual pride, saying, "for if God did not spare the natural branches, He will not spare you, either" (Rom 11:21 NASB).

That such a strong tone and attitude could be launched against the beloved in the typical revenge film is unthinkable, as it would greatly defeat its premise and moral outlook. The few instances where hostility between hero and beloved are part of the story occur *before* the bond has been established, as when *Leon* is tempted to put a bullet in Mathilda's head when she first seeks sanctuary in his apartment and disturbs his reclusive lifestyle, or when Creasy (*Man on Fire*) is first employed as Pita's bodyguard and informs her, "I'm not being paid to be your friend; I'm being paid to protect you." On the whole, revenge films consistently portray and reinforce positive displays of affection between hero and beloved, however subtle they may be. That Scripture subverts this point by including the beloved among those to be judged with violence is a critical departure from the filmic model of revenge. This cinematic framing through which we may read biblical texts may alert us to the possibility that divine loathing is not aimed at persons, villains or otherwise, *as such*. Rather, a deeper principle of wickedness is the strain common to both that elicits divine anger and the need to exact judgment.

The Avenger's Methods

It has been noted above how lethal judgments are sometimes dispensed through direct "acts of God." These are inventions that involve no human participants or natural means. The Pentateuch attests to great signs and wonders as proof of God's unique involvement in dispensing judgment (Exod 7:4-5, 14:16-18). When Korah, Dathan, and Abiram instigate a national rebellion in the wilderness, Moses declares that his vindication as prophet will be verified if God "creates something new" rather than having them die by natural deaths (Num 16:29-30). The result is the earth opens up and swallows their households and belongings (v. 31-33). During the monarchy, the Assyrians under Sennacherib invade Judah, mounting military campaigns, insults, and threats against a disheartened Hezekiah, who prays for salvation (2 Kgs 19:14-19). God vows vengeance through Isaiah:

> But I know your rising and your sitting your going out and coming in, and your raging against me. Because you have raged against me and your arrogance has come to my ears, I will put my hook in your nose and my bit in your mouth. I will turn you back on the way by which you came (19:27-28).

What follows is one of the highest kill counts recorded in Scripture in which "the angel of the Lord set out and struck down 185,000 in the camp of the Assyrians" (2 Kgs 19:35). Again, the sequence of offense, cry, vow, and annihilation exemplifies the typical revenge pattern with remarkable congruence. In the NT, Revelation features the "Rider on the White Horse" with a sword from his mouth with which to "strike down the nations" with the fury of God's wrath (Rev 19:15, 20). These images of supernatural force portray the divine figure as invincible and his enemies as pests to exterminate. This is not unlike the demonstrations of skill often employed in revenge films to highlight the extraordinary ability and legendary status of lead characters like Bryan Mills (*Taken*) or John Wick, who seem to steamroll over high numbers of low-level foes with relative ease.

This Yahweh-as-warrior motif is so replete in Scripture as can be regarded as central to many Old Testament epochs in general, including creation, exodus, and conquest accounts as well as themes of judgment and exile.[12] Perhaps the most explicit narrative involving this theme occurs in Joshua's theophany of the sword-drawn "commander of the army of the LORD," whom Joshua falls down to worship (Josh 5:13–15). This character refuses to claim immediate partisanship with either Israel or her adversaries (v. 13), but the dominant idea throughout Scripture is that the LORD of hosts fights on behalf of his people (e.g. Exod 14:13–14; Deut 1:30, 3:22; Josh 23:10; Isa 30:31–32). Often, Yahweh's warring is co-extensive with earthly military campaigns, the paradigm of which stems from the Canaanite conquests. While some victories are attributed to supernatural intervention, such as Yahweh throwing the Amorite armies into a "panic," hurling down "huge stones from heaven" (Josh 10:10–11) and causing the sun to stand still (v. 13), Yahweh's warring often aligns with the military campaigns of human agents. This is hinted in the strong link between Yahweh's kingly reign and his military status that Psalm 24:8 reinforces: "Who is the King of glory? The Lord, strong and mighty, the Lord, mighty in battle." Principally, Israel received explicit commands concerning war with the Canaanites under the concept of the "ban" as in Deut 7:1–2:

> When the Lord your God brings you into the land that you are about to enter and occupy, and he clears away many nations before you—the Hittites, the Girgashites, the Amorites, the Canaanites, the Perizzites, the Hivites, and the Jebusites, seven nations mightier and more numerous than you—and when the Lord your God gives them over to you and you defeat them,

---

12. Richard Nysse, "Yahweh Is a Warrior," *Word & World* 7, no. 2 (1987): 193.

then you must utterly destroy them. Make no covenant with them and show them no mercy.

Along with Deut 20:17, these are the most important and explicit commands to wage war on the level of complete annihilation. The point to note is that in both cases, the explicit command to wage war in the first place is absent. They are told what to do *when* they are brought into the land (7:1), *when* the LORD gives their enemies over to them (7:2), and *when* they go to war (20:1, 10).

In subsequent situations of conflict in Israel's history, such as Babylon's military role in the book of Jeremiah,[13] some commentators have insisted upon Yahweh acting in an "unmediated way," arguing that human agents are "instruments" but not "real agents."[14] In comparing the references of God engaging in wartime action vs. similar statements by Babylonian agency, Terrence Fretheim concludes "it becomes clear that God's actions are not 'stand-alone' actions; God is working in and through Babylonian agents."[15] This sharing of violent responsibility has implications for reading these texts in light of revenge films, in which protagonists very often employ allies and closely tied accomplices in their mission. Though they may function cinematically as "minor characters," allies like Robocop's partner, Lewis, and John Wick's friend, Marcus, are often crucial combatants in the hero's mission and sometimes play a role in saving the hero's life. The need for allies becomes stronger in proportion to the strength of enemy forces, as portrayed in *13 Assassins* and *Bone Tomahawk*. In *Leon*, the idea of camaraderie is especially relevant to our discussion in that a weak and troubled little girl, Mathilda, is the object of the villain's offense and joins forces with an assassin, both as a means to bond with him under his tutelage and to exact her own vengeance. Prior to him accepting her request to help him "clean" (work as an assassin), they dialogue at the dining table:

> Mathilda: I've decided what to do with my life. I wanna be a cleaner.

---

13. For example, Nebuchadnezzar is called God's "servant" in Jer 25:9; 27:6; 43:10. In Jer 27:8 God says that his punishment upon the nations with the sword, famine, and pestilence will have been completed "by his hand."

14. See Walter Bruggemann, *A Commentary on Jeremiah: Exile and Homecoming* (Grand Rapids: Eerdmans, 1996), 54, 70, 176, 193, 428, 430, 460; Robert R. Carroll, *Jeremiah: A Commentary* (Philadelphia: Westminster John Knox Press, 1986), 294 quoted in Terrence Fretheim, "Violence and the God of the Old Testament," in *Encountering Violence in the Bible*, ed. Markus Zehnder and Hallvard Hagelia (Sheffield: Sheffield Phoenix Press, 2013), 116–17.

15. Fretheim, "Violence and the God of the Old Testament," 118.

Leon: You wanna be a cleaner. Here, take it. (*Giving her a pistol*) It's a goodbye gift. Go clean. But not with me. I work alone. Understand? Alone.

Mathilda: Bonnie and Clyde didn't work alone. Thelma and Louise didn't work alone. And they were the best.

Leon (*sighs*): Mathilda. Why are doing this to me? I've been nothing but nice to you. I even saved your life yesterday. Right outside the door.

Mathilda: Right. So now you're responsible for it. If you saved my life, you must've saved it for a good reason. If you throw me out now, it's like you never opened the door, like you let me die right there in front of it . . .

Leon: Mathilda, you're just a little girl, so don't it badly, but I don't think you could do it. I'm sorry.

Mathlida then gets up, takes the pistol, walks to an open window, and starts firing random shots into the street. She returns to the dining table, places the gun down, and gives him a cocky look. "How's that?" In subsequent montages and sequences, Mathilda proves herself valuable to Leon's work, despite being young and inexperienced. This idea of training is also reflected in Scripture as part of Yahweh's rationale for leaving inhabitants in Canaan after the initial conquests. It was "to test all those in Israel who had no experience of any war in Canaan . . . to teach those who had no experience of it before" (Judg 3:1–2). To paraphrase using the language of *Leon*, God gave Israel opportunities to practice "cleaning."

How Leon and Mathilda become a great team in assassinating "clients" is by having Mathilda pose as a scared little girl in front of their doors, while Leon stands nearby with a pair of bolt cutters to breach the chain lock when the client opens the door to Mathilda's innocent-sounding voice. We noted above how in his final confrontation with Stansfield, Leon manages to pull the pin of a grenade while Stansfield gloats over him—a "ring trick" foreshadowed earlier during Mathilda's training. Likewise, Robert McCall (*The Equalizer*) employs a series of traps to take down Russian mobsters, as well as a final one by which the top crime boss, Pushkin, is electrocuted after emerging from his shower. More elaborate tricks of guile are employed as major components of plots during the pursuit of enemies in some of the Korean revenge films, like *Lady Vengeance*, *Oldboy*, and *I Saw the Devil*.

In Scripture, Ehud's killing of King Eglon (Judg 3:12–30) is a famous example of this theme that nicely fits the present framework, the offense of which is described in terms of Eglon's defeat and enslavement of the Israelites for eighteen years with the help of an alliance with the Ammonites and Amalekites (v. 13–14). The trap begins with Israel giving tribute to Eglon by way of Ehud, who conceals a cubit-long, double-edged sword hidden on his right thigh under his clothes (v. 16). By claiming to have a "secret message" for the king (v. 19), Ehud succeeds in getting a private audience with Eglon, kills him with the sword in his left hand, and escapes after locking the doors and delaying the servants (v. 21–26). Exegetes generally concur that Ehud would have met the king in a small chamber with an attached private lavatory. Thrusting his sword upwards through the belly into the heart would have caused Eglon's "dirt" to come out (v. 22), while the fat enveloped the sword preventing blood from seeping under the doors. The stench would have led the guards to believe the king was relieving himself (v. 24), giving Ehud time to escape through alternate entrance in the latrine.[16] The mission is nothing short of an assassination by a skilled operative, "raised up" by Yahweh (3:15), and most likely part of an elite breed of left-handed[17] Benjamite warriors who could "sling a stone at a hair, and not miss" (Judg 20:16; cf. 1 Chr 12:2). Judges also narrates an equally skillful display of trickery on the part of a "laywoman," Jael, who lures the fleeing Canaanite commander, Sisera, into her tent and promises him safety, only to kill him by driving a tent peg into his temple with a hammer while he slept (4:17–22). This maneuver accords well with a film like *Lady Vengeance*, in which Geum-ja, while lacking in specialized training and bodily strength, uses nurturing qualities, deceit, and keen instincts to defeat her formidable adversary.

In the final analysis, whether with the temporary help of accomplices or by means of trickery, the predominant pattern of the cinematic "final showdown" features the hero confronting the villain alone in a bitter struggle. Biblical narratives of violent finishes, I would argue, have their own way of capturing this image. In the violent deaths of Nadab and Abihu, Uzzah, and Ananias and Sapphira discussed earlier, the reader may note the repeated description of the deceased final location. The wicked sons of Aaron die "before the Lord" (Lev 10:2), Uzzah dies "beside the ark of God" (2 Sa 6:7), and Sapphira dies "at [Peter's] feet" (Acts 5:10). A similar fate befalls the spies who brought a bad report about the land and "died by a plague before the LORD" (Num 14:37) and when Samuel "hewed Agag in pieces before the LORD" (1

16. Victor H. Matthews, *Judges and Ruth* (New York: Cambridge University Press, 2004), 60–61.

17. Or, most likely, ambidextrous; cf. Barnabas Lindars, *Judges 1–5* (London: T & T Clark, 1995), 141.

Sam 15:33). The addendum functions in Scripture as a narrative trope that underscores God's personal presence and/or sanction. The spatio-locality of the phrase is significant when read in light of the close-range deaths of most villains in revenge films. Whether by firearm, blade, or hand-to-hand combat, the directness and finality of death becomes all the more clear: *the villain has been killed by my hand, right here and now.* The shot of the solitary protagonist (albeit often wounded and exhausted) standing over his vanquished enemy is commonplace in revenge films. Even Russell's semi long-distance rifle shot to the back of DeGroat's head in *Out of the Furnace* is prefaced with a conversation with him at close proximity, where the villain is made to know that this killing is personal. The interaction between cinematic and biblical motifs of presence may further suggest a sense of the avenger's *aloneness* in the final battle. Despite the great help that accomplices provide during their training, preparation, and pursuit, the avenger alone makes the decisive kill shot, and often with few or no witnesses. This, I believe, has implications when considering Jesus' sense of forsakenness in his atoning work on the cross, to be explored in the next chapter.

Aftermaths

As seen above, after the climactic "showdown" and the villain's demise, revenge films usually come to a close in one of a few ways. In some cases, the audience witnesses the typical "happy ending," in which the hero embraces the rescued beloved and bond is re-established or developed further, as in *Taken*, or in *John Wick*, where he breaks into an animal shelter to patch his wound and takes home a dog to replace his dead one. In Scripture, such positively construed epilogues may be said of the Ehud narrative. After escaping, Ehud leads the Israelites to kill ten thousand "strong, able-bodied" Moabite men and bring "rest" to the land for eighty years (Judg 3:26–30). Similarly, after Jael's killing of Sisera is the Song of Deborah (Judg 5), in which she is praised as "most blessed" among tent-dwelling women (v. 24). As a result of the defeat of Sisera and King Jabin of Canaan, the land enjoyed forty years of rest (v. 31).

Rest, of course, is a major theme in Scripture, serving theologically as a metonym for salvation and liberation, as in Isa 30:15: "In returning and rest you shall be saved; in quietness and in trust shall be your strength." In the NT, Jesus offers rest and light burden to those who are weary (Matt 11:28), and the broader continuation of the Sabbath motif in Hebrews carries deep, soteriological and eschatological implications: those who believe enter into God's rest. (Heb 4:3). Conversely, disobedience disqualifies God's people from that rest, as the author of Hebrews quotes from Ps 95:11, "in my anger I swore, 'They shall not enter my rest.'" God's anger, then, is clearly linked to the idea of not resting. That Scripture repeatedly emphasizes God's own rest from his works provides some interesting interaction with cinematic revenge in which rest is a key motivator for protagonists, who seek an end to the chaos that only they can and must create to put down powerful enemies. At the end of *The Equalizer*, Robert McCall is seated in the bathroom of the Russian crime boss, Vladimir Pushkin, and dialogues with him while flicking the light on and off:

> Pushkin: Who are you?
>
> Robert: Everybody wants to know.
>
> Pushkin: What do you want?
>
> Robert: I want the head of the snake.
>
> Pushkin (*smirking*): So it's you. And now you've come to kill me?
>
> Robert: Yes.
>
> Pushkin: And tell me, what do you gain from my death?
>
> Robert (switching the light off): Peace.

Pushkin turns on the light to find Robert gone and the sink overflowing with water, which creates a puddle under him and trips an exposed electrical wire. A loud cry is heard and Robert descends the staircase and exits the house in a slow-motion walk, the bodies of guards and henchmen strewn along his path.

We can relate this to the story of Phinehas's zealous rage elicited when he catches sight of an Israelite man taking a Midianite woman into his tent.

> When Phinehas son of Eleazar, son of Aaron the priest, saw it, he got up and left the congregation. Taking a spear in his hand, he went after the Israelite man into the tent, and pierced the two of them, the Israelite and the woman, through the belly. So the plague was stopped among the people of Israel. Nevertheless those that died by the plague were twenty-four thousand (Num 25:7–9).

If one were to imagine this narrative as a "cinematic" scene, the focused intentionality of Phinehas's movements would be immediately apparent from the play-by-play description of the act of skewering both of them with a single spear thrust. One might equivocate this with close-range bullet shots to the head or decapitation in movies. Phinehas's knee-jerk execution manages to halt the plague upon Israel, and as a result, Yahweh says: "I hereby grant him my covenant of peace . . . because he was zealous for his God, and made atonement for the Israelites" (v. 12-13).

That the two slain individuals are only named as an afterthought in verses 14-15, and not within the narrative itself, is, I believe, significant.[18] From the text, only two facts seem clear:

1. the man was Israelite and the woman was a Midianite; and
2. their deed was in "in the sight of Moses and in the sight of the whole congregation of the Israelites, while they were weeping at the entrance of the tent of meeting" (v. 6).

For Phinehas, therefore, the offense lay in their flagrant audacity in being so open about their shameful deed.[19] As individuals in this particular point in the story, he has no reason to assume that their *particular* deaths are significant. He simply witnesses a violation, gets offended, and retaliates. The scene does not demand that Phinehas's act is in calculated obedience to Yahweh's order: "Take all the chiefs of the people, and impale them in the sun before the Lord, in order that the fierce anger of the Lord may turn away from Israel" (v. 4). This logic of atonement, as Robert McCall would have it, is to kill the "head of the snake" and there will be peace. Phinehas's atoning rage is much messier and spontaneous. Rather than "chiefs," we learn later from a narrator's comment, that they were the son and daughter of tribal leaders; rather than impaling them in the sun, Phinehas impales them inside a tent. That his display of swift, reactive brutality stayed Yahweh's own hand of destruction and "made atonement" suggests something deeper at work. The "head of the snake" that needs to be killed is not immediately dependent on personality or position but is something profoundly *other*. According to Yahweh, Phinehas quenched divine wrath "by manifesting such zeal among them on my behalf" (v. 11). While this "zeal" was acted

---

18. Timothy R. Ashley, *The Book of Numbers*, NICOT (Grand Rapids: Eerdmans, 1993), 524. Ashley surmises that their insertion into verses 6-9 "would have deflected the main point of those verses, which was not connected with the specific identity of the pair but with their sin, its consequences, and Phinehas's reaction."

19. Ibid., 519. Some have debated over the exact nature of the sin, the options being illicit sex, inter-marriage, or idolatry. Probably, all three apply but textually, it seems that its wanton openness is the main motivator for Phinehas's particular response.

out against persons in this instance, it was Phinehas's passion for defending Yahweh's honor that secured peace,[20] a passion that becomes clearer when understood through the framework of cinematic revenge.

In *The Equalizer*, Pushkin's death is not captured on camera, only implied. We only see the overflowing water from the sink tripping an exposed wire, and we hear a loud cry as lights flicker over the staircase where McCall descends in a classic, slow-motion hero walk to his ominous, signature soundtrack. The arch villain is dead, thus ending the chain of criminal activity that began the conflict of the whole movie, yet we find in the end that only Robert and his specific set of traits is the point of the film. We remember Susan's charge to Robert: "*Go be him*." Peace is attained not through the killing of this or that crime boss as such, but because such a one as Robert McCall walks the streets. A comparison with Phinehas is fitting here. Phinehas has an extreme loathing for sin, that, when manifested, matched Yahweh's jealousy and wrath. The point is not that any particular individuals have been executed; it is that one can exhibit Yahweh's zeal against sin.

Biblical avenger-protagonists are often praised for acting on behalf of God or having some role in salvation history. However, many denouements of revenge films lack typical happy endings that leave viewers feeling relaxed with a sense of positive resolution and closure. Post-vengeance refractory periods are often gloomy, especially when the protagonist has sustained incredible loss, both that of the beloved and any allies along the way. With their mental acuity, emotion, and physical skill poured out fully upon the villain, there remains only emptiness after the final kill shot is made. They become fully aware that they will never be the same again. In *Sun Scarred*, Katayama sits with his back against the wall of the abandoned building where he killed his daughter's murderer, staring out in stillness as the rays of the dawn sun slowly washes over his face. Very similarly, Russell (*Out of the Furnace*) sits in his dining room staring downward while the camera slowly zooms out and fades to black to the song "Release" by Pearl Jam. Of the finale, director Scott Cooper says, "This is a man who is battling his soul and living with the consequences of violence... This is a man who, whether he is [sic] prison or not, he's in prison for the rest of his life. Hopefully he will find peace and contentment at some point."[21]

At the extreme end of the spectrum, the darkness faced after finally unleashing one's wrath can lead to moments of emotional breakdown (e.g. Su-hyeon, *I Saw the Devil*), or even suicide (e.g. U-jin, *Oldboy*). The

---

20. Ibid., 522.

21. Christopher Rosen, "What Really Happens At The End Of 'Out Of The Furnace'?," *The Huffington Post*, September 12, 2013, http://www.huffingtonpost.com/2013/12/09/out-of-the-furnace-ending_n_4365572.html.

protagonist's own death is figuratively portrayed in a spellbinding final sequence in *Oldboy*, in which Dae-su is helped by a hypnotist to kill off his alter-ego, "The Monster," allowing the resulting Dae-su to go on living without the memory of his secret incestuous moment with his daughter. After the hypnosis, he awakens in a snowy field and gives an ambiguous smile while embracing her. Lighting design in the final scenes of *Man from Nowhere* is particularly suggestive of Tae-sik's "redemption." With his head tilted down after killing his villain, the cone of light above him casts a dark shadow on his face as he puts a pistol to his head. After So-mi emerges and embraces him, he lifts his head up, reflecting a bright glow off his face. The final scene in *Lady Vengeance* employs the image of falling snow to achieve a similar idea, as Geum-ja's daughter prompts her to lift her head to consume the falling flakes. To reinforce the idea of her return to purity, she comically mashes her face in a plate of tofu seconds later. In these films, the reunion, if it occurs, is the only redemption the character receives. It counteracts the darkness of their souls in the aftermath of their vengeance. This situation concurs with God's prophetic insistence: "I have no pleasure in the death of the wicked, but that the wicked turn from their ways and live" (Ezek 33:11, cf. 18:23, 32).

Analysis and Conclusion

By allowing biblical narratives to be read alongside examples of revenge films, several resonances and dissonances are discernable in the texture of the narratives that serve to challenge and supplement our understanding of the scenes presented in both media. In the course of these comparisons, a few important things have been learned about biblical retribution that informs its use as a theological idea. First, avengers are depicted in both as being extremely skilled and decisive in their killing techniques. Whether it is a consuming fire from Yahweh's altar or a brilliantly rigged electrocution; whether a spear that runs through two people in a single thrust or a rifle headshot from several hundred yards, protagonists in these narratives have both the will and the skill for a successful kill. Mistakes or ambiguities in the avenger's final takedown of an enemy are foreign to both texts, and any interpretations of the kill are almost always narrated, either visually or textually, with unflinching approval. Second, and similarly, villains are portrayed as fully deserving their violent demise. Narrators take some effort to adequately explain the gross depravity of villains, and in some colorful cases, paint them with unsavory physical features and mannerisms. At the same time, however, an imbalance lies in the Bible's "overkill" in some narratives of divine killing. The deaths of Uzzah as well as that of Ananias and Sapphira evoke shock and fear among its witnesses rather than peace and satisfaction. One is also made to wonder what "the nations" have done to deserve a wholesale slaughtering of its inhabitants by the sword proceeding from the Rider on the White Horse (Rev 19:15).

This leads to an important third aspect of the cinematic and biblical narratives, the beloved. The identity of the beloved may range from an individual, to whole groups, to abstract concepts like family honor or nationhood. Regardless, the motivations for a hero to spring into action and engage the enemy with such violence tends to be proportional to the threat posed to this beloved entity. These are either imminent threats, leading to protectionist interventions, or threats already accomplished, leading to acts of retaliation. Cinema helps to clarify the personal aspect of these threats: violating the hero's beloved means violating the hero. Interestingly, however, Scripture again transcends this theme by presenting situations where the hero inflicts violence *upon* the beloved. Such a scenario *never* happens in revenge films. The only harm that might be reasonably incurred on the beloved is the psychological pain of separation when the hero must die or depart in order to secure her safety. The question that arises is profound: Who or what, exactly, is the target of wrath? Fourthly, the aftermath of retribution upon abominable villains in both Scripture and cinema demonstrate the necessity for the violent intervention and portray some sense of closure if not complete tranquility. By and large, however, it is the revenge film that tends to close with a moral question mark, a feeling that the vengeful act, while necessary, was by no means pleasurable. Some indelible wound has left a scar upon the avenger, and in some sense, a part of him has died. In contrast, biblical narratives exalt avengers who are deemed as divinely-sanctioned actors, and in some cases, the actors are reprimanded for not being thorough enough in their annihilation (e.g. Judg 2:1–5; 1 Sam 15:17–23).

On the surface, it seems that cinema is simply more ethically straightforward and therefore enjoys the moral high-ground against biblical "problem texts." To a certain extent, this is true. As discussed previously, genre films in general, and revenge films in particular, set up blatant contrasts and minimize moral ambiguity in keeping with its nature as fiction and in propagating heroic myth. The emotional payoff that makes cinematic revenge so satisfying depends on the clarity of the film's moral vision achieved in large part by the uniformity of the audience's responses. What can be made of the fact that biblical acts of revenge seem more outrageous and unjustified than those of movies, or that Scripture often portrays the beloved receiving retributive violence when movies do not, or that films portray a sense of the hero's pain when all is accomplished?

If we allow the notion that cinematic and biblical revenge narratives are, in fact, a common story, the "intensifications" seen in Scripture may not be incongruent deviations as they are paths to a deeper story. We have observed how well-meaning members of the covenant community, like Uzzah and Ananias and Sapphira, can be struck down in the same manner as villains, whose moral depravity is often visualized to portray them as loathsome beasts, like King Eglon and Goliath. With the seeming lack of evidence that these figures are hopelessly depraved felons, one can only conclude that something apart from their person bears the brunt of God's extreme prejudice. Tentatively positing this "entity" as sin requires us to begin engaging the subject as a theological concept.

6.

Narrative Reconfigurations of Atonement Dogmatics

IN THE PRECEDING CHAPTER, I have attempted to demonstrate how the stories of retributive judgment against sinner-villains in cinema and biblical narratives track with each other with a strong degree of congruence, and even instances of dissonance between the texts have the function of disclosing ideas that are not obvious without the help of its dialogue partner. If successful, the resulting theo-cinematic synthesis can be regarded as stemming from Scripture's own narratives, a vital element to this study as a work of evangelical theology. It remains to be seen within this chapter whether the components of a revenge framework of atonement is relevant to and compatible with dogmatic treatments of these themes. Among the central issues that need to be worked out theologically are:

1. the possibility of identifying sin in an objective sense;
2. the nature and operation of trinitarian relations with respect to Christ's mission; and
3. the mechanism of vengeful atonement with respect to the crucifixion.

Sin as Villain

An atonement model that retains violence while diverting it from *direct* human harm hinges upon identifying the object of God's wrath specifically as sin as a radical other and not any particular individual or community. Is this a theologically valid option? In the course of what follows, I will argue that sin as an objective reality—that is, distinct from agents who commit it—is a valid, Christian way of speaking about sin in light of scriptural precedent and dogmatic formulation. Once the plausibility of sin as an object is established, we may call upon cinematic resources to imagine the nature of this reality as a "villain" within a narrative model of the atonement.

Scriptural evidences

The Bible repeatedly employs metaphor to describe sin as though it were an isolated *entity*. First, sin is described using spatio-temporal language. One can sin "against" God, individuals (e.g. 1 Sam 19:4), and heaven (Luke 15:21), and even more dynamically, God tells Jonah that the wickedness of the Ninevites "has come up before me" (1:2). This image of sin making an ascent to God is figured in Genesis as a disturbing "outcry" that prompts Yahweh to "go down" and verify the gravity of Sodom and Gomorrah's sin (18:20–21). In a similar way, Yahweh tells Abram that the "inquity of the Amorites is not yet *full*" (KJV). Reciprocally, actions can be done *to* sin, as though it were an object taking up space. God may "hide" his face from sin (Ps 51:9) or "visit" it throughout generations (Exod 34:7). Paul warns the Romans not to "present your members to sin as instruments of wickedness" (6:13).

Going further, Scripture's spatio-temporal mode of speaking of sin suggests transmissibility. The chief OT reference is found in Lev 16:21–22, where Aaron is commanded to lay both hands on the head of a live goat and "confess over it all the iniquities of the people of Israel." In so doing, the goat "shall bear on itself all their iniquities to a barren region." Of the Suffering Servant, Isaiah would later declare, "All we like sheep have gone astray; we have all turned to our own way, and the Lord has laid on him the iniquity of us all" (53:6; also, v. 11–12). In the NT Paul hints at transmission when relating how "one man's trespass" has led to condemnation for all (Rom 5:15–21)—the idea of imputation, to be discussed later.

Second, the way sin is handled within the OT cultic system suggests the idea of sin as a stain that lingers long after a deed has been committed. Defilement through physical contact with unclean objects was often met with severe consequences, as when, for example, Kohathite-Levites who looked at or touched sanctuary vessels were to be executed (Num 4:13, 20), or when an animal raped by a human was to be killed (Lev 20:16). Nazirites were forbidden from coming into contact with corpses, even those of family members, and prescriptions for accidentally "defiling the consecrated head" on account of a sudden death nearby included the Nazirite shaving his head and offering a expiatory sacrifice (Num 6:9–11). Defilement was pronounced for incidents that are unintentional and even natural, such as pelvic emissions (nocturnal emission, ejaculation of semen during intercourse, and periodic menstruation;

Lev 15:16-30), and met with regulations including removal from the camp, laborious cleansing procedures, and a waiting period (Num 5:1-4; Lev 15). For complex and urgent procedures to be enforced for infractions of cultic ritual—*whether intentional or not*—suggests a significant dissociation of sin from volitional acts of disobedience or malice.[1]

It becomes reasonable to conclude that sin "triggers the creation of some sort of thing . . . a stain is spontaneously generated once the fateful act has been accomplished."[2] Common to many Near Eastern cultures, impurity was a form of spiritual pollution that posed a significant threat to the community. As Jacob Milgrom writes: "Impurity was feared because it was considered demonic. It was an unending threat to the gods themselves and especially to their temples . . . Thus for both Israel and her neighbors impurity was a physical substance, an aerial miasma which possessed magnetic attraction for the realm of the sacred."[3]

A third way that Scripture unabashedly uses language that circumscribes sin as a distinct entity is by personifying it as possessing malicious agency. In the primeval history, sin is "crouching" (NIV; "lurking," NRSV) at the door lying in wait for Cain (Gen 4:7). James speaks of sin as capable of being born and growing to maturity (1:15). As a representative for sin, the untamed tongue is a "fire" placed among our members to be a "world of iniquity," which "stains the whole body, sets on fire the cycle of nature, and is itself set on fire by hell" (3:6). In Romans 5-7, we find the most protracted exposition of sin's "active agency." For Paul, sin "came into the world" (5:12) and "exercised dominion" both corporately "from Adam to Moses," (5:14) and individually to "exercise dominion in your mortal bodies, to make you obey their passions" (6:12). In Paul's (debatably) autobiographical narrative, sin "seized" opportunity and "produced" covetousness (7:8), "revived" (7:9), "deceived" and "killed" him (7:11). E. P. Sanders, among others, is open to a "modified dualism" in Paul, influenced by a cultural and religious consensus regarding the existence and activity of evil forces.[4] Elsewhere, Paul refers

---

1. Robin C. Cover, "Sin and Sinners (OT)," in *The Anchor Yale Bible Dictionary, Si–Z: Volume 6* (New Haven; London: Yale University Press, 1992), 34.

2. Gary A. Anderson, *Sin: A History* (New Haven: Yale University Press, 2009), 4.

3. Jacob Milgrom, *Cult and Conscience: The Asham and the Priestly Doctrine of Repentance* (Leiden: Brill, 1976), 392, quoted in Cover, "Sin and Sinners (OT)," 35.

4. This is even in light of his preference for his own view, put forward in E. P. Sanders, *Paul and Palestinian Judaism: A Comparison of Patterns of Religion* (Philadelphia: Fortress, 1977), 442-47; 474-75. In brief, Sanders argues that Paul's strong conception of sin in Rom 5-7 does not square with his earlier remarks in Rom 1-2 regarding the gravity and universality of Jewish and Gentile sin so as to place both "under sin" (3:9). To explain this, Sanders suggests that Paul came to Christianity knowing that salvation was in Christ, but he did not have a fully worked-out conception of humanity's plight

to "god(s)" (2 Cor 4:4; 8:5), "rulers"(1 Cor 2:6), or "demons" (1 Cor 10:20) at work in this world or age.

The above sampling of texts prompts the question of which label for this mode of describing sin is most apt. Röhser argues that "superhuman being" is perhaps too strong, while "only a metaphor" is too weak. Thus he proposes "a certain form of hypostatizing" for which the term "personification" is perhaps best.[5] Here it must be emphasized that Paul cannot be said to be a dualist in any absolute sense of the term. His is a high view of divine sovereignty; it is by God's will that "creation was subjected to futility" (Rom 8:20). However, at the same time, for Paul to speak at length of sin as a personification that renders one impotent to counter its effects (Rom 7:14–20) is surprising and bold. It is worth noting, finally, that Paul nowhere discusses repentance in this passage. This absence, beyond reinforcing his argument on the universality of sinfulness amongst Jews and Gentiles (Rom 2:17–3:20), serves to elevate sin's radically active character in contrast to humanity's passive impotence to resolve its plight.

The theological feasibility of sin as object

Moving from scriptural language to theology, we can find Christian tradition accommodating the notion of sin as an objective reality. The Greek fathers tended to locate sin in something external to humans insofar as it helped to secure Adam's initial innocence. Irenaeus attributed Adam's sin to the limitations placed upon him by virtue of his creaturely and childlike state, which made him particularly susceptible to the devil's power.[6] Athanasius blames the inherently corruptible materiality from which Adam was made and which momentarily took Adam's gaze away from God.[7] In Gregory of Nyssa, there are echoes of an earlier patristic link between sin and sexuality such that Eve bears a greater portion of blame for original

---

that called for a solution. That all were under bondage to sin, then, is deduced "backward" from his clarity about soteriology. For response, see Frank Thielman, *From Plight to Solution: A Jewish Framework for Understanding Paul's View of the Law in Galatians and Romans*, Reprint edition (Eugene, OR: Wipf & Stock, 2008).

5. See Günter Röhser, *Metaphorik und Personifikation der Sünde: antike Sündenvorstellungen und paulinische Hamartia* (Tübingen: J.C.B. Mohr Siebeck, 1987); cf. E.P. Sanders, "Sin and Sinners (NT)," in *The Anchor Yale Bible Dictionary, Si–Z: Volume 6* (New Haven; London: Yale University Press, 1992), 45. Also Venter, "Romans 8:3–4 and God's Resolution," 3 n12, sin as "slave master."

6. Irenaeus, *Proof the Apostolic Preaching*, 12; cf. *Against Heresies*, III.23.1.

7. Athanasius, *On the Incarnation*, I.4–5

sin.[8] To safeguard human free will, there is in these writers a suggestion of sin as a kind of "potential force." While the devil is typically blamed for inducing sin, what is evident is that in the "original" sense, sin is understood as something external to Adam.

It is not until Augustine's battle with Pelagius that harmatiology reaches an epochal plateau. Pelagius believed sin to be located completely within the free actions of individual responsibility and that its universal character is a matter of a habitual repetition and imitation. Augustine opposed this thesis, arguing for original sin as transmitted to humanity through Adam's guilt on the basis of Romans 5. The catholic position seems to settle on a balance between the internal and external aspects of sin. On the one hand, sin is internal to the sinner and in no way a part of God's created order; humans perform acts of sin and are fully culpable. On the other hand, the transmutability of original sin leaves open the possibility of dissociation between sin and *mere* volitional action.

This delicate balance, or some might say indecision, is palpable within the Augustinian tradition. In his chapter on the essence of sin, G. C. Berkouwer prefaces his discussion with a sobering reminder that we are not dealing with mere theory or speculative riddle but a recognition of "a very vicious and mortal enemy, an irascible and persistent power, which must certainly be *known* in order to be *overcome*."[9] Although he notes a distinct "unclarity" in understanding the nature of sin, he affirms "there is always a *contra*-element in sin" that manifests itself in a "strategy of deceit."[10] This leads him to an initial assertion that evil "has no thesis in itself but only antithesis." This follows from the Augustinian concept of *privatio*, already present in Athanasius[11] and taken up by the Reformed tradition to deny that sin has substance and independent existence. Bavinck defends that sin as *nihil* is uncontestably orthodox, arguing: "If sin were a substance, there would exist an entity that either was not created by God or was not caused by God."[12] Augustine's need to combat the dualistic worldview of the Manicheans, as well as the Reformers' need to uphold the meticulous sovereignty of God

---

8. Gregory of Nyssa, *On the Making of Man*, 16.

9. G. C. Berkouwer, *Studies in Dogmatics: Sin* (Grand Rapids: Eerdmans, 1971), 235 (emphasis in original).

10. Ibid., 237.

11. Athanasius, *On the Incarnation*, I.4.

12. Herman Bavinck, *Reformed Dogmatics Vol. 3: Sin and Salvation in Christ*, ed. John Bolt, trans. John Vriend (Grand Rapids: Baker, 2006), 330. He cites such works as Athanasius, *Against the Heathens*, Gregory of Nyssa, *The Catechetical Oration*; Pseudo-Dionysius, *The Divine Names*; and John of Damascus, *Exposition of the Orthodox Faith*.

in all of existence undergirds the push to understand sin as parasitic—a corruption, distortion, or abuse of good, creaturely reality.

And yet, the potency and obvious reality of sin drove even Reformed scholastics to acknowledge an active element in the nature of sin *in some sense*. In their terminology, they were quick to deny sin as *mera privatio* ("mere privation") and opted for the stronger designation *privatio actuosa* ("actualized or active privation"). Bavinck observes how Scripture often speaks of sin in a very positive sense and the impossibility of certain sins, such as blasphemy and idolatry, to ever assume a "good form."[13] Thus, he concludes: "Certainly [sin] is not a mere lack, pure nonbeing, but an active and corrupting principle, a dissolving, destructive power."[14] For Berkouwer, the ubiquity and concreteness of sin in everyday experience "can almost be touched" and observes, as many do, how it is often personified in Scripture.[15] He admits that the difficulty in upholding an ancient tradition while appreciating a daily reality is an "ecumenical problem" in which both Catholic and Protestant theology has a stake.[16] On the one hand, Christian dogma unreservedly announces Augustine victorious over the Manicheans in his project to demythologize evil.[17] On the other, we can and should, as Berkouwer favors, "use the language of Scripture itself" in speaking of sin's "demonic effrontery."[18]

The modern era, in many ways, has challenged the idea of inherited guilt or being *in a state of sin*. Schleiermacher understood sin as an aspect of a lower human nature that resists moral development and universal God-consciousness. He believed humanity's desires need to be transformed by God imparting a "blessedness" that elevates our "God-consciousness" to that which Christ possessed, thus causing our sensuous consciousness to gradually wane.[19] In Barth, we find a resurgence of an Augustinian framework. His disagreement with Emil Brunner surrounding man's inability to know his fallen state and need of saving grace accented the pervasiveness and potency of sin among theological conservatives. While Brunner allowed for some "capacity for revelation," Barth vehemently denied that one can have knowledge of sin anymore than one have knowledge of God, revelation, or

13. Ibid.
14. Ibid.
15. Berkouwer, *Sin*, 264.
16. Ibid., 263.
17. See Charles T. Mathewes, *Evil and the Augustinian Tradition* (Cambridge: Cambridge University Press, 2006), 63.
18. Berkouwer, *Sin*, 265.
19. Friedrich Schleiermacher, *The Christian Faith*, ed. H. R. Mackintosh and J. S. Stewart (London: T&T Clark, 1999), 350.

faith apart from the explicit presence and action of Jesus Christ.[20] For him, sin is "absurd," and although "the man of sin becomes someone other than himself, that his nature is altered in all its elements when he commits sin,"[21] he is not in a state of "absolute and ontological godlessness."[22]

In late modern and postmodern theology, it can be said that sin is understood less in terms of a principle and more in terms of a *process*. Twentieth-century American theologians, like Reinhold Niebuhr and Paul Tillich, spoke of sin in terms of tensions and estrangements between our current state and our true, or fully actualized selves. Liberation and postcolonial theologians have understood sin in terms of oppressive and exploitative political and economic structures rigged against the poor and marginalized to benefit the rich and powerful. Closely associated are feminist theologians, who view sin in terms of self-contempt and the perpetuating cycle of patriarchal subjugation.

This being the case, however, even in contemporary and context-dependent theologies that take issue with Augustinian categories, we still find sin spoken of in abstract ways that distance it from the *mere*, volitional acts of individual agents. Be it estrangement, oppressive socio-political structures, or patriarchy, there is in modern and postmodern thought a view of sin as a movement operating in some supra-material sphere and possessing its own active potency. While human participation in and culpability for sin is never negated, there also remains a strong sense in which sin is believed to be at work in abstract dimensions such as systems, regimes, and cultural attitudes. These "forces" (or as Walter Wink names "powers") are capable of permeating society and enslaving populations *against their will*; hence the need for supernatural *liberation*. On this point, the liberationist interpretation of sin is in agreement, surprisingly, with more traditionally catholic harmartiology. Even if a precise metaphysics of sin eludes us, the experiential dimension of sin's otherness is palpably felt by all sides of the aisle.

---

20. Barth writes that "only when we know Jesus Christ do we really know that man is the man of sin, and what sin is, and what it means for man," *Church Dogmatics*, IV.1, 389; cf. Brandon L. Morgan, "The Absurdity of Sin and the Creaturely Life of Faith in Karl Barth's Theological Epistemology," *Pacifica: Journal of the Melbourne College of Divinity* 27, no. 2 (June 2014): 159.

21. *CD*, IV.1, 406, quoted in ibid., 160.

22. *CD*, IV.1, 480, quoted in ibid., 161.

"In the likeness of sinful flesh"

The final component of my argument for an objective view of sin as distinct from the mere temporal actions of human beings considers the question: How did Christ relate with sin in his incarnation? I will show how the orthodox understanding of Jesus' participation in sinful humanity supports a supra-temporal notion sin, or sinfulness, as an isolated phenomenon.

According to Romans 8:3, God sent his own son "in the likeness of sinful flesh" (*en homoiōmati sarkos harmartias*). Of obvious interest to exegetes has been the meaning of the word translated as "likeness". Vincent Branick holds that it means full identification such that "sinful flesh is fully visible in the flesh of Christ,"[23] while Gillman argues that linguistically, and in Paul's own usage in his epistles, *homoiōma* can denote both similarity *and difference*.[24] Taken together with similar phraseology in Phil 2:7, a broad conclusion may be drawn that Christ's "likeness with sinful flesh" is meant to express his full humanity.[25] Theologically, it is probably no more significant than to say, as Martin Scharlemann sums up: "St. Paul's phraseology is designed, on the one hand, to reject the notion that the life of Jesus Christ as a man only seemed to be human, and on the other, to forestall any conception of Jesus as being no more than a man."[26]

While there has been some doctrinal development regarding what is meant that Jesus was "in the likeness of sinful flesh," a general consensus can be detected.[27] Defending the sinlessness of Christ has traditionally occupied the foreground in interpreting this and other pertinent verses. A minority position among early patristic writers leaned docetic. For example, Clement of Alexandria believed Jesus' body was "supported by holy power" such that he only ate food to prevent false notions about him and that he was "untroubled by passion," much less sin;[28] and Cassian argued that he did not experience inner vice "but only the appearance of it."[29] The need to respond to heresy

23. Vincent P Branick, "The Sinful Flesh of the Son of God (Rom 8:3): A Key Image of Pauline Theology," *CBQ* 47, no. 2 (April 1985): 250.

24. Florence Morgan Gillman, "Another Look at Romans 8:3: 'In the Likeness of Sinful Flesh,'" *CBQ* 49, no. 4 (October 1987): 598–600.

25. Ibid., 602.

26. Martin H. Scharlemann, "'In the Likeness of Sinful Flesh,'" *CTM* 32, no. 3 (March 1961): 134.

27. Much of this historical survey is drawn from primary source quotations in Part II of Thomas G. Weinandy, *In the Likeness of Sinful Flesh: An Essay on the Humanity of Christ* (Edinburgh: T & T Clark, 1993).

28. Clement of Alexandria, *Stromateis*, 6.9, quoted in Ibid., 24.

29. Cassian, *Conlationes* 5.5.3, quoted in Dominic Keech, "John Cassian and the Christology of Romans 8.3," *Vigiliae Christianae* 64, no. 3 (2010): 286.

prompted more theologians to lock on to the maxim attributed to Gregory of Nazianzus, "What is not assumed is not saved," and assert that Christ took on sinful humanity while denying any propensity toward sin. Ambrosiaster took a strong position arguing that Christ had been made sin from his very incarnation: "It says that God the Father made his Son, Christ, sin; because having been made flesh he was not altered but became incarnate and so was made sin . . . On account of this his entire flesh is under sin, therefore since it has been made flesh, it has also been made sin."[30]

Post-Augustinian theology tended to confirm that Christ did not inherit original sin or the penalty accrued by taking on sinful flesh. Anselm appealed to the virgin birth to argue strongly against the idea that Christ's nature had "anything pertaining to the sin of the sinful mass either could have, or should have, affected the man who was conceived from the Virgin alone."[31] This includes Christ's sufferings and death, which were not part of the humanity he assumed but was undertaken voluntarily. Aquinas, however, provided corrective, arguing that "the penalties, such as hunger, thirst, death, and the like, which we suffer sensibly in this life flow from original sin. And hence Christ, in order to satisfy fully for original sin, wished to suffer sensible pain, that He might consume death and the like in Himself."[32] In short, Christ was of the quality but not the cause of sin-inherited defects, and he entered into them by his own will.[33]

In what way did Christ possess the taint of sin without participating in it as an active agent? Ian McFarland proposes that we distinguish between "fallenness" and "sinfulness" when speaking of Christ's humanity. By appealing to the Chalcedonian categories of nature and hypostasis, it is possible for Christ to have a fallen nature, that is, "the damaged condition of postlapsarian humanity,"[34] while remaining sinless in terms of hypostasis (person). The key to establishing this distinction rests on the nature of will. He draws on Maximus the Confessor to argue for the difference between Christ's will and ours:[35] Our wills and desires are perverse and make us sin-

---

30. Ambrosiaster, *In ad Corinthios Secunda*, 5.21, quoted in Weinandy, *In the Likeness of Sinful Flesh*, 30.

31. Anselm, "The Virgin Conception and Original Sin," in *Complete Philosophical and Theological Treatises of Anselm of Cantebury*, trans. Jasper Hopkins and Herbert Richardson (Minneapolis: The Arthur J. Banning Press, 2000), XV, 448.

32. Aquinas, *ST* III.1.4 ad. 3

33. Aquinas, *ST* III.14.3; ibid., ad. 3

34. Ian A McFarland, "Fallen or Unfallen?: Christ's Human Nature and the Ontology of Human Sinfulness," *IJST* 10, no. 4 (October 2008): 408.

35. "But as for the Savior's willing according to his human nature, even though it was natural, it was not bare like ours, any more than his humanity as such is, since

ners, but Christ's will as hypostatically divine is perpetually turned toward and shaped by God's will.[36] Thus Jesus is capable of having a fallen nature without undermining his status as sinless: "A nature can be damaged (and thus fallen); but a nature cannot sin, because sin is ascribed to agents, and thus is a matter of the hypostasis."[37] He locates the will as "the place where my sinfulness is experienced and known."[38] Our status as sinners, therefore, is a function of the fallenness of our wills.[39]

While the emphasis on will does create the logically tenable distinction between fallenness and sinfulness, the question remains as to whether this position requires that we severely downplay Paul's insistence that sin "dwells within me, that is, *in my flesh*" (7:17-18). Moreover, he says, "I see in my *members* another law at war with the law of my mind, making me captive to the law of sin that dwells in my members" (v. 23). Paul's "body language" is unfortunately at odds with McFarland, who prefers that the inner conflict be viewed "as evidence of the will's incapacity to determine the desires by which it is shaped."[40] Of course, Paul is speaking on behalf of sinners, which Christ is not. However, only a few verses later, we find him declaring that Christ has, in fact, come "in the likeness of *sinful flesh*" and "for sin," "condemned sin *in the flesh*" (8:3). There is simply not enough room within the flow of Paul's flesh-laden discourse to introduce the individual will as the true locus of sin's presence and activity, either in the sinner or in Christ. In fact, Paul proffers the exact opposite: "but I see in my members another law at war with the law of my mind, making me captive to the law of sin that dwells in my members" (7:23).[41] Reasonably, the "law of my mind" and "inmost self" (v. 22) most closely equates with the will—and it is at *war* with the flesh. If Paul is in fact talking about physical flesh (and I think he is), and if there is no warrant to suggest Paul makes a distinction between his flesh (and that of humanity) and Christ's, then the implication is profound: Jesus fully participates in our sinful humanity—at a level as intimate as our own bodily flesh, thus giving place to violence—and yet is without sin.

---

it has been perfectly deified above us in union, because of which it is actually sinless." Maximus the Confessor, *Opuscula Theologica et Polemica*, quoted in ibid., 409.

36. Ibid., 409-10.

37. Ibid., 413.

38. Ibid.

39. Ibid., 415.

40. Ibid., 70.

41. The debate over whether Paul's "I" is referring to a pre-fall or post-fall state does not factor here. My consideration is only in the contrast between flesh/members and mind, which Paul is clearly setting up.

But even if we dismiss Paul's language as metaphorical rhetoric, McFarland's proposal, though it blurs the connection between fallenness and sinfulness due to an emphasis on will, helpfully provides some theoretical basis for regarding Christ's simultaneous association with, and dissociation from, sin. This could only be possible if sin possesses some supra-temporal character that touches Christ in some manner that does not involve individual agency. In fact, like many other balanced theologians surveyed in this chapter, McFarland is unwilling to dislodge sin completely from this "ontological" sense:

> In sharing our nature without sharing our sin, Christ reveals sin as a function of the will that is nevertheless *prior* to any act of the will, and thus allows it to be understood as an *ontological* rather than an axiological category. Far from letting us off the hook, however, the revelation that sin is a matter of who rather than what we are reveals the depth to which we are implicated in sin even as it vindicates the ineradicable goodness of our created whatness.[42]

Theo-cinematic synthesis

We now consider the ways in which elements of the revenge film distilled in earlier chapters may help to cast fresh light and offer new vocabularies for thought regarding how sin as a character the story of atonement as envisioned in this study.

Human, but not

Exegetes and theologians have consistently emphasized the role that human volition plays in any doctrine of sin. Berkouwer writes: "The dreadful horror of sin is evident in that it is both uncreaturely and *still finds place* in the central disposition of man's heart. Sin is not a peripheral phenomenon. Though it remains an "alien force" it is completely pervasive and wells up from the heart of man himself."[43] While debates abound regarding the degree to which it affects human nature, all agree that sin finds its native habitation in and around human beings and their behaviors. The cinematic villain's depiction as a human being (usually male) is the first obvious affirmation of sin as intimately tied to mundane, creaturely agency. Villains

---

42. McFarland, *In Adam's Fall*, 131. Emphasis added.
43. Berkouwer, *Sin*, 265.

have bodies, emotions, desires, aspirations, and they participate fully in their cinematic worlds alongside other individuals. They are motivated to get what they want in no *fundamentally* different way as protagonists are.

At the same time, if the scriptural evidences above are to inform our theology, one cannot ignore the biblical suggestion that sin also operates at some distance to mere human volition. As observed earlier, the depictions of villains, though typical and generalized, are uniquely set apart from other characters in ways that are significant to our discussion of sin.

First, villains are absolute. They are as abominable as possible within the "realistic" limits of a film and never show signs of moral progress. In narrative terms, they rarely possess any *character arc*, which in a way strips them of humanity. Likewise, Louis Berkof identifies sin as possessing "an absolute character," that is, a lack of "gradations" that mark the transition between good and evil.[44] While he repudiates a dualistic view of sin, he still affirms: "A moral being that is good does not become evil by simply diminishing his goodness, but only by a radical qualitative change, by turning to sin. Sin is not a lesser degree of goodness, but a positive evil."[45]

We can relate this with the concept of concupiscence. Recalling Augustine's conception of evil as privation, all created things including flesh are therefore inherently good. Materiality, however, is corruptible and flesh is the lower part of the self that contains a "defect" that has desires opposed the spirit.[46] It is this defect that Augustine attributes as the "nothing good" that dwells in the flesh (Rom 7:18), and "when it ceases to exist, there will still be flesh, but it will no longer be defecting or sinful."[47] Specifically, this "defect" should properly be understood as *concupiscentia carnis*, a post-fall condition of desire, which, according to Lamberigts, "ultimately strove in its indeterminateness towards the unlawful, that the human person,

---

44. Louis Berkhof, *Systematic Theology* (Grand Rapids: Eerdmans, 1941), in his chapter entitled "The Essential Nature of Sin. It is the second of six headings outlining aspects of the "The Scriptural Idea of Sin." The dualism he repudiates here is of the Gnostic sort, namely, the belief in an "eternal principle of evil" and which holds that "in man the spirit represents the principle of good, and the body, that of evil." He objects to this for three reasons: (1) there is nothing outside of God that is eternal or independent of His will; (2) it reduces evil to something physical and independent of human willing, thereby removing its ethical character; and (3) it removes human responsibility by representing sin as a "physical necessity," ibid., 238.

45. Ibid., 232.

46. Augustine, *Marriage and Virginity*, ed. John E. Rotelle, trans. Ray Kearney (Hyde Park, NY: New City Press, 1999), 204.

47. Ibid.

person—even under grace—loved what ought to be shunned and shunned what ought to be loved"[48]—in short, an impulse toward sin.

The revenge villain illustrates this nicely. Consider the showdown scene of *Taken 2*. Bryan Mills offers leniency to the crime boss, Murad Hoxha (Rade Šerbedžija), and bids him return home to Albania and enjoy his remaining sons (Bryan had killed his son Marko in *Taken*), saying, "I'm tired of it all," as he drops his gun to the floor and begins to walk away. Murad pretends to acquiesce, only to grab the gun and attempt to shoot Bryan in the back. After an empty click (Bryan had taken the bullet out), Bryan finishes him off. This may serve to show the inadequacy of understanding sin as *mera privatio*, as pure *nihil*, and affirms Berkouwer's suggestion of a "contra-element" in sin. Murad, even when granted a merciful stay of execution, is incapable of persuasion but manages to corrupt a benevolent act. Such a decided and consistent orientation toward evil could not be said of pure nothingness.

Second, villains are powerful. They are often heads of crime organizations, gangs, or occupy political office. As individuals who are independently wealthy, they have their hands in more than one criminal venture and employ henchmen and lackeys to perform low-level tasks. Although they are matchless in their intelligence and brutality and occupy a sphere of dominance over their subordinates, in many cases they command an army of thugs who work in coordinated fashion, and they bring their personal influence to bear on their criminal businesses. This has some bearing on an often-neglected aspect of sin inhering not only in human beings and behaviour but also extending its influence into institutions, mindsets, and power structures. We are reminded of revenge films like *Ajuma*, *Sun Scarred*, and *Out of the Furnace*, where the incompetence, politics, and red-tape of the police and civil authorities function as kind of "indirect villain" hindering the cause of justice and at times acting grossly unjust. Paul speaks of "rulers," "authorities," "cosmic powers of this present darkness," and "spiritual forces of evil in the heavenly places" (Eph 6:13), so the temptation to lump this together with his discussion of sin's active agency in Romans 7 is an understandable one. For one thing, assigning sin's power to the realm of demonic creatures avoids the confounding metaphysical problem of how a non-entity could seem to possess positive agency, which the majority of exegetes and theologians continue to affirm.

---

48. Mathijs Lamberigts, "A Critical Evaluation of Critiques of Augustine's View of Sexuality," in *Augustine and His Critics*, eds. Robert Dodaro and George Lawless (New York: Routledge, 2000), 180. He identifies at least three forms of *concupiscentia* in Augustine: (1) *concupiscentia bona*, the desire for things of the spirit; (2) *concupiscentia naturalis*; and, (3) *concupiscentia carnis*, associated with sinful desire, ibid.,178–80.

While this remains a distressing conundrum for philosophical theology, cinema playfully revels in paradox when portraying villains—our final observation. One manifestation of this is the inappropriateness of their behavior. They often laugh when mortally wounded or fly into a rage in serene environments. Another is the filmmakers' choice of a villain's physical appearance as either attractively clean-cut (e.g. U-jin, *Oldboy*) or morbidly unkempt (e.g. troglodytes, *Bone Tomahawk*). The two extremes can also merge into one, as in *The Equalizer*, where Teddy (Marton Csokas) sports a clean appearance and slicked black hair but also brandishes gruesome tattoos of demons that cover his body in scenes where he is shirtless. In *Oldboy*, the audience is intentionally made to mistake U-jin's uncontrolled laughter as remorseful weeping when Dae-su stoops to lick his shoes. Likewise, Stansfield (*Leon*) listens to soft classical music while murdering Malthida's entire family. In these examples, one is immediately reminded of paradox as a vexing problem in Augustine's grappling with the concept of sin: If it has no being, how is it so evident? Why do we fear it? How is it afforded the enslaving power that it has?[49] He uses the image of a "twisted and tangled knottiness" to describe the confusion surrounding sin's nature and effects.[50] Like cinematic villains, sin attracts by joining itself to desirable things.[51] It is sometimes hard to tell whether the characters are weak, silly, and simple or if they are extremely complex.

Ridding the land of pollution

The presence of the cinematic villain supports what can be considered as a "narrative" of ritual pollution in Israel's cult. Initial dread comes upon (usually) a community in the light of the threat of a villain and his murderous designs. Such is the case with the appearance of Harlon DeGroat in city of North Braddock (*Out of the Furnace*), the cannibals in the town of Bright Hope (*Bone Tomahawk*), and the Russian mob on the streets of Boston (*The Equalizer*). The community feels the stain or wound that has been left after an offense has been committed. It is simply not enough that the defiling act cease and the people move on. A mark has been left, a deep and festering *han*, as it were, that calls for cleanup. Not only must the community heal

---

49. Augustine, *Confessions*, xii.5.7. For an excellent study on how the 17th c. poet and divine, John Donne, also grappled with this theme, see Gillian R. Evans, "John Donne and the Augustinian Paradox of Sin," *The Review of English Studies* 33, no. 129 (1982): 1–22.

50. Augustine, *Confessions*, ii.10.18.

51. Evans, "John Donne and the Augustinian Paradox of Sin," 14.

from the damages already inflicted, it must vigilantly protect itself from subsequent incursions of evil. As long as the stain remains, threat is imminent. An important feature of the entire process is its physicality. In both Scripture and cinema, a violating offense activates a set of responses and procedures for expunging it with utmost tenacity. In dealing with ritual pollution in ancient Israel, objects must be scrubbed, washed, burnt, sprinkled, removed, broken, covered, etc. Likewise, heroic avengers embark on the arduous task of surveying terrains, obtaining armaments, recruiting allies, torturing accomplices, and defeating goons. Finally, the process comes to an end with the complete extermination of the villain. Like Robert McCall storming Pushkin's Moscow home and wiping out every resident, the Israelite cleansing procedure for territorial uncleanness is inconveniently thorough, ridding the land once for all of its pollution and averting divine wrath.

The reaction evoked from the imagery of stain finds a counterpart in the physicality of cinematic villainy. Regarding impurity in the Hebrew Bible, Joseph Lam writes: "Stain elicits dread, not evaluation—our need for their elimination stems not as much from a process of conscious deliberation as from an instinctual preference for purity, homogeneity, and cleanness."[52] The value of the metaphor is that it appeals to a "visceral reaction" and "sense of aversion" as the basis for sin's rejection.[53] Similarly, Thomas Kazen attempts to bridge the gap between ritual and moral impurity by focusing on the notion of disgust as "the basic corporeal aspect" of morality."[54] If tenable, it fosters greater connection between the physical and spiritual dimensions of purification and atonement rituals. Revenge cinema nicely visualizes and narrates the revulsion that victims and avengers have for villains and the necessary lethal force required to remove their threat. On another front, it seems that cultic impurity, by and large, is generated from *within* the community, as a result of their acts, and not as a result of some external entity. The eating of unclean animals and performing idolatrous practices are perhaps the exception as they identify impurity in reference to foreign cultures. In the black and white ethos of the revenge film, however, the threat is an invader, an enemy from outside. The insider/outsider dynamic reinforces the claim that purity laws operate within the sphere of the holy and may go some distance in advancing the case for sin's radically alien nature.

52. Joseph Lam, *Patterns of Sin in the Hebrew Bible: Metaphor, Culture, and the Making of a Religious Concept* (New York: Oxford University Press, 2016), 180.

53. Ibid.

54. Thomas Kazen, "Dirt and Disgust: Body and Morality in Biblical Purity Laws," in *Perspectives on Purity and Purification in the Bible*, ed. Baruch J. Schwartz et al. (New York: Bloomsbury T&T Clark, 2008), 52.

The avenger-villain

It is when we consider Jesus' relationship to sin in the incarnation that cinematic contributions helps the present atonement theory to make a break from traditions that very closely associate—or even equate—sin with the devil or demonic powers. Many revenge films play with the idea that although the avenger is the protagonist and hero, he/she in many ways either possesses or takes on sinister traits. Chris Deacy suggests that from an audience perspective the criminal traits of "anti-heroes" in *film noir* help make the case that "only a tainted individual can, meaningfully and authentically, speak to, and be in a position to address the needs of, a tainted sinful humanity."[55] As touches revenge films and atonement theology, the theme of identification goes one step further. Instead of identifying with sinful humans, the hero identifies with evil itself. Thus, the gunslinging "Preacher," who rescues the mining settlement from evil land developers, is himself the *Pale Rider*, whose name is Death (Rev 6:8); Dae-su's alter ego is the "Monster," who he must kill even after his nemesis is long dead (*Oldboy*); John Wick is known among his former mobster associates as "Baba Yaga," the Boogeyman, or more comically, according to Viggo, "the one you send to *kill* the fuckin' Boogeyman." The recurrent idea is that this nefarious identity is part of the person's past, whom the avenger has since walked away from but must resurrect in order to exact vengeance on the true villain.

It is here that cinematic considerations challenge the impulse within *Christus Victor* and its contemporary analogues to identify the devil as the villain in the story of atonement. Films associate the protagonist with the villain in a very intimate way; they make the "argument" that the protagonist's close identification and familiarity with the "realm" of his enemy is necessary to destroy the villain.[56] However, Jesus' identification and collusion with demons at the level of his own ontology is far too theologically problematic. In Christian tradition, his identification is with fallen, sinful humanity and not other creatures, not to mention the devil! To be fair, Scripture does attest to images that associate Christ with the "serpent" (John 3:14), the "curse" (Gal 3:13), and "sin" itself (2 Cor 5:21). If, by drawing upon cinematic insights, we retain the narrative of a strong association between the hero and

---

55. Christopher Deacy, ed., *Screen Christologies: Redemption and the Medium of Film* (Cardiff: University of Wales Press, 2001), 99.

56. The overlap between the sin-bearer and demons might be seen in idea of the scapegoat that is sent "for Azazel" (Lev 16:8, 10, or "to" Azazel vv. 10, 26). While the meaning of the word is uncertain, the argument that it refers to some demonic personality is fairly strong. David P. Wright, "Azazel," ed. David Noel Freedman, *ABD, Vol. 1: A–C* (New Haven; London: Yale University Press, June 1, 1992), 536.

his nemesis, then identifying the villain as the non-creaturely entity of sin is a much better option than to imagine the reprehensible idea that Christ is intimately familiar with and participates in the demonic realm.

Revenge films often end on an ambiguous note that leaves the audience wondering whether the hero is no different from the villain in the close associating that is forged in their mutual identities. Once the hero exacts vengeance there is a sense in which he/she has permanently crossed a line and cannot come back. In the face of criticisms that satisfaction theories inadequately address the resurrection, this cinematic feature intensifies the need for the hero to be vindicated. There is no other way to know that the character is not in fact another deplorable villain other than through some form of vindication that the audience is made aware of.

Analysis and summary

Through a consideration of the testimonies of Scripture, Christian theology, and cinema, I have attempted to defend an objective notion of sin as distinct from the mere individual actions of human beings. In light of the impossibility of speaking univocally about the nature of sin as it is, that is to say, in an unmediated way, I follow Ricoeur's injunction that we attend not to "speculative" rationalizations of evil but "spontaneous" expressions imbibed in such things as myth. Once stripped of its pretensions (demythologized), "the myth reveals its explanatory significance and its contribution to understanding, . . . its symbolic function."[57] Thus, in seeking to model theology in a narrative mode, I submit the claim of sin as a character, a villain, an object of God's vengeance. Its primary expression in the world is in the deviant, volitional acts of individual human beings, but at the level of God's redemption of the cosmos, there is sufficient warrant, I think, to regard it as objectively isolatable, transmittable, and condemnable in its own right. Attention must be given to its complex and multifaceted character. While it is true that sin is associated to some volitional trespass occurring in time, it is not necessarily true that a given instance of volitional trespass encapsulates everything that sin entails. Thus, there are instances where sin exists and operates *at some distance* to willful infraction, such as in the idea of sin placing the individual in a state of debt, or cases of defilement in which sin causes impurity to linger and requires expiation long after offenses have been committed, or when sin seems to exercise a power to enslave. Perhaps the strongest argument for sin's potential detachment from human transgression is the incarnation,

---

57. Paul Ricoeur, *The Symbolism of Evil*, trans. Emerson Buchanan (New York: Beacon, 1967), 4–5.

which suggests that Christ takes on flesh that is somehow touched by sin while he never himself performs a sinful act. Only at his final moments upon the cross (as I will argue in the next chapter) does he "become sin" in the fullest sense of the term. Prior to that, a certain *solubility* between his "tainted" nature and the sin he plans to condemn is logically required to accomplish expiation. Edward Irving helpfully imagines the flesh of Christ as the "fit field of contention," the "middle space on which the powers of the world contended with the Holy Spirit dwelling in his soul."[58] This was because his flesh was "linked unto all material things, devil-possessed" and being of the same kind over which the devil had triumphed.[59]

Once isolated, we begin to appreciate sin's radical *otherness*. Ontologically, we are forced to agree with Bavinck that sin is neither an entity created by God (making God the author of sin) nor an uncreated entity (God himself). Yet even Bavinck hesitates to call it *mere* privation or simple non-being. Is it a creature, then? *Christus Victor* proponents, ancient and modern, obviously prefer this option. A major problem is that the atonement story being put forward demands an intimate association between Christ and his enemy, which is feasible when we imagine the villain in terms of sin, but problematic when a link is forged between Christ and the devil. Furthermore, in *Christus Victor*, we are led to equate one single creature with the totality of evil in the world and forced to adopt a "the-devil-made-me-to-it" posture in reference to our own moral failures and every other calamity befalling the cosmos. Even theologies that prefer identifying the enemy as demonic creatures keep close at hand the notion of sin as an abstract principle. Walter Wink understands "powers" as the spiritual "interiority" of epochs, nations, systems, etc., which (at least to ancient peoples) were capable of being personified as entities.[60] We should keep in mind (at least tradition assumes) that the devil himself sinned at some point in time. Heinrich Schlier, while seeming to vacillate on the objective status of principalities and powers, nonetheless emphasizes: "The principalities always have an ally within us, the *sin* derived from Adam."[61]

Where philosophical language faces a vexing contradiction and inhibits further discussion of sin's essence, narrative (with the help of cinema) enfleshes this paradox as a character in the divine drama. This character is absolute in that it *always* orients itself in the direction of evil and actively

---

58. Edward Irving, *The Collected Writings of Edward Irving: In Five Volumes*, ed. Gavin Carlyle (London: Alexander Strahan, 1865), 161.

59. Ibid.

60. Walter Wink, *Unmasking the Powers* (Philadelphia: Fortress, 1986), 4.

61. Heinrich Schlier, *Principalities and Powers in the New Testament* (New York: Herder and Herder, 1961), 60. Emphasis mine.

pulls its prey into destruction, yet, paradoxically, it shares a deep connection with us, speaks our language, and occupies our very own space and thoughts. The portrayal—indeed *enjoyment*—of paradox is an example of art's capacity to sidestep complex philosophical debate while still contributing meaningfully by way of imaginative modeling. While logical argumentation might demand that either *nihil* or demonic powers be chosen to label sin, sin as imagined through cinematic appropriation allows us to *visualize* the absurdity and observe its function within a dramatically-modeled explanation of the atonement. The visual representation sustains the concept in a tension that we can work with and learn from.

Preparation and Pursuit

Having provided some groundwork for the possibility of isolating sin as a target for divine action, we will now turn to consider the motivation that makes atonement necessary and the means that aid its accomplishment. If sin is the ultimate target that God intends to vengefully repay, it seems apt to locate divine motivation *prior* to the fall of human beings (and perhaps of angels as well). The Reformed concept of the covenant of redemption (also called *pactum salutis* or "counsel of peace," hereafter CR) serves as a well-suited device that establishes the conditions prior to the climactic work of the cross. It provides some theological language for *narrating* the progress of atonement from inception to fulfillment in positive terms.

The covenant of redemption: a relevant framework

The CR is a product of late sixteenth century Reformed federalism. The puritan divine, Samuel Willard, in his 1693 treatise on the topic states it in simple terms as "an everlasting compact clearly made, and firmly ratified, between God the Father and God the Son, about the redemption and salvation of a number of the children of men."[62] More technically, it posits a pretemporal agreement, or pact, within the "meta-history"[63] of God's trinitarian life concerning the working out of the covenant of grace (*foedus gratiae*), which would be put to effect in space and time. Through it, the triune persons enter into the economic mode of relation in which the Father

---

62. Samuel Willard, *The Doctrine of the Covenant of Redemption In Which Is Laid the Foundation of All Our Hopes and Happiness, Briefly Opened and Improved*, ed. Therese B. McMahon (Coconut Creek, FL: Puritan Publications, 2014), 22–23.

63. John Von Rohr, *The Covenant of Grace in Puritan Thought* (Wipf & Stock, 2010), 43.

appoints and commissions the Son to be the mediator of humanity, and the Son guarantees the fulfillment of all righteousness and the payment of the debt on account of humanity's sin. The doctrine was established within Reformed orthodoxy as a means of securing the eternal and trinitarian foundation for salvation by grace alone, as seen in the prominent use of the language of the "counsels" of God. Although a seemingly speculative discourse, federal theologians are convinced that it is rooted in Scripture as an appropriate inference of various texts, one classic reference being Zec 6:13: "It is he that shall build the temple of the Lord; he shall bear royal honor, and shall sit upon his throne and rule. There shall be a priest by his throne, with *peaceful understanding between the two of them*." Other texts along the "narrative" concerns the economic relationship between the Father and Son (e.g. Ps. 22:2; John 20:17, Isa. 49f), the tasks assigned to the Messiah (e.g. Isa. 53:10; John 6:38–40; 10:18; 12:49; 14:31; 17:4), the promises of reward (e.g. Ps. 2:8; Isa. 53:10; John 17:4, 11, 17, 24; Eph. 1:20f.; Phil. 2:9f.), and the fulfillment of obedience (e.g. Matt. 26:42; John 4:34; 15:10; 17:4–5; 19:30).

Some points within this doctrine are worth highlighting for their relevance when we later bring them into dialogue with themes in revenge cinema. First, theologians have been quick to distinguish the persons of the Trinity, especially the Father and the Son, with respect to their roles in redemption rather than subsume the divine decree under a single head. In other words, they find it more fitting to say, "the Father does X, the Son does Y, and the Spirit does Z" than to say, "God does X, Y, and Z." Bavinck, for instance, lauds the *pactum* as the "divine work par excellence" in the way it demonstrates the coordinated operation of each member of the Trinity engaged in a specific task. This is in contrast to other decrees, like predestination, where only the "one will of God occupied the foreground."[64] A further distinction is perceived in how the covenant relates within the Godhead compared with God's actions *ad extra*. The CR flows from the trinitarian life of "consummate self-consciousness and freedom," whereas covenants made between God and humanity, on account of the infinite distance between them, takes on the character of a one-sided sovereign grant.[65] It is the Second Person of the Trinity as specifically divine, who willingly takes on the Father's charge. The decree for the Son to become man is subservient to the initial act of entering into the CR. The incarnation is "a *condition* of redemption (or a thing requisite in him who was to be a redeemer, in order to his

---

64. Bavinck, *Reformed Dogmatics Vol. 3: Sin and Salvation in Christ*, 346.

65. Ibid. Cf. Willard, *Covenant of Redemption*, 31: "The Father no sooner proposed it to him than he readily complied with it."

fitness to go through with that great undertaking) than a *quality* needed to render him a party."[66]

Second, as regards the order and place of the CR within the divine will, Willard proposes that the decrees be spoken of in terms of ends and means and that this distinction be appreciated. The end for which the decrees are ultimately designed is, straightforwardly, the demonstration of the glory of God's grace. The means pertain to all that is required in the redemption of humanity to achieve this end, which includes the CR as subsumed within the divine decree to elect persons to salvation. Having been crafted in eternity, the motivation lies in God alone as an "arbitrary" and "voluntary" undertaking.[67] Willard takes no small pains to remove any external or antecedent grounds that *cause* God to act redemptively. Both the ends and means, then, must necessarily fall within a single divine intention, lest two wills be present for which two ends must be assigned, thereby undercutting the praise of God's glory.[68] Willard therefore insists that though they are put in order, the decreeing acts must be seen as "coordinate" and happening inseparably together.[69]

Although God occupies central place in the means and ends of the outworking of the CR, sin is discussed as the main problem that the covenanting Son is tasked to deal with. Drawing from Olevianus, Heinrich Heppe writes: "Accordingly, the Father declared the Son to be His Anointed, who as such was to come into the world in His name and by His commission, and who was promised that his sacrifice and his intercession would be accepted by the Father as a perfect satisfaction for the sins of the elect."[70] An early British covenant theologian, David Dickson, in refuting the charge that the CR only involves the Father and Son, speaks of each member of the Trinity being "offended" at human sin:

66. He writes: "Though the Son of God could not actually redeem us unless he was in our nature, yet without our nature he could *covenant* to redeem us. Though he could not perform obedience, active or passive, to the law unless in our nature (which was only concerned in this obedience, as to the actual performance of it), yet he could undertake without, to obey the law in it. That is sufficient with respect to his covenanting about it." Willard, *Covenant of Redemption*, 40–41.

67. Ibid., 44. The word "arbitrary" here should be taken to mean random or devoid of rationale. Willard uses the term to highlight that the covenant was not a "natural" or "necessary" act.

68. Willard, *Covenant of Redemption*, 51–52.

69. Ibid., 52.

70. Heinrich Heppe, *Reformed Dogmatics: Set Out and Illustrated from the Sources*, ed. Ernst Bizer, trans. G. T. Thomson (Grand Rapids: Baker, 1978), 376. He cites Gaspar Olevianus, *De Substantia Foederis Gratuiti inter Deum et electosa itemque de mediis, quibus ea ipsa substantia nobis communicator, libri duo*. Geneva, 1585, 23.

> When we name the Father as the one party and His Son Christ as the other party in this covenant, we do not seclude the Son and holy [sic] Spirit from being the party offended; but do look upon the Father, Son and Spirit, one God in three Persons, as offended by mans sin; and yet all three contented to take satisfaction to divine justice for man sin in the Person of the Son . . . [71]

In an exposition of Matt 26:39 ("let this cup pass from me"), Dickson expands Jesus' words into language that accords with the CR:

> The love that our Lord hath to our redemption, and his special covenant made with the Father, for the paying of our ransome, made him to subject his holy nature and Will to that which otherwise is abhorred; therefore looking to the Fathers will, thus to expiate the sins of the Redeemed, he sayeth . . . I voluntarily doe choose it . . . Let mee drink this cup: and heer the merit of sin, the strictness of Divine Justice, the horrour of the wrath of God, with the weight of the curse, the mercy of God toward sinners, and the unspeakable love both of GOD and CHRIST toward the Elect, is to be seen vively set foorth before us in our Lords passion.[72]

Two points are noteworthy in the above passage: First, the love of God is featured as the primary motivator for the redemption of the elect and the "passion" demonstrates it. Second, by giving added content and "characterization" to Jesus' words, Dickson shows how the doctrine weaves seamlessly with Scripture in a narrative form.

Later theologians gave a more metaphysical account, presumably, to emphasize the absoluteness of God with respect to the CR. For Willard, the object of the covenant (that to which the covenant benefits) was *ens possibile* (possible being). Having not yet become an "offspring of time," humanity, and all that is entailed in their creation, sinless state, fall, curse, and need for redemption, exists in the eternal mind of God only as a possibility.[73] While he does not expound further on this, it opens up the question of justice and mercy within the divine perfections and where sin enters into the ordering of the CR. Patrick Gillespie in his 1677 treatise on the subject answers the question of whether there was any "natural essential justice in God" serving

---

71. David Dickson, *Therapeutica Sacra*, I.4.24, quoted in Carol A. Williams, "The Decree of Redemption Is in Effect a Covenant: David Dickson and the Covenant of Redemption" (Unpublished Ph.D Dissertation, Calvin Theological Seminary, 2005), 209.

72. Dickson, *A Brief Exposition of the Evangel of Jesus Christ According to Matthew*, quoted in ibid., 183.

73. Willard, *Covenant of Redemption*, 51.

as the "efficient cause" in dealing with sin. He enlists the extreme position of the Socinians, who deny justice as an essential property of God and make justice "the meer voluntary effect of his Will," to illustrate the necessity of God punishing sin as a function of his nature.[74] At the same time, he refutes the other extreme: because justice is natural to God, he *cannot but* punish it or demand satisfaction lest he cease to be God. First, he uses the analogy that just because it is natural for humans to laugh or speak, it does not mean that humans do so *necessarily*; the individual, rather, does so freely. Thus to argue that God absolutely *must* punish sin means it would have to be so "without any moderation" and "to the utmost degree."[75] Second, he argues that natural properties of God do not require any objects much less the "exercise of acts" *ad extra*. In this way, God is rightfully said to be wise, good, just, etc. prior to having created anything. This being the case, all that is required is a "hypothetical necessity."[76]

The main contributions of this Reformed doctrine for this study are twofold: First, it unifies the Triune members in the work of redemption and eliminates the caricature of an angry Father inflicting violence on his innocent Son. Second, even though the ultimate ends and means for redemption arise in, and is driven by, God alone, the perception of sin and humanity's plight, even as a "possibility" or "hypothetical" object, is unambiguously named as the offending agent that motivates and mobilizes the Trinity's plan for redemption.

The question of honor

Aspects of the CR have deeper relevance when considering the divine "honor" that is supposedly lost due to humanity's sin in Anselm's model of satisfaction. In *Cur Deus Homo*, I.xii, honor expresses the justice or "uprightness of will" that creatures rightfully owe to God. One who fails to render this honor "robs God of his own and dishonours him." Furthermore, it is not sufficient merely to repay what has been taken away: rather, he ought to pay back more than he took, in proportion to the insult which he has inflicted. For just as, in the case of someone who injures the health of another, it is not sufficient for him to restore that person's health, if he does not pay some compensation for the painful injury which has been inflicted, similarly it

---

74. Patrick Gillespie, *The Ark of the Covenant Opened: Or, A Treatise on the Covenant of Redemption between God and Christ, as the Foundation of the Covenant of Grace* (London: Tho. Parkhurst, 1677), 36.

75. Ibid., 38.

76. Ibid.

is not sufficient for someone who violates someone else's honor, to restore that person's honor, if he does not, in consequence of the harmful act of dishonor, given, as restitution to that person whom he has dishonored, something pleasing to that person.[77]

Rachel Erdman urgently offers two points to note. First, honor should not be understood as "God's ego." "Offending God's honor is not equivalent to insulting an aristocrat. In Anselm's thinking, the stakes are infinitely higher. The entirety of the universal order rests on God's honor being upheld."[78] Second, she quotes Anselm to show that God's honor cannot actually be harmed:

> . . . when a rational being does not wish for what is right, he dishonors God, with regard to himself, since he is not willingly subordinating himself to God's governance, and is disturbing, as far as he is able, the order and beauty of the universe. *In spite of this he does not harm or besmirch the honor of God to the slightest extent.*[79]

While Erdman's reading is sound, we should be careful not to quench the potency of Anselm's anthropomorphism here. On denying that God's honor cannot be subject to injury Anselm is, of course, alluding to the divine attribute of immutability *as God is in himself*. As such, God cannot be dishonored—*nor honored*, technically speaking—as Anselm recognizes in that same passage. He ends this line of discussion saying, "but the creature, as far as he is concerned appears to do this when he submits or opposes his will to the will of God." In other words, the act of sin *should be regarded as* dishonor. Erdman takes the fact that God is unaffected by dishonor and concludes (too hastily I think): "Sin cannot hurt God; it hurts humans. The need for satisfaction is not to exact vengeance, but to restore harmony."[80] For Erdman, that God requires compensation is not "economic," that is, a transactional payment of a debt, but a demonstration that God's justice means something.[81] Again, while Anselm does speak of the need for God to punish sinners in order to uphold the "consistency" of his governance (I.xii), he does not diminish the need to demand punishment or satisfaction *on a personal level*. In fact, apart from invoking immutability to deny the

---

77. Anselm, *Anselm of Canterbury: The Major Works*, ed. Brian Davies and G. R. Evans (Oxford: Oxford University Press, 2008), 283.

78. Rachel Erdman, "Sacrifice as Satisfaction, Not Substitution: Atonement in the Summa Theologiae," 463.

79. *Cur Deus Homo, I.xv*, in Anselm, *Major Works*, 288 Erdman's emphasis.

80. Erdman, "Sacrifice as Satisfaction," 464.

81. Ibid., 464–65.

possibility for God to "lose honor," Anselm argues that God receives his due even if it means taking it by force:

> This is because either a man of his own free will demonstrates the submission which he owes to God by not sinning, or alternatively by paying recompense for his sin, or else God brings him into submission to himself against his will, by subjecting him to torment, and in this way he shows that he is his Lord, something which the man himself refuses to admit voluntarily. In this connection, it needs to be borne in mind that, just as a man by sinning seizes what belongs to God, likewise God, by punishing him, takes away what belongs to man.[82]

Erdman's attempt to reconfigure satisfaction unfortunately depersonalizes the offense as something that affects humans and our dignity within God's ordered universe. This is true but should not be asserted at the expense of God being personally affected and wanting personal compensation. Erdman's project involves recasting satisfaction in a way that distances itself from penal substitution and the violence with which it is associated. She argues that the impetus for satisfaction should not be understood as a transactional payment of debt but a restored "*relationship* with God that was fractured by human sin."[83] By recruiting Aquinas' understanding of sacrifice as a "superabundant gift" that "*creates and intensifies* the internal experience of love within us,"[84] she develops this into the means by which the obstacle of sin is overcome and communion with God is restored.

The endeavor to avoid drawing violence against sinners (or against Christ for that matter) into God's atonement logic is, of course, the theological task at hand. It may very well be that Anselm's God, who requires the payment of honor at the hands of sinners, is simply too brutal. Given the assumption that God is rightly regarded as a potentate and we his subjects, however, the notion of honor remains appropriate and helpful.

The way that honor is construed within the CR, I would argue, retains this meaning while simultaneously affirming Erdman's vision of atonement as a restoration of relationship rather than a punishment. In the promissory content of the covenant, theologians stress a deep sense of honor that marks the relationship. Along with appointing and sending the Son, the Father endows the Son with the authority appropriate to his role as prophet, priest, and king; he prepares for him the body (Heb 10:5) to which he would be hypostatically united in order to fulfill active and passive obedience; and he

---

82. *Cur Deus Homo*, I.xiv, in Anselm, *Major Works*, 287.
83. Erdman, "Sacrifice as Satisfaction," 465 Erdman's emphasis.
84. Ibid., 472.

anoints and sanctifies him (Isa 61:1–2). Because the undertaking was "a great work" wherein the Son would bear infinite wrath upon his frail nature, he was given the constant support of the Father's "mighty arm" so as not to be broken under its weight.[85]

As a reward for his obedience, the Father promises the Son a kingdom and inheritance, and that he would judge the cosmos and be exceedingly exalted (Phil 2:6–11). The work of God in redemption ratified in eternity by the CR and ultimately accomplished in time by the Mediator culminates in the "declarative glory" of God (as the Puritans put it). This glory is manifested not so much *by* creatures as "*in* God's dealings with creatures."[86] Where the Anselmic sense of honor can be thought of as humanity's "debt" due to God for committing sin, the covenantal sense is of a "reward" bestowed to members of the Triune Godhead, especially Christ, for the defeat of sin.[87] Honor that is foreordained in God's good pleasure and dispensed by all creation, seen and unseen (Eph 3:10–11), is of a higher order and more substantial than honor originally lost by the fall. In light of this, Isa 53:11 ("Out of his anguish he shall see light; he shall find satisfaction through his knowledge") and Heb 12:2 ("looking to Jesus the pioneer and perfecter of our faith, who for the sake of the joy that was set before him endured the cross, disregarding its shame, and has taken his seat at the right hand of the throne of God") fills out this alternative understanding of "satisfaction" entailed in the atonement. God is satisfied not in the sight of blood paid as a debt for lost honor; rather, God is satisfied in the honor and glory mutually bestowed within the Godhead in celebration for the victory over sin.

Theo-cinematic synthesis

The lone hero

We have observed how revenge films are ultimately about the avenger, not the villain nor his offense, nor even ultimately about the beloved object. The avenger as hero occupies center stage in the plot, which is essentially a showcase of his/her abilities and resolve. Apart from rare cases, the avenger fights alone at the final showdown. Far from a haphazard and "lucky"

---

85. Willard, *Covenant of Redemption*, 73.
86. Gillespie, *Covenant of Redemption*, 39.
87. Gillespie lists the various ways in which "peculiar glory" was rendered to the members of the Trinity respecting their person and roles, e.g. from the Son to the Father (Jn 8:49); from the Son to the Spirit (Heb 9:14; I Cor 6:11; Gal 4:6). Ibid., 42.

pursuit of the villain, there is a strong sense that the avenger's success is due to pre-planning and superior strategy. Although the process is bloody and brutal, the hero traps and kills the villain in the way that was intended. This reinforces the idea of a united effort on the part of the Trinity against a common foe and pushes back against caricatures of divine "abuse" between the Father and the Son.

The unity of the Godhead also raises points of debate with Moltmann's attempt of locating the cross *within* the Trinity. The godforsakenness of the Son and the grief of the Father at the loss of the Son are essential aspects of intratrinitarian relationship expressed in his dictum: "The form of the crucified Christ is the Trinity."[88] Although this state of despair within the Trinity issues unconditional love and secures peace for humanity, it is at the expense of introducing creaturelines, death, and contradiction into the Trinity *ad intra*. The motif of preparation and pursuit keeps these spheres separate while safely celebrating that truth that Christ is slain "before the foundation of the world" (Rev 13:8). Further, that the Trinity is in united opposition against sin as a foreign entity reinforces the impossibility of it being derived from, or located in, God.

Vows and pacts

The idea of the CR as a pact is particularly relevant in light of the "vow" wherein the avenger verbally pledges and plans to destroy the villain. Instances that show maximum congruity are those in which a vow is made either to equals (e.g. John Creasy vowing to Pita's mother, *Man on Fire*; Katayama to his friend, *Sun Scarred*), to oneself (Will Graham, *Manhunter*), or when a vow is a response to a request from an authority figure (Shinzaemon and the band of samurai in response to the Justice Minister, *13 Assassins*). Aligning with an important point in covenant theology, the avenger is completely free to enter the mission or not. In *Bone Tomahawk*, the decision for Sheriff Hunt and O'Dwyer to embark on their mission is predicated on the assertion, "there isn't a choice." One could say that while the members of the Trinity are under no *necessary* obligation to redeem creatures, they are obligated to one another as united members of the Godhead. The Sheriff goes because the townsmen are going; where one goes, all go. Just as the CR "officially" makes Christ the Surety and Mediator, it is at the moment of the vow that the mission begins and the film protagonist is "robed" with vengeance.

---

88. Jürgen Moltmann, *The Crucified God: The Cross of Christ as the Foundation and Criticism of Christian Theology* (New York: HarperCollins, 1974), 246.

That vows in revenge films are most often spoken directly to villains is dissonant but with possible fruitful theological returns. In the CR, the content and tone of the "dialogue" between the triune persons is, not surprisingly, heavily inward as it points to their plan, their roles, and their glory. After all, at this point in the divine "meta-history," creaturely existence is yet only "hypothetical." In much the same way that Will Graham (*Manhunter*) vows vengeance by speaking aloud to himself, God in effect makes a pact by talking to Godself. At the same time, virtually all renderings of the CR include the element of sin and some describe the offense felt by the triune persons at the thought of sin and its devastating effect upon humanity. Vows and threats of vengeance carry the potential of contextually challenging the doctrine to place more emphasis on the divine rage that elicits their action.

The satisfaction of honor

Through a deeper consideration of the film, *Hara-Kiri*, the common feudal context of Anselm's eleventh century British serfdom and the Japanese shogunate system affords an interesting opportunity to re-enter these worlds and reappropriate the ideas of honor and satisfaction. In the film, a feudal lord is offended at Motome's ploy to obtain charity by feigning *seppuku* on their hollowed grounds, so he demands his life as a price for their lost honor; thus, a fairly typical feudal notion of satisfaction. Enter Motome's father-in-law, Hanshiro, who is enraged at their merciless interpretation of honor and seeks vengeance upon the house. His strategy of gaining audience with the lord involves performing the exact ploy that his son-in-law had attempted. The inexperienced army of samurai finally suppresses him, but not before he unveils the sheared topknots of the warriors who killed Motome, wreaks havoc on the grounds with a bamboo sword, and topples their Shogun's ceremonial red armor, which the lord calls the "pride of our noble house."[89] Hanshiro's "satisfaction" in this case lies in vindicating the honor of his son-in-law while utterly stripping the feudal house of theirs. His final death is striking in that instead of taking his own life, he raises his arms in a cruciform position as the surrounding horde of samurai slash him with their swords, further solidifying their extreme lack of true honor. So we see that, while not discounting the idea of satisfaction as a debt paid toward Hanshiro, another interpretation of satisfaction is possible: Hanshiro receives satisfaction through the dishonor and defeat of his foes.

---

89. The top-knots of samurai at that time were considered sacred and having it cut off was extremely disgraceful to the point of performing Hara-Kiri

This film as considered alongside themes in covenant theology raises another important point. Although Motome has winded up in his predicament as a result of his willful mistake, Hanshiro's rage is targeted externally *unto those who abused his son-in-law*. Likewise we find in the CR the Trinity does not "react" to humanity's rebellion, at least not in the first place. Within the Reformed framework, the elect are eternally beloved and destined for salvation. As previously discussed, God's glory is first in priority, followed by the concern that sinners be redeemed to achieve that end. The implication is a vital one for conceiving the "direction" of God's anger: wrath is not aimed at humanity because of their sin; it is aimed at sin *itself*. There is a strong sense, then, that redemption does not immediately flow from rebellion *by* sinners but from damage done *to* sinners. As Athanasius writes: "It was our sorry case that caused the Word to come down, our transgression that called out His love for us, so that He made haste to help us and to appear among us."[90]

Suiting for battle

A final fruitful product of this cinematic narrativizing of doctrine is the place that the avenger's allies fit into the story. The avenging hero, while alone at the final showdown, makes his way through the fray with no little help from faithful accomplices. As covenant theologians routinely affirm, the persons of the Trinity all engage in specific tasks that lead to a unified outcome. In particular, the Holy Spirit plays an important role of "furnishing" the Son with all the physical and spiritual gifts and capacities to accomplish his mission. Similarly, "supporting characters" assist their avenger-friend by providing affirmation (Susan, *The Equalizer*), knowledge (Sam, *Taken*), armaments (Rayburn, *Man on Fire*), companionship (Ned, *Unforgiven*), and combat support (Marcus, *John Wick*). Where much of the recent response to the relative absence of the Holy Spirit in atonement turns to the Spirit's involvement in sanctifying or gifting the believer for Christian living post-conversion, there is in the concept of the avenger's "ally" a substantial place for the Holy Spirit in Christ's working of atonement proper. This has implications for the role of violence in Jesus' sufferings. Far from being left as a purely passive victim, much less *God's* forsaken victim, Jesus is equipped and enabled *by God* to be victorious through the sufferings that will come as a result of his own embittered engagement with sin.

---

90. Athanasius, *On the Incarnation*, I.4.

Analysis and summary

Recalling Hans Boersma's concern to remove violence from the "heart of God," his strategy is to condemn double predestination and opt for a historical understanding of election as a mode of divine "hospitality." The CR pulls the plan of atonement even further back and reconstructs the rationale and methods involved in a way that is essentially positive. As it stands, the identification of "the beloved" within this model presupposes the doctrine of election, which is generally embraced by those for whom the current model is under severe criticism. The doctrine is not only present but helps to foreground the personal nature of sin's offensiveness and solidifies the Godhead's motivation for doing what God does. Furthermore, Christ's expiation of sin as an isolated entity requires that it be understood as the sin of an elected mass of individuals.

Additionally, the often-neglected doctrine of the covenant of redemption is relevant as a framework, which, when seen through the lens of cinema, effectively displays the preparation and pursuit of the villain as essential aspects of atonement. We discover the mutual and satisfying honoring of the persons of the Trinity as the motivation, the redemption of humanity as the means, and God's offense at sin as the main obstacle. This construal challenges the claim of inherent disunity and despair in the Godhead with respect to the cross and places the violence of the atonement one step removed from the idea that God is attacking persons as such, be it the Son or humanity in general.

The Showdown at Calvary

We come now to the central event in our narrative of atonement where we consider a narrative model for how the violent death of Christ vengefully expiates sin. The paradigmatic texts are Paul's words Rom 8:3, which says, ". . . by sending his own Son in the likeness of sinful flesh, and to deal with sin, he condemned sin in the flesh . . . " and 2 Cor 5:21, speaking of how God made Jesus "to be sin." I will show how Paul's christology infers the isolation and imputation of sin that can be imagined as punished in the *crucible* of Christ's flesh by his deliberate self-sacrifice. As an alternative to the idea of a pure substitution, the sinner (in Christ) participates in this death through union with him (Gal 2:20). Interacting with cinema on this point will help to explicate how self-sacrifice may produce victory as well as reconfigure our typical understandings of Christ's "forsakenness" on the cross (Matt 27:46).

"He condemned sin in the flesh"

Much of the discussion concerning the sinful/fallen nature of Jesus surrounds his incarnation, giving the impression of an unchanged state until the resurrection. However, more needs to be made of the fact that Scripture suggests a temporal progression leading up to the cross in which God "has laid on him the iniquity of us all" (Isa 53:6) and where he *becomes* sin (2 Cor 5:21; cf. Gal 3:13). Were it the case that Jesus is cursed with the sin of the world in its fullest measure *throughout his earthly life*, it becomes more difficult to understand the Father's early announcement that he delights and takes pleasure in him (Matt 3:17; Mark 1:11) and the violent death that befalls him as a result of God's condemnation of sin in his flesh (Rom 8:3). The image evoked in Rom 8:3 is one in which sin seems "concentrated" upon the flesh of Christ and is subsequently accursed and removed by divine wrath. Although, as we have seen, Christ takes on "sinful flesh" in his incarnation, there is the sense that another, alien sin (*peccatum alienum*) "comes upon him" at some point in time and is condemned. Visualizing this in narrative form is indeed possible. The concept of imputation is helpful for squaring the fact that Christ did not inherit or incur guilt and yet is the one who "takes away the sin of the world" (John 1:29; cf. 1 John 3:5).

Reinstating imputation

Imputation, essentially "to reckon," means ascribing to someone an act he/she has not committed as though they committed it and to treat that person accordingly.[91] It is primarily found in three related but distinct atonement ideas:

1. universal culpability for Adam's sin;
2. the bestowing of Christ's "alien righteousness" to believers by faith; and
3. the laying of the sin of the world upon Christ.

The first two have dominated the discussion over the centuries, but it is the third aspect that is most relevant for this present study. At its core is the image of transferring or crediting something. Paul in regard to Onesimus' debt, instructs Philemon: "If he has wronged you in any way, or owes you anything, charge that to my account" (v. 18). That Paul is, in effect,

---

91. Joshua Lacy Wilson, *Imputation of Sin and Righteousness: A Sermon from Rom. 5:18,19* (Hanover College Press, 1835), 8.

penning an "IOU" (v. 19)[92] shows that the concept is fairly mundane and uncontroversial.

As applied to Christ as he "bore our sins in his body on the cross" (1 Pet 2:24), matters are complicated. Christian tradition has generally read Paul as straightforwardly taking up this imagery in his description of Christ becoming "sin" (2 Cor 5:21), a "curse" (Gal 3:13), and being sent "in the likeness of sinful flesh" (Rom 8:3). Some recent exegetical treatments have attempted to dismiss this interpretation but have been either unconvincing or unable to reinterpret all of the many references addressing it.[93] Perhaps the most astute theological critique, however, came from the radical sixteenth century cleric, Faustus Socinus, who deemed it unjust to impute sin to Christ and exact punishment when he did not deserve it. Among his many criticisms is his argument that if imputation had taken place, then God had every right to kill him; but this is contradicted by the fact God extolled honors on Christ for his act.[94] Furthermore, Socinus reasoned that two conditions must be met before sin might be imputed on someone:

1. that there be a sufficient connection between the sinner and recipient; and
2. that the recipient imitate the sinner's wickedness.[95]

For Socinus, what would be unjust with regard to punishment is equally unjust with regard to imputation.

Without getting into this protracted debate, it is sufficient to hear John Owen on the matter, who responded to similar (though not as vitriolic) objections from William Twisse.

> God may inflict the punishment due to one on another, after,—in consequence of his own right and the consent of that other,—he

---

92. F. F. Bruce, *The Epistles to the Colossians, to Philemon, and to the Ephesians*, 2nd Ed. (Grand Rapids: Eerdmans, 1984), 220.

93. For example, N. T. Wright, "On Becoming the Righteousness of God: 2 Corinthians 5:21," in *Pauline Theology*, vol. 2, ed. David M. Hay (Minneapolis: Augsburg Fortress, 1993), 200–208 in which he argues that 2 Cor 5:21 must be read in the context of Paul's defense of his ministry; for Paul the righteousness of God refers to God's covenant faithfulness to his people, not a transfer of righteousness as though it were a substance: "The 'earthen vessel' that Paul knows himself to be (4:7) has found the problem of his own earthiness dealt with, and has found itself filled, paradoxically, with treasure indeed: "for our sake God made Christ, who did not know sin, to be a sin-offering for us, so that in him we might become God's covenant-faithfulness," 205. For response, see J. V. Fesko, "N.T. Wright on Imputation," *RTR* 66, no. 1 (April 2007): 2–22.

94. Faustus Socinus, *De Jesu Christo Servatore*, III.9.

95. *De Jesu*, III.10. Socinus cites Gen 18:25 as an example of God not willing to destroy Lot and his family along with Sodom as this would be wicked.

hath laid the sins upon that other on account of which he inflicts the punishment. He might punish the elect either in their own persons, or in their surety standing in their room and stead; and when he is punished, they also are punished: for in this point of view the federal head and those represented by him are not considered as distinct, but as one; for although they are not one in respect of personal unity, they are, however, one,—that is, one body in mystical union, yea, *one mystical Christ*;—namely, the surety is the head, those represented by him the members; and when the head is punished, the members also are punished. Nor could even he himself be called a surety absolutely innocent: for although he was properly and personally innocent, he was imputatively and substitutively guilty . . . "[96]

Owen argues from within his Reformed federalism, which positions Adam and Christ as the only two representatives for humanity. The concentric logic, drawn principally from Romans 5, is as follows:

1. Adam commits spiritual treachery and is guilty (recall, "the law is spiritual," Rom 7:14; cf. v. 12)

2. Humanity pays physically with death (Rom 5:12)

3. Christ pays physically with death and is innocent (5:16)

4. Humanity reaps the spiritual benefits of justification and eternal life (5:18)

The relationship of Adam's disobedience leading to death is the inverse of (i.e. "not like," vv. 14–16) Christ's "free gift" that leads to eternal life. Physical punishment can justly fall upon Christ, but only insofar as he federally represents actual sinners who deserve it. Furthermore, that sin is capable of wreaking social havoc beyond the boundaries of individual liability is evidence of its metastatic nature. If misfortune can befall those outside the immediate sphere of the evildoer, then it can operate on an independent domain and transferability of sin becomes possible.[97]

The idea of the sinner's mystical union with Christ supplies the intimate connection needed to justify Christ as a representative but not a replacement. As Paul writes: "We know that our old self was crucified with him so that the body of sin might be destroyed" (Rom 6:6; Gal 2:19-20). Furthermore, Christian baptism symbolizes, among other things, our burial

---

96. John Owen, *The Works of John Owen, D.D.*, vol. 10, ed. William H. Goold (New York: Robert Carter & Bros., 1852), 598.

97. Wolfhart Pannenberg, *Jesus—God and Man*, trans. Lewis L. Wilkins and Duane A. Priebe (Philadelphia: Westminster Press, 1977), 266.

"into his death" (Rom 6:3-4; Gal 3:27). The charge of injustice on God's part begins to dissipate in light of this union that—astonishingly—renders Christ as a mediator who is not "absolutely innocent." It must be stressed that wrongdoing on Christ's part is outrightly denied; it is the believer's imputed sin that is condemned by virtue of her mystical union with him. Within the union, our sin (in the absolute, as concerns atonement) is "decoupled" from our flesh where it normally resides to destroy us and it is communicated unto Christ's "sinful flesh" that ably receives it but where no personal sin dwells. His flesh, then, functions as the *crucible* for the wrath of God—not the object thereof—and can be likened to Irving's apt image of a "field of contention" and "middle space" in which sin is expunged.

Violence as condemnation

Once we are able to establish that imputed sin gives a ground for divine condemnation, the question before us is: why was Jesus' death so violent? As argued earlier by Calvin, God providentially reinforces the atonement as a condemnation. Modern interpretations of the crucifixion have tended to view Jesus' trial and execution as a sham and tragedy that should never have happened. Postcolonial writers have been quick to point out the role of empire and their practices of domination that led to Jesus' trial and execution, and theologians influenced by Girardian mimetic theory highlight the problem of the myth of scapegoating that perpetuates the sanctioning of such violence. Writing perceptively before his time, Berkouwer foresaw a tendency in these attempts toward the "rehabilitation" of justice to its pristine state. "The objective of such a rehabilitation is the 'revival' of justice and morality, or the self-correction of the Jewish people or of mankind, and," he writes, "it is exactly for this reason for this reason that it misses the core of the gospel concerning the suffering of Jesus Christ."[98]

That Jesus is repeatedly recognized as innocent is clear and should never be minimized, but Berkouwer rightly fears that an overemphasis on Jesus' innocence may obscure the theme of guilt surrounding the crucifixion. Guilt, even though it is mistakenly or vindictively attributed to Jesus, courses through the gospel narrative and subsequent apostolic reflections. The biblical writers did not labor to complain about the injustice of the sentence; they were concerned to relate the fact that *it happened* and that it happened at the hands of sinful men. Jesus himself was convinced that he was

---

98. G. C. Berkouwer, *Studies in Dogmatics: The Work of Christ* (Eerdmans, 1965), 138.

"to be delivered into the hands of men" (Mark 9:31, ESV),[99] "undergo great suffering, and be rejected by the elders, the chief priests, and the scribes" (Mark 8:31), who will "condemn him to death" (Mark 10:33). The apostolic preaching in Acts reinforces the idea that Jesus died at the hands of the people in general (e.g. Acts 2:36; 4:10) and named authority figures, Herod and Pontius Pilate, in particular (Acts 4:27).

Girard insists, "There is nothing in the Gospels to suggest that God causes the mob to come together against Jesus . . . Those responsible for the Passion are the human participants themselves."[100] We must here charge Girard with a highly selective reading of Scripture, for if we consider that the Gospels often speak of the things Christ "must" suffer (e.g. Matt 16:21; Mark 8:31; Luke 9:22), or the urgency with which the Scriptures concerning him are to be fulfilled (e.g. Matt 26:54, 56; Luke 24:44), these are clearly suggestive of a divinely orchestrated plan. Most explicitly, the Acts community was convinced that the massive project of wicked scheming and large-scale corruption occurred precisely because the conspirators had all done "whatever [God's] hand and [God's] plan had predestined to take place" (Acts 4:28). Furthermore, Jesus said, "No one takes [my life] from me, but I lay it down of my own accord. I have power to lay it down, and I have power to take it up again. I have received this command from my Father" (John 10:18). The idea is repeated when Jesus corrects Pilate's claim to authority over his life: "You would have no power over me unless it had been given you from above; therefore the one who handed me over to you is guilty of a greater sin" (John 19:11).

Jesus' response to Pilate is especially striking at it seems to minimize his culpability. The Heidelberg Catechism's question 38 which asks why Jesus suffered under Pontius Pilate as judge, the answer being: "That he, being innocent, and yet condemned by a temporal judge, might thereby free us from the severe judgment of God to which we were exposed." Berkouwer notes that Herod or Caiaphas might have otherwise been mentioned in the creed, yet Pilate alone is named. The suggestion of the Reformed on this point is compelling. In the "judicial homicide"[101] pronounced by a temporal judge, God is in effect "crossing the activity of man in the historical identity between Pilate's act in his capacity of a judge and God's act."[102] In other words, God uses the occasion of Jesus' judicial sentence to declare an abso-

---

99. The NRSV translates παραδίδοται ("delivered") as "betrayed," which is more dynamic than is necessary.

100. Girard, *I See Satan*, 21.

101. Berkouwer, *Studies in Dogmatics*, 158 n36, borrowing from Kuyper.

102. Ibid.

lute condemnation upon sin, which only an absolute judge can and should do. It seemed expedient in the divine wisdom that Jesus' death *be seen as* the result of the punishment of a criminal—someone that worldly authorities would have deemed deserving of execution. Hence the discussion in which the Jewish leaders tell Pilate that Jesus is a "criminal" (John 18:30), Pilate's suggestion to judge him "according to your law" (v. 31), and the final recognition that the Jews "are not permitted to put anyone to death" (v. 32). Of course, this does not excuse the unfathomable foul play that had to occur in order for someone as innocent as Jesus to be executed. But the fact that this mistake of herculean proportions is divinely orchestrated to look like a judicial process demonstrates the significant link between Jesus' death and the law. If intended, the arrangement of events in such a manner could not be more brilliant, for in so doing, the meaning of atonement (the condemnation of sin) and the method of atonement (the condemnation of a criminal) coalesce into one.

On the most superficial level, violence, far from being the tragic happenstance of imperial brutality, is, more accurately, the physical outworking of judicial condemnation ("for [the governing authority] is a minister of God to you for good. But if you do what is evil, be afraid; for it does not bear the sword for nothing; for it is a minister of God, an avenger who brings wrath on the one who practices evil" Rom 13:4 NASB). The repeated predictions and descriptions of Jesus' being beaten, mocked, scourged, spit on, and pierced are not to be understood merely as torture methods put to random and sadistic use. Rather, they all fall within the purview of state-sanctioned punishment under the law performed by people with the *authority* to do so. Physical deprivation as a mode of retributive punishment is endemic to society and intuitive to relationships of authority, so while it is horrific, it is not surprising that Jesus suffered physically as a result of being condemned as a criminal. In the case of Roman crucifixion, it might be asked whether it was excessively violent? Perhaps. The Romans were experts in the craft of killing. But, even the "excruciating" suffering could still providentially be made to further underscore the heinousness and offense of sin as we have already explored. What would make much less sense, however, is if Jesus died by old age or accident, for the element of coming under the condemnation of the law would altogether be lost. I surmise that while sin could still be imputed and expunged in Christ's dying body regardless of the mode, Paul could not easily say that God had *condemned* sin in Christ's flesh or that he is the cursed one who hangs upon the tree.

In order for atonement to actually effect something, we must move beyond the pedagogical reasons for linking condemnation with violence and explore the uniqueness of Jesus' own suffering and death. Paul had argued that the law was incapable of condemning sin because it was weakened by the flesh. In fact, as John Murray puts it, the law, "rather than depriving sin of its power, only provides the occasion for the more violent exercise of its power."[103] We note the dual problems of the incapability of the law and the weakness of the flesh that provides the context in which God must act.[104] What "God has done" contrasts with this incapability and weakness in way that highlights the need for Christ to overcome natural human inability with superior strength.

That Jesus appears in the "likeness of sinful flesh," we may discover a new form of the ancient idea of "divine deception" emerging. His human nature had all the characteristics of the weakened flesh that sin had so successfully enslaved before. But in a house "swept clean" (i.e. Christ's intrinsic holiness), seven even more wicked spirits may rush in, or be *imputed* (Luke 11:25–26; Matt 12:44–45). To indulge in yet further allegorization, one who is stronger can now storm the house and bind the "strong man" in order to plunder his goods (Matt 12:29; Mark 3:27). The superior strength of Jesus lies in his absolute sinlessness. With such an upper hand, the power of sin collapses and condemnation is reversed. The principle of Rom 6:7, "For whoever has died is freed from sin" applies, but in Jesus' case, he does not "free himself" from sin by dying; *he dies with it*, thus killing it in his body. Like a virus that dies when its host dies, sin, trapped in the crucible of sin-like flesh perishes as Jesus' body perishes.

Within this model, it cannot be stressed enough that the flesh of Jesus is not the *direct object* of the wrath of God as Judge. The condemnation falls upon sin that has been imputed on Jesus and is located "in his flesh" (Rom 8:3), but the execution of that condemnation is carried out by the death itself that Jesus undergoes by his own authority and power. Death is intrinsic to the essence of sin as a desire for ultimate separation from God (the "origin of life") and is therefore not extrinsic as an "arbitrary punishment" subsequent to it.[105]

Theo-cinematic synthesis

The potential contributions of revenge films to theological themes discussed above are numerous. The following are some that touch on the themes of imputation, self-sacrifice, and abandonment.

---

103. John Murray, *Epistle to the Romans: The English Text with Introduction, Exposition, and Notes* (Grand Rapids: Eerdmans, 1997), 278.

104. Venter, "Romans 8:3–4 and God's Resolution," 3.

105. Pannenberg, *Jesus—God and Man*, 265.

Victory through self-inflicted violence

The final demise of the villains in *Bone Tomahawk*, *John Wick*, and *Leon* come as a result of a trap that involves self-inflicted violence. The variations of these climactic scenes come together to help form a fully-orbed picture of Christ's vengeful payback upon sin. *Bone Tomahawk* depicts the classic case of noble self-sacrifice. Sheriff Hunt lies mortally wounded and orders the other three compatriots to flee the cave while he remains to ambush the rest of the advancing troglodytes. With his three friends safely out of the dark cave and in broad daylight, three rifle shots echo in the background. They are free indeed. In *John Wick*, we are spectators to a final hand-to-hand battle. At the moment of an apparent stalemated arm lock with the knife-wielding Viggo, John Wick plunges Viggo's knife into his own body. Viggo's shock and surprise momentarily loosens his arm and John manages to gain the upper hand to finish him off. That John "receives" the very weapon that may kill him is modestly analogous to the idea of imputation: Christ takes on a foreign and destructive object, but he does so voluntarily and with his own might, thus offering some illumination to Jesus' words concerning his life: "I have *power* to lay it down" (John 10:18).

In *Leon*, the villain, Stansfield, hovers over Leon's body and gloats over his supposed victory but is surprised to see that Leon has managed to pull a pin from a grenade strapped to his chest. "This is from Mathilda," he says slowly, before both of them are consumed in a massive explosion. Leon's death particularly enhances the interpretation of Romans 5:15–17 that Christ's moment of death is the "free gift" and "act of righteousness" (5:18) that abounds to many. Interestingly, Leon, in fact, says the gift is *"from"* Mathilda. The viewer might have expected Leon to say that the death is "for" Mathilda, and certainly it was. He ultimately kills Stansfield so that she might be safe. That he says the grenade pin, a symbol of their imminent deaths, is "from" Mathilda underscores the theological concept of mystical union. In the single sacrificial death of Leon is the manifestation of both his *and Mathilda's* revenge upon Stansfield. Furthermore, at the moment of the grenade explosion, Mathilda has already fled the scene. She does not yet know that the two have died and certainly never comes to know of her "gift." But this does not make it any less potent for Stansfield or poetic for Leon and for us, the viewers. Similarly, one criticism about the sinner's union with Christ in his crucifixion could be that it is merely poetic fiction, and if it is true, we are completely nonexistent or at best passive in the process. However, this does not diminish the profound meaning that it has, if not for us, then for spiritual entities that have witnessed it (Eph 3:10).

In each of these films, the protagonist allows himself to be inflicted, and in so doing, the villain meets his final doom. As a narrative model, it finds some similarities with *Christus Victor*'s analogy of the fish-hook trap where Jesus allows his flesh to be "swallowed up" by Leviathan while concealing his immortal deity. The significant difference is that within *Christus Victor*, triumph over the enemy is not accomplished at the cross *per se* but only in the subsequent resurrection. The death of Jesus, in and of itself, is a win for the devil. The biblical images of decisive victory suggested in sin being "condemned" in the flesh (Rom 8:3) or God removing the record of sins, "nailing it to the cross" (Col 2:14) are lost within *Christus Victor*.

The cinematic model is capable of retaining the idea of strategic deception in a way that makes the death of Christ on the cross as a *completed* victory over his foe. In *John Wick* and *Leon*, the hero brings down the villain by forming an actual physical bond or forced attachment with them. John Wick grabs Viggo's hand and plunges it into his mid-section, and Leon grips Stansfield's hand as he reveals the released grenade pin. In these instances, the hero pulls his foe into his dying self. Viewing the death of Christ from this narrative frame allows love, judgment, victory, and death to all converge on a single point.

One last narrative synthesis may be made in reference to the "final moments" of suffering that lead up to the definitive defeat of the villain. The sequences of imminent death portrayed in revenge films very often involves a clichéd, drawn-out scene of suffering, but is nonetheless juxtaposed with jump cuts to pleasant images of the beloved. Maximus (*Gladiator*) has a vision of his wife and son awaiting him in the afterlife; Mathilda (*Leon*) runs away from the scene in safety; Hanshiro (*Hara-Kiri*) remembers happy moments with his daughter and son-in-law; Sheriff Hunt and Chicory (*Bone Tomahawk*) exchange parting words about their beloved wives. These juxtapositions communicate that the hero by no means dies defeated and overcome. He is the *overcomer*. As he gasps his final breaths while bleeding out, he perishes in a state of peace. He dies satisfied. A glimpse of positivity becomes infused in a crucifixion that heretofore was looked upon by contemporary critics of atonement with horror and disgust.

Rethinking the dereliction of the Son of God

A final way in which film contributes to a theology of the cross is in offering a fresh interpretation of Christ's cry of abandonment, "My God, my God, why have you forsaken me?" (Matt 27:46; Mark 15:34). Traditionally, it is understood as an expression of Christ's human nature in response to his hellish passion as well as a means of identifying with sinful humanity in relation to the holiness of God.[106] A positive interpretation of the cry is usually viewed in light of the full Psalm 22 reference, which ends with an affirmation of dependence upon God,[107] but commentators often complain that this requires too much reading between the lines and suggests a level of insincerity. Recent theological proposals have taken the cry very seriously and have even sought to draw this anguish into the divine nature with respect to intratrinitarian relations.[108]

Most radically has been Moltmann's push to see the experience of Christ's God-forsakenness as the center of authentic Christian theology in a way that brings about a revolution in our thinking about the Trinity. For him, the paradox of the crucified Christ compels us to go beyond theology *via negativa* or discussion of the two natures. Such theories make it impossible to take the suffering of Christ seriously when in fact the cross should be viewed in trinitarian terms as "an event concerned with a relationship between persons in which these persons constitute themselves in their relationship with each other."[109] He boldy asserts:

> In the forsakenness of the Son the Father also forsakes himself. In the surrender of the Son the Father also surrenders himself, though not in the same way... The Son suffers dying. The Father suffers the death of the Son. The grief of the Father here is just as important as the death of the Son. The fatherlessness of the Son is matched by the Sonlessness of the Father, and if God has constituted himself as the Father of Jesus Christ, then he also suffers the death of his Fatherhood in the death of the Son.[110]

The position rests on the presupposition that genuine love means having the ability to suffer and be affected. Thus, the positive swing occurs in that the Father and Son are "deeply separated in forsakenness and at the

---

106. France, *The Gospel of Matthew*, 1076–77. For France, the cry does not indicate a loss of faith but a temporary "loss of contact."

107. For example Curtis Mitch et al., *The Gospel of Matthew*, ed. Kevin Perrotta, Catholic Commentary on Sacred Scripture (Grand Rapids: Baker, 2010), 360; Craig S. Keener, *A Commentary on the Gospel of Matthew* (Grand Rapids: Eerdmans, 1999), 682–83.

108. For example, Kazoh Kitamori, *Theology of the Pain of God* (Richmond: John Knox Press, 1965); Jürgen Moltmann, *The Crucified God: The Cross of Christ As the Foundation and Criticism of Christian Theology* (New York: HarperCollins, 1974); Choan-Seng Song, *Jesus, the Crucified People* (New York: Crossroad, 1990).

109. Moltmann, *The Crucified God*, 1974, 245.

110. Ibid., 243.

same time are most inwardly one in their surrender,"[111] and what results from this event is the Spirit "justifies the Godless, fills the forsaken with love and even brings the dead to life."[112] The Trinity, then, becomes the "history of God" as well as "eschatological process" that is open to and includes the history of human suffering and forsakenness.[113]

Moltmann's cruciform trinitarianism rooted in the paradox of the cross is chiefly responsible for explaining how death and grief turns into love and hope. Richard Bauckham helpfully summarizes: "The Trinity is therefore a dialectical historical process, inaugurated by the Son's identification with the world in all its negativity on the cross, and taking, through the work of the Spirit, all human history into itself in order to open it to the eschatological future."[114] As it operates within the mode of divine identification with human suffering, this love extends outward and is primarily meant for the eschatological liberation of humanity. Thus, a panentheistic worldview is required for negativity to subsist in the Godhead, which Moltmann himself admits:

> Understood in pantheistic terms, that would be a dream that would have to ignore the negative element in the world. But a trinitarian theology of the cross perceives God in the negative element and therefore the negative element in God, and in this dialectical way is panentheistic. For in the hidden mode of humiliation to the point of the cross, all being and all that annihilates has already been taken up in God and God begins to become "all in all."[115]

The difficulty comes in locating intratrinitarian love among the triune persons when their relations are so bound up with the negativity of death and abandonment. As far as I can see, there is no reason why a theology of the cross with division and despair at its center should be preferable over one in which the persons of the Trinity eternally love and honor each other in unity.

The cinematic narrative of revenge offers an alternative interpretation of the so-called "cry of dereliction." In most films, as we have observed, there is a point where the hero must face the villain alone. Allies aid and accompany the avenger at various moments along the pursuit, but only up to a point. Eventually, they are either absent (e.g. *True Grit*, *13 Assassins*), ineffective (e.g. *Ajuma*, *Sun-Scarred*), held captive (e.g. *The Equalizer*,

111. Ibid., 244.
112. Ibid.
113. Ibid., 255–56; cf. 249.
114. Richard Bauckham, *The Theology of Jürgen Moltmann* (Edinburgh: Bloomsbury T&T Clark, 1995), 154–55.
115. Moltmann, *The Crucified God*, 1974, 277.

Oldboy), fleeing (*Leon, Bone Tomahawk*), or already dead (e.g. *John Wick, Unforgiven*). Viewers are reminded that not just anyone—not even a trained accomplice—is capable of taking down the powerful villain. It is the destiny of the hero and the hero alone. The image, then, is not one of forsakenness or abandonment but a freeing of the hero to finish the job that only he can perform. In terms of the inner workings of the narrative of atonement, it might be said that prior to the cross the Father and Spirit have "done their part" to commission, send, affirm, and equip the Son for his mission of redemption. As the incarnate God in the likeness of sinful flesh and with the sin of the world imputed upon him, he is absolutely unique and must be left to do what only the God-man can do: die. We might be able to go so far as to posit that it is not *necessarily* the Father who unleashes his wrath upon Christ's "sinful flesh" but Christ himself, who functions as both the crucible and the consuming fire (Heb 12:29) that annihilates sin. Christ alone is "obedient to death" (Phil 2:8, NIV), and he alone lays down his own life by the authority commanded of him by his Father (John 10:18).

This is not to say that it is *impossible* for the Father's wrath to have been the expunging force, for we have already submitted that the violence is one step removed from an attack upon the person. But what *does* become possible is that from this perspective Jesus' cry of dereliction does not demonstrate intratrinitarian forsakenness or fatherly abuse, but rather, a deep and recognizable expression of unity and love. "Why have you forsaken me?" is the relational acknowledgement that the hour of glory has finally come. All that the triune persons had planned for and pursued approaches completion. Jesus must now be let go to make the final "kill shot" by himself. The satisfaction of receiving glory, honor, and an inheritance of redeemed people await him for performing this "act of obedience" (Rom 5:19), so it is only right that he be freed to take hold of it. In a sense, the Father and Spirit (poetically in the dual address, "My God, My God") "forsake" him not because their wrath is about to strike him but because their wrath *could not*. Intratrinitarian love could never allow the Son to come under fire by any of the members even in the midst of him becoming sin. The wrath of the triune God is fully aimed at sin, and at the final moment of truth, it is the Son of God who makes the kill by expiating sin in his dying flesh.

Analysis and summary

A major issue for contemporary theologians reflecting on the cross is the degree to which Christ was a passive victim. From the solidarist and invalidationist perspectives, the effort to bring to light issues that remain relevant for present-day victims under unjust systems of power often means construing the cross in terms of Jesus being swept up by the socio-political forces of imperial domination that opposed his ministry of mercy and nonviolence. However, rather than opt for pure passivity on Jesus' part, proponents insist that the cross produces a counteracting force by way of protest and subversion. In this way the efficacy of the cross lies in its nature as proclamation; it "speaks" solidarity to victims and rebuke to persecutors. Actual change in status quo that demonstrates the practical outworking of redemption comes only as people *heed* the proclamation and repent of their previously unenlightened mindsets: victims must see that God is "on their side," and oppressors must cease their victimization. In short, the passivity of the crucifixion possesses the action of *persuading*. But this also means that whatever effect the cross might have can only be actualized, hopefully, at some future time. The same future-orientedness is true of *Christus Victor's* dependence on resurrection. A gap is left in the narrative that leaves the question of whether the cross, as such, has accomplished any immediate good.

A *Christus Ultor* model sees no mutual exclusivity between the unjust condemnation of Christ under imperial dominators and his fully active and definitive removal of humanity's plight. In this narrative, Jesus arrives at the cross equipped with a nature that truly accords with fallen humanity and which associates closely with the nature of sin. This body becomes the trap and crucible into which sin is imputed by way of our mystical union with him and is condemned in the only the only way that humanity understands punishment: violence. This wrath that encapsulates the full notion of divine judgment, however, does not flow from the Father unto the Son but one that flows principally from the Son unto sin. The last of his gasping breaths is "given up"[116] in a sigh of satisfaction, knowing that the inheritance of his beloved is secure.

---

116. Matt 27:50; Luke 23:46; John 19:30.

7.

Conclusions: *Christus Ultor* as Cinematic Soteriology

Re-contextualizing the Atonement Story

IN AN AGE WHEN our societies are more diverse than ever and where ideology and technology are not only capable but have already inflicted massive harm, the recent sensitivity toward violence is pervasive and understandable. The traditional understanding of the cross as the center of Christian faith is naturally embroiled in controversy and has become a cause for embarrassment. The charge of complicity in violent victimization "crouches at the door" of most atonement models based on the notion of satisfaction where God requires blood at the hands of sinners to atone for their sin. In light of this, recent adaptations of the atonement have tended to veer in one of two opposite directions: the first understands God's redemptive work in terms of victory over cosmic agents; the second repudiates redemptive violence altogether urging an end to notions of sacrifice. In neither of these broad tendencies in atonement theory is the actual suffering and death of Christ fully appreciated as integral to a *positive* redemptive work of God on behalf of humanity.

The modest attempt of this study has been to offer an alternative rendering of the cross that incorporates the concerns and contributions of recent theological formulations on the atonement while retaining much that Christian tradition has confessed with regard to the centrality of the cross and its benefits.

The essential product of this study is a narrative of the atonement that may be summarized in the following way: In eternity past, the Father, Son and Holy Spirit foresaw the entrance of sin into the world. It had polluted the perfection of creation and brought sickness, violence, and death. Worst of all, it enslaved under its power all of humanity, beloved beings created in the image and likeness of God. It violated and executed them one by one throughout history without remorse or escape. Deeply offended and enraged at so vile an enemy, the Trinity vowed to annihilate the sin that threatened to destroy God's beloved. The Father commanded and commissioned the Son to be the avenger-warrior with promise of eternal glory, and the Spirit resolved to equip and aid the Son in his mission. The Son took upon himself fallen human flesh, where sin resides in humanity, but lived out a life of perfect obedience as part of his pledge to fulfill all righteousness. At the same time, so consumed had he become to punish evil, that he spared no opportunity to wreak havoc upon the domain of evil during his earthly life. As part of the pedagogical move to overlap earthly and divine justice, he was condemned to die by a human judge. He endured violent chastisement and crucifixion as the physical representation of the cosmic act he was about to perform against sin. Upon the cross, the trap was set. The Father imputed the sin of the beloved upon his flesh by mystically uniting them to him, at which point the Father and Spirit released the Son to undergo death so he might fulfill his glorious destiny. In the full fury of divine vengeance, the Son, *Christus Ultor*, exhausted his wrath upon sin and consumed it in the crucible of his own flesh as he dragged it *ad infernos*. His flesh perished, but the beloved's flesh was spared and liberated, destined to rise with him as the righteousness of God, a promised figured in baptism. In his act, the Son was fully satisfied: he was exalted to the highest place of honor, the beloved was liberated from her enslavement, and the sin hanging over the elect was eliminated. As a result of sin's removal, forgiveness and acceptance rushes upon the sinner and she is atoned.

If successful, a *Christus Ultor* theory of the atonement presents a coherent story of God's redemptive work that allows one to "glory in the cross" while sufficiently dissociating oneself from complicity in abuse, punishment, torture, and the like upon actual persons. Such a framework is extensive enough so as to unite the images of cosmic warfare, ransom, satisfaction, penal debt, ritual cleansing, redemption, propitiation, expiation, and sacrifice, for each of these find a valued place along the narrative of God's vengeful repayment to sin. This is in contrast to the current push for atonement theology to function as an eclectic "kaleidoscope" of unrelated metaphors, which usually results in either the unintentional domination of one option over others and/or the direct suppression of an unsavory metaphor.

It seems intuitive that the gospel, of which atonement is central, is most suitably told as a recognizable story. By employing the popular genre of the revenge film, whose narrative is well understood and largely satisfying, it has become possible to frame the story of atonement in a way that is doctrinally robust, culturally relevant, and emotionally resonant. Furthermore, that the story finds it ultimate basis in Scripture itself may quell the anxious hearts of those who might fear that this story of atonement is a product of a foreign, untranslatable concept or an isolated cultural context. In a cinematic theology, the story-shaped world of the Bible comes into contact with the contemporary experience of the masses. Within this theory the themes of retributive justice and violence are taken seriously while avoiding the charge that God inflicts violence upon human persons as such. This, in turn, allows readers of Scripture to go back and understand so-called "problem texts" as types and shadows of a more profound reality and not arbitrary episodes of violence that need to be deconstructed or disregarded.

Christus Ultor among Contemporary Soteriologies: Distinctives, Gains, and Limits

The view that I have laid out in this book positions itself as an evangelical alternative to current atonement theologies. In terms of its basic premise, it aligns most with the duality framework that understands God's work of redemption in a combative mode. The most obvious and important difference is that in most *Christus Victor* models the villains are demonic creatures or systems, whereas in *Christus Ultor*, the villain is sin. To be sure, naming Satan as God's chief enemy that Jesus engages in his atoning work is well attested in the tradition, and because Satan is a personal creature, the cosmic battle is more easily understood as literal.

There are several reasons, however, why Jesus' defeat of the devil *per se* is inadequate as an atonement model that evangelicals could comfortably call their own. Defeating the devil, while greatly minimizing malicious evil in the world does not, in itself, make anyone right with God. Sin fundamentally places an individual in a state of debt, which works death and corruption in the created order regardless of the Satan's direct intervention. The demonic realm, though powerful, is not as ubiquitous a force in cosmic and earthly history as is sin. After all, popular Christian tradition surmises that Satan and his minions *themselves* fell into sin at some point in time. At best, killing the devil brings humanity to a state of pre-fall neutrality inviting us to live in perfect, perpetual obedience; but this only serves to re-instate Pelagianism as the model for salvation. From another angle, it would seem that destroying the devil presumably liberates all of creation in one fell swoop, thus leaning in the direction of a universalistic soteriology, which is, as it stands, outside the bounds of evangelical theology. Also, harking back to J. Denny Weaver's insistence on radical nonviolence, killing the devil would simply be another instance of God violently executing one of his creatures.

Granted, there is generally little sympathy for the Prince of Darkness among reasonable minds, but if the atonement depends on God's act of destroying a creature with his wrath, then we have not progressed from an essentially violence-dependent paradigm. Atonement violence in this case would differ only in degree from that which has prompted the modern revulsion in the first place. In sum, if the atonement is to be regarded as that final and glorious work performed at the expense of the God-man's very life, it ought to be situated at a step logically prior to even the person of the devil.

In relation to the framework of solidarity, there are some points of fruitful contact as well as obvious divergence. Morna Hooker suggests "it is arguable that for Paul the idea of human solidarity is a vitally important factor in the substructure of his thought, more fundamental than all the images he uses . . . "[1] Within modern liberationist theologies solidarity is usually spoken of in terms of Christ's identification with our experience of physical suffering, oppression, and marginalization. A helpful (but culturally distant) concept here is the idea of "*han*-filled" cry of despair that alerts and mobilizes the God who identifies with the afflicted. In so doing, systems of domination and injustice are exposed, and freedom from sin results as the apparatus of accusation is dismantled. Affirming Gregory Boyd on this point, there is a need to take more seriously the "cosmic" dimension of redemption. *Christus Ultor* serves to intensify the idea of sin by locating it at a more fundamental level. Liberationist solidarity is manifested through a psychological cohesion between a group's experience of oppression and injustice caused by earthly systems and Christ's own analogous experience of those same systems. Mystical union manifests solidarity in the sphere of the cosmic, in battle with sin as the slave-master/oppressor *par excellence*. Where modern solidarity garners sentimental comfort through Christ's "coming down" to relate with our earthly problems, mystical union translates us "up" into "heavenly places" to participate in his death by which the true enemy is defeated. As Hooker writes: "It is not only that Christ shares our death, but that we deliberately share his—and in doing so are enabled to share in his resurrection."[2]

Finally, a Christ-as-avenger model, at one level, resonates quite deeply with Girardian mimetic rivalry. His theory gives support to retaliation as endemic to humanity's narrative thereby transcending contextual categories for understanding basic truths. The action-reaction mechanism of

---

1. Morna D. Hooker, "Interchange and Atonement," in *From Adam to Christ: Essays on Paul* (Eugene, OR: Wipf & Stock, 2008), 41.

2. Ibid., 33.

vengeance either between individuals or societies is in fact the driving force of this scheme. As Girard explains:

> At the level of the blood feud, in fact, there is always only one act, murder, which is performed in the same way for the same reasons, in vengeful imitation of the preceding murder. And this imitation propagates itself by degrees . . . In such cases, in its perfection and paroxysm mimesis becomes a chain reaction of vengeance, in which human beings are constrained to the monotonous repetition of homicide.³

However, it is when this vengeance manifests on the stage of human affairs and actual violence is committed that invalidationists may rightly reject it as the poison of history and religion. *Christus Ultor* likewise confronts the idea that the atonement is *essentially* violence upon human flesh; rather, Christ punishes sin—a non-creaturely but *active* force of deviance. At the level of the cosmic, sin is not the scapegoat in the sense of a misplaced victim; rather, it is the root of all that is evil, and it *must* be put to death. The ultimate persecution of evil could only be the most benevolent of acts performed by the all-good God of the Bible. Once the question of bodily infliction is removed the discomfort in admitting God's involvement in such violence should vanish as well. As it stands, however, the main point of contention is over the role of the divine will. While both see the death of Christ as ultimately good, invalidationists are not in the position of acknowledging that it is good *by design*.

In terms of the limits of my proposal, perhaps the aspect of soteriology that receives the least attention within a *Christus Ultor* model is that of eschatology. First, one might discern a relative lack of discussion concerning the resurrection, which all soteriologies, ancient and modern, want to see closely tied together with the cross. In contemporary thought, the resurrection seems to be *the* definitive work of atonement. The present model envisages the resurrection more in terms of the first step in Christ securing his satisfaction of honor and the inheritance of a redeemed and sanctified people. This Godward perspective on the resurrection is likely to leave sinners feeling "left out," which can be mitigated when one keeps in full view the emphasis on the sinner's union with God, a reality that includes both our dying and rising with him.

Second is the related problem of the continued presence of sin in the world and the Christian's persistent lack of victory over it. Within an atonement that stresses God's vengeful annihilation of sin at the cross, what are

---

3. René Girard, *Things Hidden Since the Foundation of the World*, trans. Stephen Bann and Michael Metteer (Stanford: Stanford University Press, 1987), 12.

we to make of the reality of indwelling sin and its powerful influence here and now? Oscar Cullmann's analogy illustrating his thesis concerning the eschatological "already and not yet" tension of life after the cross event is helpful. He writes:

> The decisive battle in a war may already have occurred in a relatively early stage of the war, and yet the war still continues. Although the decisive effect of that battle is—perhaps not recognized by all, it nevertheless already means victory. But the war must still be carried on for an undefined time, until "Victory Day." Precisely this is the situation of which the New Testament is conscious, as a result of the recognition of the new division of time; the revelation consists precisely in the fact of the proclamation that that event on the cross, together with the resurrection which followed, was the already concluded decisive battle.[4]

That Cullmann employs a combat metaphor is particularly apt within the frame of the present work. Decisively winning a war and the need to fight remaining battles are not necessarily exclusive. *Christus Ultor*, and perhaps any theory involving the combat metaphor, it must be admitted, continually runs the risk of an over-realized eschatology. But as we have seen in the gloomy epilogues of many revenge films, ongoing uncertainty and struggle is factored into the genre. Although the villain is defeated, the beloved continues to live in a world already damaged by his influence. The two sequels to *Taken* make this plain in that Bryan must continue to use his "particular set of skills" to protect his wife and daughter against new villains. In the case where the hero dies, as in *Leon*, the beloved (Mathilda) has at least become equipped through the mentorship of her deceased hitman friend to fend for herself. This reality of the ongoing struggle against sin may provide the much-needed corrective and caution when an objective view of sin, as espoused in this book, is emphasized over and against the continued need to look no further than our own hearts for the source of sin. G. C. Berkouwer wisely warns against rational speculations about the origin of sin: "The very forms of causal thinking are peculiarly adaptable to our own self excuse. They are congenial to papering over the deepest depths of our own guilt."[5]

As atonement theology moves into the future, the theme of violence is likely to resurface. If this study has contributed anything to the discussion, it is the possibility of embracing the idea of violence in a non-naïve way and redirecting violence away from the natural sphere and into the absurdity

---

4. Oscar Cullmann, *Christ and Time: The Primitive Christian Concept of Time and History*, 3rd ed., trans. Floyd V. Filson (London: SCM, 1962), 84.

5. Berkouwer, *Sin*, 16.

that is evil. In light of the limitation of words and reason, I would expect that art may become more influential in exploring and expressing theological paradox. It is unlikely that theologians and philosophers will positively arrive at any satisfying metaphysical formulations about sin's substance, but it may be possible to begin considering sin as the very ontological manifestation of evil. At any rate, theology with a narrative shape, as this study has modestly attempted to sketch, will probably continue to have meaning and require reworking in generations to come, just as it has in the past.

Some Practical Implications

In this study, I have argued for the positive potential for a cinematic model of the atonement. Yet, even though the discipline of theology and film dialogue approaches its half-century mark, suspicion continues to surround the use of film in theology especially where the ethics of screen violence is concerned. It is worth reiterating my foundational justification for this framework: the revenge theme is inherently scriptural, and scriptural precedents are the *sina qua non* of evangelical theologizing. The revenge film is the cultural analogue that helps to reframe and recontextualize the scriptural theme, but only when it is appreciated within certain parameters, the chief of which is the self-contained nature of film stories. Movies operate within, and are enjoyed because of, its own inherent logic that belongs properly to its own world. Because that world overlaps with ours at typical and strategic junctures, the logic is understood and our own experience guides meaning. Danger lurks when we do not adequately separate the worlds in terms of its material and physical content, but act out in our world the attitudes and actions of figures in the cinematic world. In such cases, the caution of contemporary atonement theologians is well-taken: violent models can make us complicit in violent behavior.

That said, I have argued that films and their corresponding biblical parallels come with their own "safety mechanism" when understood as localized instances of a broader theological narrative. Using film as a resource for considering atonement violence affords theologians the opportunity to engage liberally on the subject while avoiding any implication of harm at a material level. Cinematic worlds are inherently fictional and unreal, while at same time, powerfully visceral. Just like the benefits of "play fighting" among predatory animals, the dialogue between cinema and theology is a safe work space for dealing candidly and experimentally with violence without physically participating in the morbidity of an actual moment of carnage. Where biblical texts of violence seem problematic, cinema can helps to "repackage" the violence within the framework of self-contained narratives that point beyond mere physical realities. Although it is unable to completely dissipate the uneasy feelings surrounding visual or narrated gore, a cinematic rendering of such scenes helps in some small measure to suspend and re-contextualize our disgust and deal with their reality on alternative fronts.

One such front is a dissociated form of violence that might be redirected for the purpose of societal critique. José Miguez Bonino has suggested two ways that violence can be put to positive use within the context of liberation theology. The first is built upon the recognition of the inherent order of the universe and a "natural law" whereby "whatever disturbs it is irrational and evil and ought to be countered through the rational use of coercion."[6] The second perspective understands violence as a fight against "the objectifications given in nature, in history, in society, in religion" so as to "conceive history as a dialectic in which the negation of which the new can emerge implies always a certain measure of violence."[7] Here, the revolutionary spirit that characterizes so much of Jesus' own ministry, and which draws the admiration of solidarists and invalidationists, finds yet another contextualized expression in the form of active resistance. Where in the first instance, violence is negatively construed as a "rupture" in the harmony of the status quo, the second may be a "positive manifestation of the situation that requires righting."[8] In short, it simply will not do to reduce every type of violence as belonging to the aegis of tyrants and rapists when so much of theology and human relations has a positive place for it.

Another practical outworking involves re-casting sin as a tangible reality with the aim of supplementing daily strategies for personal piety and sanctification. Although sin has been vanquished definitively and objectively at the cross, it continues its work in our lives as an almost tangible, coercive power. Whether it possesses metaphysical substance is still up for debate, but if we allow Scripture to tell its story of sin and echo back its substantive language, we might develop a renewed appreciation for the positive benefits of Christian anger. In John Owen's work, *Of the Mortification of Sin in Believers*, he writes: "Be killing sin, or sin will be killing you."[9] Likewise, the dramatic and retributive tone imbibed in expressions such as Bryan Mills's, "I will find you, and I will kill you" (*Taken*), when

---

6. Robin Gill, *A Textbook of Christian Ethics*, 3rd ed. (London: T & T Clark, 2006), 259.

7. Ibid.

8. Ibid., 260.

9. John Owen, *Overcoming Sin and Temptation* (Crossway Books, 2006), 50.

lived out as a means toward sanctification, can become part of a strategy for personal piety and manifest itself in concrete ways that foster more robust—indeed *material*—ways of engaging it in the daily struggle of faith. This could contribute to challenging the Western overemphasis on will and reason and shape a holistic and embodied spirituality that takes seriously the role of prayer, sacrament, fasting, repentance, ritual, spiritual warfare, and social engagement. We can thus agree with Gregory Boyd, who writes: "The church, ministering within the interval between the 'victory achieved' and the 'victory manifested,' is therefore called to bear witness against the diabolic corruption of these forces, and thereby work to restore them to their original God-created place."[10]

Finally, seeing Christ in terms of heroic avenger potentially adds a new dimension to our perspective on, and relationship to, God and the nature of the Trinity's dealings with humanity. As weak and often frightened souls, there is still much comfort to be had from knowing we have an avenger-servant with a holy anger against all that ravages against our dignity[11] and that much of his intercession on our behalf at the Father's right hand continues in a combative mode. A certain, unspoken, intimacy resides in the realm of the viscious that is often missed in the genteel "niceness" all too common to our modern understandings of love. Alastair Campbell, in his pastoral theology, *The Gospel of Anger*, writes:

> To know love is to know fire—and the deeper the love the stronger the fire. We find it in our relationships with fellow human beings intimacy can be painful and that the arousal of strong feelings of mutual attraction in mutual trust carries the obverse, a sense of vulnerability to hurt and anger.[12]

A deeper familiarity with this "darker" side of love naturally flows into our practice of neighborly love. As Mark Galli writes: "True love is robust. It includes compassion *and* confrontation, empathy *and* truth-telling, kindness *and* sternness. When we enter such relationships, we must enter them not with our sentimentality but with full-orbed love. This takes not only compassion but courage."[13]

---

10. Boyd, *God at War*, 272.

11. See Alastair V. Campbell, *Gospel of Anger* (London: SPCK, 1986), 95–102 where he discusses the positive, pastoral contribution of a theology of anger in light of vulnerability, loss, and oppression.

12. Ibid., 94.

13. Mark Galli, *Jesus Mean and Wild: The Unexpected Love of an Untamable God* (Grand Rapids: Baker, 2008), 80.

CONCLUSIONS: CHRISTUS ULTOR AS CINEMATIC SOTERIOLOGY

The fourteenth century mystic, Julian of Norwich, models for us this spirituality during a particular despairing moment of conflict with temptation in which "the Fiend came again with his heat and with his stench, and made me much ado, the stench was so vile and so painful, and also dreadful and travailous." After contemplating the cross and being comforted by God's presence, she reflects: "For I thought soothly were I safe from sin, I were full safe from all the fiends of hell and enemies of my soul." She finally concludes: "And thus was I delivered from him by the virtue of Christ's Passion: for therewith is the Fiend overcome, as our Lord Jesus said afore."[14] For Julian, and perhaps for us, the courage to live can come through the comfort of Christ's death, a death prior to which he might well have said, on our behalf, "It is mine to avenge. I will repay."

---

14. Julian of Norwich, *Revelations of Divine Love* (Mineola, NY.: Dover Publications, 2006), 141–42.

Bibliography

Anderson, Gary A. *Sin: A History*. New Haven: Yale University Press, 2009.
Anker, Roy M. *Catching Light: Looking for God in the Movies*. Grand Rapids: Eerdmans, 2004.
Anselm. *Anselm of Canterbury: The Major Works*. Edited by Brian Davies and G. R. Evans. Oxford: Oxford University Press, 2008.
———. "The Virgin Conception and Original Sin." In *Complete Philosophical and Theological Treatises of Anselm of Cantebury*, translated by Jasper Hopkins and Herbert Richardson. Minneapolis: The Arthur J. Banning Press, 2000.
Ashley, Timothy R. *The Book of Numbers*. New International Commentary on the Old Testament. Grand Rapids: Eerdmans, 1993.
Augustine. *Marriage and Virginity*. Edited by John E. Rotelle. Translated by Ray Kearney. Hyde Park, NY: New City Press, 1999.
Aulén, Gustaf. *Christus Victor: An Historical Study of the Three Main Types of the Idea of Atonement*. Translated by A. G. Herbert. Eugene, OR: Wipf & Stock, 2003.
Austin, Michael Ridgwell. *Explorations in Art, Theology and Imagination*. London ; Oakville, CT: Routledge, 2005.
Axmaker, Sean. "'Bone Tomahawk' on Amazon Prime." *Stream On Demand*, December 31, 2015. http://streamondemandathome.com/bone-tomahawk-on-amazon-prime/.
Bailie, Gil. *Violence Unveiled: Humanity at the Crossroads*. New York: The Crossroad Publishing Company, 1996.
Baker, Mark D., ed. *Proclaiming the Scandal of the Cross: Contemporary Images of the Atonement*. Grand Rapids: Baker, 2006.
Balthasar, Hans Urs von. *Glory of the Lord VOL 1: Seeing The Form*. A&C Black, 1982.
———. *The Glory of the Lord. A Theological Aesthetics*. Edited by Joseph Fessio and John Riches. Translated by E. Leiva-Merkakis. San Francisco: Ignatius Press, 1982.
Barth, Karl. *Letters, 1961–1968*. Grand Rapids: Eerdmans, 1981.
Bauckham, Richard. *The Theology of Jürgen Moltmann*. Edinburgh: Bloomsbury T&T Clark, 1995.
Bavinck, Herman. *Reformed Dogmatics Vol. 3: Sin and Salvation in Christ*. Edited by John Bolt. Translated by John Vriend. Grand Rapids: Baker, 2006.
Beck, Jeff. "Leon: The Professional: A Wonderful Character Study." *Examiner.com*, November 17, 2015. http://www.examiner.com/article/leon-the-professional-a-wonderful-character-study-blu-ray.

Beilby, James, and Paul R. Eddy, eds. *The Nature of the Atonement: Four Views*. Downers Grove: IVP Academic, 2006.
Bell, Richard H. "Sacrifice and Christology in Paul." *The Journal of Theological Studies* 53, no. 1 (April 2002): 1–27.
Belousek, Darrin W. Snyder. "The Crucified King: Atonement and Kingdom in Biblical and Systematic Theology." *The Conrad Grebel Review* 33, no. 1 (2015): 96–97.
Berkhof, Louis. *Systematic Theology*. Grand Rapids: Eerdmans, 1941.
Berkouwer, G. C. *Studies in Dogmatics: Sin*. Grand Rapids: Eerdmans, 1971.
———. *Studies in Dogmatics: The Work of Christ*. Grand Rapids: Eerdmans, 1965.
Boersma, Hans. "Response to J. Denny Weaver." In *Atonement and Violence: A Theological Conversation*, edited by John Sanders. Nashville: Abingdon, 2006.
———. *Violence, Hospitality, and the Cross: Reappropriating the Atonement Tradition*. Grand Rapids: Baker, 2006.
———. "Violence, the Cross, and Divine Intentionality: A Modified Reformed View." In *Atonement and Violence: A Theological Conversation*, edited by John Sanders. Nashville: Abingdon, 2006.
Boyd, Gregory A. *God at War: The Bible & Spiritual Conflict*. Downers Grove: IVP Academic, 1997.
Brakel, Wilhelmus à. *The Christian's Reasonable Service*. Edited by Joel R. Beeke. Translated by Bartel Elshout. Vol. 1. 4 vols. Rotterdam: D. Bolle, 1999.
Branick, Vincent P. "The Sinful Flesh of the Son of God (Rom 8:3): A Key Image of Pauline Theology." *The Catholic Biblical Quarterly* 47, no. 2 (April 1985): 246–62.
Brant, Jonathan. *Paul Tillich and the Possibility of Revelation through Film*. Oxford ; New York: Oxford University Press, 2012.
Brock, Rita Nakashima. *Journeys by Heart: A Christology of Erotic Power*. Eugene, OR: Wipf & Stock, 2008.
Brown, Frank Burch, ed. *The Oxford Handbook of Religion and the Arts*. New York: Oxford University Press, 2014.
Bruce, F. F. *The Epistles to the Colossians, to Philemon, and to the Ephesians*. 2nd Ed. Grand Rapids: Eerdmans, 1984.
Brueggemann, Walter. *Isaiah 40–66*. Louisville: Westminster/John Knox Press, 1998.
———. *A Commentary on Jeremiah: Exile and Homecoming*. Grand Rapids: Eerdmans, 1996.
Busch, Eberhard. *Karl Barth: His Life from Letters and Autobiographical Texts*. Wipf and Stock Publishers, 2005.
Calvin, John. *Institutes of the Christian Religion, 1536*. Translated by Henry Bevridge. Peabody, MA: Hendrickson, 2008.
———. *[New Testament] Commentaries*. Edited by David W. Torrance and Thomas F. Torrance. 12 vols. Grand Rapids: Eerdmans, 1960–72.
Carroll, Noel. *The Philosophy of Horror: Or, Paradoxes of the Heart*. New York: Routledge, 1990.
Carroll, Noël E. *Philosophical Problems of Classical Film Theory*. Princeton, NJ: Princeton University Press, 1988.
Carroll, Robert R. *Jeremiah: A Commentary*. Philadelphia: Westminster/John Knox Press, 1986.
Carson, D. A., Peter T. O'Brien, and Mark A. Seifrid, eds. *Justification and Variegated Nomism: The Paradoxes of Paul*. Grand Rapids: Baker, 2004.

Carson, Donald A. "God, the Bible and Spiritual Warfare: A Review Article." *Journal of the Evangelical Theological Society* 42, no. 2 (June 1999): 251–69.
Carter, Warren. *Matthew and the Margins: A Socio-Political and Religious Reading*. London: T&T Clark, 2004.
Cavell, Stanley. *The World Viewed: Reflections on the Ontology of Film*. Cambridge: Harvard University Press, 1979.
Chapp, Larry Scott. "The Theological Method of Hans Urs Von Balthasar." Unpublished Ph.D Dissertation, Fordham University, 1994. http://fordham.bepress.com/dissertations/AAI9425189.
Charnock, Stephen. "A Discourse of God's Being the Author of Reconciliation." Christian Classics Ethereal Library. Accessed May 26, 2016. http://www.ccel.org/c/charnock/reconcil/reconciliation.html.
Christianson, Eric S. "A Fistful of Shekels: Ehud the Judge (Judges 3.12–30) and the Spaghetti Western." In *Cinéma Divinité: Religion, Theology And The Bible In Film*, edited by Eric S. Christianson, Peter Francis, and William R. Telford. London: SCM, 2005.
Christianson, Eric S., Peter Francis, and William R. Telford, eds. *Cinéma Divinité: Religion, Theology and the Bible in Film*. London: SCM, 2005.
Cover, Robin C. "Sin and Sinners (OT)." In *The Anchor Yale Bible Dictionary, Si–Z: Volume 6*. New Haven; London: Yale University Press, 1992.
Crysdale, Cynthia S. W. *Embracing Travail: Retrieving the Cross Today*. New York: Continuum, 1999.
Cullmann, Oscar. *Christ and Time: The Primitive Christian Concept of Time and History*. Translated by Floyd V. Filson. Revised 3rd edition. London: SCM, 1962.
Daniels, T. Scott. "Passing the Peace: Worship That Shapes Nonsubstitutionary Convictions." In *Atonement and Violence: A Theological Conversation*. Edited by John Sanders. Nashville: Abingdon, 2006.
Deacy, Christopher, ed. *Screen Christologies: Redemption and the Medium of Film*. Cardiff: University of Wales Press, 2001.
Deacy, Christopher, and Gaye Williams Ortiz. *Theology and Film: Challenging the Sacred/Secular Divide*. Malden, MA ; Oxford: Wiley-Blackwell, 2008.
Desilet, Gregory. *Our Faith in Evil: Melodrama and the Effects of Entertainment Violence*. Jefferson, NC: McFarland & Company, 2006.
Detweiler, Craig. *Into the Dark: Seeing the Sacred in the Top Films of the 21st Century*. Grand Rapids: Baker, 2008.
Detweiler, Craig and Taylor, Barry. *A Matrix of Meanings: Finding God in Pop Culture*. Grand Rapids, Baker, 2003.
Dixon, John W. *Art and the Theological Imagination*. New York: Seabury Press, 1978.
Ebert, Roger. "True Grit Movie Review & Film Summary (2010)." http://www.rogerebert.com/reviews/true-grit-2010.
Erdman, Rachel. "Sacrifice as Satisfaction, Not Substitution: Atonement in the Summa Theologiae." *Anglican Theological Review* 96, no. 3 (2014): 461–80.
Erp, Stephan Van. *The Art of Theology: Hans Urs Von Balthasar's Theological Aesthetics and the Foundations of Faith*. Leuven ; Dudley, MA: Peeters, 2004.
Evans, Gillian R. "John Donne and the Augustinian Paradox of Sin." *The Review of English Studies* 33, no. 129 (1982): 1–22.
Fesko, John V. "N.T. Wright on Imputation." *The Reformed Theological Review* 66, no. 1 (April 2007): 2–22.

Finlan, Stephen. *Problems With Atonement: The Origins Of, and Controversy About, the Atonement Doctrine*. Collegeville, MN: Liturgical Press, 2005.
Forsyth, Peter Taylor. *The Cruciality of the Cross*. Eugene, OR: Wipf and Stock, 1997.
France, R. T. *The Gospel of Matthew*. New International Commentary on the New Testament. Grand Rapids: Eerdmans, 2007.
Francis, Peter. "Clint Eastwood Westerns: Promised Land and Real Men." In *Cinéma Divinité: Religion, Theology And The Bible In Film*. Edited by Eric S. Christianson, Peter Francis, and William R. Telford. London: SCM, 2005.
Fraser, Peter. *Images of the Passion: The Sacramental Mode in Film*. Westport, Conn: Praeger, 1998.
French, Philip. "True Grit – Review." *The Guardian*, February 13, 2011, sec. Film. https://www.theguardian.com/film/2011/feb/13/true-grit-coen-brothers-review.
Fretheim, Terrence. "Violence and the God of the Old Testament." In *Encountering Violence in the Bible*, edited by Markus Zehnder and Hallvard Hagelia. Sheffield: Sheffield Phoenix Press, 2013.
Galli, Mark. *Jesus Mean and Wild: The Unexpected Love of an Untamable God*. Grand Rapids: Baker, 2008.
Gilbert, Sophie. "John Wick: An Idiot Killed His Puppy and Now Everyone Must Die." *The Atlantic*, October 24, 2014. http://www.theatlantic.com/entertainment/archive/2014/10/john-wick-an-idiot-killed-his-puppy-and-now-everyone-mustdie/381921/?single_page=true.
Gill, Robin. *A Textbook of Christian Ethics*. 3rd ed. London: T & T Clark, 2006.
Gillespie, George. *Notes Of Debates And Proceedings Of The Assembly Of Divines And Other Commissioners At Westminster: From February 1644 To January 1645*. Kessinger Publishing, 2008.
Gillespie, Patrick. *The Ark of the Covenant Opened: Or, A Treatise on the Covenant of Redemption between God and Christ, as the Foundation of the Covenant of Grace*. London: Tho. Parkhurst, 1677. https://archive.org/stream/arkofcopeoogill#page/n62/mode/1up.
Gillman, Florence Morgan. "Another Look at Romans 8:3: 'In the Likeness of Sinful Flesh.'" *The Catholic Biblical Quarterly* 49, no. 4 (October 1987): 597–604.
Girard, René. *Deceit, Desire, and the Novel*. Baltimore: Johns Hopkins University Press, 1965.
———. *I See Satan Fall Like Lightning*. Maryknoll, NY: Orbis Books, 2001.
———. *The Scapegoat*. Baltimore: Johns Hopkins University Press, 1986.
———. *Things Hidden Since the Foundation of the World*. Translated by Stephen Bann and Michael Metteer. Stanford: Stanford University Press, 1987.
———. *Violence and the Sacred*. Baltimore: Johns Hopkins University Press, 1977.
Godawa, Brian. *Hollywood Worldviews: Watching Films with Wisdom & Discernment*. Updated and Expanded edition. Downers Grove: IVP, 2009.
Goldberg, Michael. *Theology and Narrative: A Critical Introduction*. Philadelphia: Trinity Press International, 1991.
Gorringe, Timothy. *God's Just Vengeance: Crime, Violence and the Rhetoric of Salvation*. New York: Cambridge University Press, 1996.
Gouwens, David J. "Mozart Among the Theologians." *Modern Theology* 16, no. 4 (October 2000): 461–74.
Grant, Barry Keith, ed. *Film Genre Reader III*. Austin: University of Texas Press, 2003.

Grasmick et. al., Harold G. "Protestant Fundamentalism and the Retributive Doctrine of Punishment." *Criminology* 30, no. 1 (March 2006): 21–46.

Greenspahn, Frederick E. *When Brothers Dwell Together: The Preeminence of Younger Siblings in the Hebrew Bible*. New York: Oxford University Press, 1994.

Guest, P. Deryn. "Judges." In *Eerdmans Commentary on the Bible*, edited by James D. G. Dunn. Grand Rapids: Eerdmans, 2003.

Gunton, Colin E. *The Actuality of Atonement: A Study of Metaphor, Rationality and the Christian Tradition*. London: T&T Clark, 2003.

Hamerton-Kelly, Robert G. *Sacred Violence: Paul's Hermeneutic of the Cross*. Minneapolis: Fortress, 1991.

Harnack, et. al., Adolf. *The Atonement in Modern Religious Thought: A Theological Symposium*. Miami: HardPress Publishing, 2013.

Hay, Andrew R. "The Heart of Wrath: Calvin, Barth, and Reformed Theories of Atonement." *Neue Zeitschrift für Systematische Theologie und Religionsphilosophie* 55 no. 3 (2013): 361–378.

Heim, S. Mark. *Saved from Sacrifice: A Theology of the Cross*. Grand Rapids: Eerdmans, 2006.

———. "A Cross-Section of Sin: The Mimetic Character of Human Nature in Biological and Theological Perspective." In *Evolution and Ethics: Human Morality in Biological and Religious Perspective*, edited by Philip Clayton and Jeffrey Scholss. Grand Rapids: Eerdmans, 2004.

Heppe, Heinrich. *Reformed Dogmatics: Set Out and Illustrated from the Sources*. Edited by Ernst Bizer. Translated by G. T. Thomson. Grand Rapids: Baker, 1978.

Hill, Charles E., and Frank A. James III, eds. *The Glory of the Atonement: Biblical, Theological & Practical Perspectives*. Downers Grove: IVP Academic, 2004.

Hodge, Charles. *Systematic Theology Vol. 2*. Reprint ed. Peabody, MA: Hendrickson Publishers, 1981.

Hoffman-Han, Alison. "'You Can't Help But Feel Uncomfortable, Even Though You're Smiling': An Interview with Park Chan-Wook." *Journal of Japanese and Korean Cinema* 4, no. 2 (January 1, 2012): 185–93. doi:10.1386/jjkc.4.2.185_7.

Hooker, Morna D. "Interchange and Atonement." In *From Adam to Christ: Essays on Paul*. Eugene, OR: Wipf & Stock, 2008.

Hoover, Stephen. *Payback: The Essential Revenge Thriller Films*. San Bernardino, CA: Stephen Hoover, 2013.

Hurley, Neil P. *Theology Through Film*. London: Harper & Row, 1970.

Irving, Edward. *The Collected Writings of Edward Irving: In Five Volumes*. Edited by Gavin Carlyle. London: Alexander Strahan, 1865.

Jeffery, Steve, Michael Ovey, and Andrew Sach. *Pierced for Our Transgressions: Rediscovering the Glory of Penal Substitution*. Wheaton: Crossway, 2007.

Jennings, Theodore W. *Transforming Atonement: A Political Theology of the Cross*. Minneapolis: Fortress, 2009.

Jeong, Kelly Y. "Towards Humanity and Redemption: The World of Park Chan-Wook's Revenge Film Trilogy." *Journal of Japanese and Korean Cinema* 4, no. 2 (January 1, 2012): 169–83.

Jewett, Robert. *Saint Paul at the Movies: The Apostle's Dialogue with American Culture*. Louisville: Westminster/John Knox Press, 1993.

———. *Saint Paul Returns to the Movies: Triumph over Shame*. Milwaukee: Eerdmans, 1998.

Johnson, Elizabeth A. *She Who Is: The Mystery of God in Feminist Theological Discourse.* 10th ed. New York: The Crossroad Publishing Company, 2002.
Johnson, John F. "Analogia Fidei as Hermeneutical Principle." *Springfielder* 36, no. 4 (March 1973): 249–59.
Johnston, Robert K. *Reel Spirituality: Theology and Film in Dialogue.* 2nd edition. Grand Rapids: Baker, 2006.
———. *Useless Beauty: Ecclesiastes through the Lens of Contemporary Film.* Eugene, OR: Wipf & Stock Pub, 2011.
Jones, Gareth, ed. *The Blackwell Companion to Modern Theology.* Malden, MA: Wiley-Blackwell, 2004.
Julian of Norwich. *Revelations of Divine Love.* Mineola, NY.: Dover Publications, 2006.
Kandinsky, Wassily. *Concerning the Spiritual in Art.* Translated by M. T. H. Sadler. Revised edition. New York: Dover Publications, 1977.
Kazen, Thomas. "Dirt and Disgust: Body and Morality in Biblical Purity Laws." In *Perspectives on Purity and Purification in the Bible,* edited by Baruch J. Schwartz, Naphtali S. Meshel, Jeffrey Stackert, and David P. Wright, 43–64. New York: Bloomsbury T&T Clark, 2008.
Keech, Dominic. "John Cassian and the Christology of Romans 8,3." *Vigiliae Christianae* 64, no. 3 (2010): 280–99. doi:10.1163/157007210X498664.
Keener, Craig S. *A Commentary on the Gospel of Matthew.* Grand Rapids: Eerdmans, 1999.
King, Stephen. *Danse Macabre.* New York: Berkley, 1981.
Kitamori, Kazoh. *Theology of the Pain of God.* Richmond: John Knox Press, 1965.
Kline, Meredith G. *By Oath Consigned: A Reinterpretation of the Covenant Signs of Circumcision and Baptism.* Grand Rapids: Eerdmans, 1968.
———. *Kingdom Prologue: Genesis Foundations for a Covenantal Worldview.* Eugene, OR: Wipf & Stock, 2006.
Knight, Deborah. "Making Sense of Genre." *American Studies at the University of Virginia.* Accessed May 3, 2016. http://xroads.virginia.edu/~DRBR2/knight.html.
Kostas, John. "Windows into Heaven: The Role of Icons in the Greek Orthodox Church." *Word & World* 28, no. 4 (September 2008): 366–72.
Kraft, Charles H. *Christianity in Culture: A Study in Dynamic Biblical Theologizing in Cross-Cultural Perspective.* Maryknoll, NY: Orbis Books, 1979.
Kreitzer, Larry J. *The New Testament in Fiction and Film: On Reversing the Hermeneutical Flow.* Sheffield: Sheffield Academic Press, 1993.
———. *The Old Testament in Fiction and Film: On Reversing the Hermeneutical Flow.* Sheffield, UK: Sheffield Academic Press, 1994.
———. *Gospel Images in Fiction and Film: On Reversing the Hermeneutical Flow.* London; New York: Bloomsbury T&T Clark, 2002.
———. *Pauline Images in Fiction and Film: On Reversing the Hermeneutical Flow.* Sheffield, UK: Bloomsbury T&T Clark, 1999.
Kuyper, Abraham. *Wisdom & Wonder: Common Grace in Science & Art.* Edited by Jordan J. Ballor and Stephen J. Grabill. Translated by Nelson D. Kloosterman. Grand Rapids: Christian's Library Press, 2011.
Kydd, Elspeth. *The Critical Practice of Film: An Introduction.* New York: Palgrave Macmillan, 2011.
Lackey, Douglas P. "Reflections on Cavell's Ontology of Film." *The Journal of Aesthetics and Art Criticism* 32, no. 2 (1973): 271–73.

Lam, Joseph. *Patterns of Sin in the Hebrew Bible: Metaphor, Culture, and the Making of a Religious Concept*. New York: Oxford University Press, 2016.
Lamberigts, Mathijs. "A Critical Evaluation of Critques of Augustine's View of Sexuality." In *Augustine and His Critics*, edited by Robert Dodaro and George Lawless. New York: Routledge, 2000.
Lawrence, John Shelton, and Robert Jewett. *The Myth of the American Superhero*. Eerdmans, 2003.
Leeuw, Gerardus van der. *Sacred and Profane Beauty: The Holy in Art*. Translated by David E. Green. New York: Oxford University Press, 2006.
Lim, Sung Uk. "Biopolitics in the Trial of Jesus (John 18:28–19:16a)." *The Expository Times* Februray 2016, no. 127 (2015): 209–16. doi:10.1177/0014524615574665.
Lombardo, Nicholas E. *The Father's Will: Christ's Crucifixion and the Goodness of God*. New York: Oxford University Press, 2014.
Luther, Martin. *Luther's Works, Volume 47: Christian in Society IV*. Edited by Franklin Sherman and Helmut T. Lehmann. Philadelphia: Fortress, 1971.
Luz, Ulrich. *Matthew 21–28: A Commentary*. Edited by Helmut Koester. Translated by James E. Crouch. Minneapolis: Augsburg Fortress, 2005.
Lyden, John C., ed. *The Routledge Companion to Religion and Film*. London ; New York: Routledge, 2009.
———. *Film as Religion: Myths, Morals, and Rituals*. New York: NYU Press, 2003.
Lynch, Gordon. *Understanding Theology and Popular Culture*. Malden, MA: Wiley-Blackwell, 2005.
Malone, Peter. *Screen Jesus: Portrayals of Christ in Television and Film*. Lanham: Scarecrow Press, 2012.
Malone, Peter, and Sr Rose Pacatte. *Lights, Camera, Faith: A Movie Lectionary Guide to Scripture, Cycle C*. Boston, MA: Pauline Books & Media, 2003.
Marsh, Clive. *Cinema and Sentiment: Film's Challenge to Theology*. Eugene, OR: Wipf & Stock, 2014.
———. "Religion, Theology and Film in a Postmodern Age: A Response to John C. Lyden." *Journal of Religion and Film* 2, no. 1 (1998). http://www.uno-maha.edu/jrf/marshrel.htm.
Marsh, Clive, and Gaye Ortiz, eds. *Explorations in Theology and Film: An Introduction*. Malden, Mass: Wiley-Blackwell, 1997.
Marshall, I. Howard. *Aspects of the Atonement: Cross and Resurrection in the Reconciling of God and Humanity*. London: Paternoster, 2007.
Martin, Joel. *Screening The Sacred: Religion, Myth, And Ideology In Popular American Film*. Edited by Conrad E. Ostwalt Jr. Boulder: Westview Press, 1995.
Mathewes, Charles T. *Evil and the Augustinian Tradition*. Cambridge: Cambridge University Press, 2006.
Matthews, Victor H. *Judges and Ruth*. New York: Cambridge University Press, 2004.
May, John R., ed. *New Image of Religious Film*. Kansas City, MO: Sheed & Ward, 1997.
McCarthy, Todd. "Review: 'Man on Fire.'" *Variety*, April 21, 2004. http://variety.com/2004/film/markets-festivals/man-on-fire-2-1200533909/.
McCauley, Clark. "When Screen Violence Is Not Attractive." In *Why We Watch: The Attractions of Violent Entertainment*, edited by Jeffrey Goldstein. New York: Oxford University Press, 1998.

McFarland, Ian A. "Fallen or Unfallen?: Christ's Human Nature and the Ontology of Human Sinfulness." *International Journal of Systematic Theology* 10, no. 4 (October 2008): 399–415. doi:10.1111/j.1468-2400.2008.00382.x.

McFarland, Ian A. *In Adam's Fall a Meditation on the Christian Doctrine of Original Sin*. Maldon, MA: Wiley-Blackwell, 2010.

McGrath, Alister E. *The Genesis of Doctrine*. Grand Rapids; Vancouver: Eerdmans; Regent College Publishing, 1997.

McIntyre, John. *The Shape of Soteriology: Studies in the Doctrine of the Death of Christ*. Edinburgh: T&T Clark, 1992.

McKinney, Devin. "Violence: The Strong and the Weak." In *Screening Violence*, edited by Stephen Prince. New Brunswick, NJ: Rutgers University Press, 2000.

Milgrom, Jacob. *Cult and Conscience: The Asham and the Priestly Doctrine of Repentance*. Leiden: Brill, 1976.

Mitch, Curtis, Peter Williamson, Mary Healy, and Edward Sri. *The Gospel of Matthew*. Edited by Kevin Perrotta. Catholic Commentary on Sacred Scripture. Grand Rapids: Baker, 2010.

Moltmann, Jürgen. "The Cross as Military Symbol for Sacrifice." In *Cross Examinations: Readings on the Meaning of the Cross Today*, edited by Marit Trelstad. Minneapolis, MN: Augsburg Fortress, 2006.

———. *The Crucified God: The Cross of Christ as the Foundation and Criticism of Christian Theology*. New York: HarperCollins, 1974.

Moore, Roger. "Movie Review: 'I Saw the Devil.'" *Movie Nation*, January 13, 2013. https://rogersmovienation.com/2013/01/13/movie-review-i-saw-the-devil/.

Moore, Susan Hardman. "For the Mind's Eye Only: Puritans, Images and 'The Golden Mines of Scripture.'" *Scottish Journal of Theology* 59, no. 3 (2006): 281–96. doi:10.1017/S0036930606002274.

Morgan, Brandon L. "The Absurdity of Sin and the Creaturely Life of Faith in Karl Barth's Theological Epistemology." *Pacifica: Journal of the Melbourne College of Divinity* 27, no. 2 (June 2014): 149–69. doi:doi:http://dx.doi.org/10.1177/1030570X14544928.

Murray, John. *Epistle to the Romans: The English Text With Introduction, Exposition, and Notes*. Grand Rapids: Eerdmans, 1997.

Nachbar, John G. *Focus on the Western*. Englewood Cliffs, NJ.: Prentice-Hall, 1974.

Nelson, Richard D. *Deuteronomy*. Louisville: Westminster/John Knox Press, 2002.

Niebuhr, H. Richard. *Christ and Culture*. San Francisco: Harper & Row, 1975.

Nysse, Richard. "Yahweh Is a Warrior." *Word & World* 7, no. 2 (1987): 192–201.

O'Kelley, Aaron. *Did the Reformers Misread Paul?: A Historical-Theological Critique of the New Perspective*. Eugene, OR: Wipf & Stock, 2014.

Olyan, Saul M., ed. *Ritual Violence in the Hebrew Bible*. New York: Oxford University Press, 2015.

Owen, John. *Overcoming Sin and Temptation*. Wheaton: Crossway, 2006.

———. *The Death of Death in the Death of Christ: A Treatise of the Redemption and Reconciliation That Is in the Blood of Christ, with the Merit Therof, and Satisfaction Wrought Thereby*. Reprint ed. Carlisle, PA: Banner of Truth, 2013.

———. *The Works of John Owen, D.D.* Edited by William H. Goold. Vol. 10. New York: Robert Carter & Bros., 1852.

Packer, J. I., and Mark Dever. *In My Place Condemned He Stood: Celebrating the Glory of the Atonement*. Wheaton: Crossway, 2008.

Packer, J.I. "What Did the Cross Achieve? The Logic of Penal Substitution." *TynBul* 25 (1974): 3–45.
Pannenberg, Wolfhart. *Jesus — God and Man*. Translated by Lewis L. Wilkins and Duane A. Priebe. Philadelphia: Westminster Press, 1977.
Park, Andrew Sung. *Triune Atonement: Christ's Healing for Sinners, Victims, and the Whole Creation*. Louisville: Westminster/John Knox Press, 2009.
Pelikan, Jaroslav. *The Christian Tradition: A History of the Development of Doctrine, Vol. 4: Reformation of Church and Dogma*. Chicago: University Of Chicago Press, 1985.
Peterson, Robert A. *Calvin's Doctrine of the Atonement*. Philipsburg, NJ: P & R, 1983
Prince, Stephen, ed. *Screening Violence*. New Brunswick, NJ: Rutgers University Press, 2000.
Ricoeur, Paul. *Time and Narrative, vol. 1*. Trans. Kathleen McLaughlin and David Pellauer Chicago: University Of Chicago Press, 1984.
Riley, Thomas Robin. *Film, Faith, and Cultural Conflict: The Case of Martin Scorsese's The Last Temptation of Christ*. Westport, CT: Praeger, 2003.
Roan, Brian, Amanda Waltz, and Bill Graham. *Bone Tomahawk and Krampus*. The Film Stage Show, n.d. https://thefilmstage.com/features/the-film-stage-show-ep-167-bone-tomahawk-and-krampus/.
Rohls, Jan. *Reformed Confessions: Theology from Zurich to Barmen*. Louisville: Westminster/John Knox Press, 1998.
Rohr, John Von. *The Covenant of Grace in Puritan Thought*. Eugene, OR: Wipf and Stock, 2010.
Röhser, Günter. *Metaphorik und Personifikation der Sünde: antike Sündenvorstellungen und paulinische Hamartia*. Tubingen: J.C.B. Mohr Siebeck, 1987.
Romanowski, William D. and Vander Heide, Jennifer L. "Easier Said than Done: On Reversing the Hermeneutical Flow in the Theology and Film Dialogue" in *Journal of Communication and Religion* 30 (March 2007): 40–64.
Rosen, Christopher. "What Really Happens At The End Of 'Out Of The Furnace'?" *The HuffingtonPost*, September 12, 2013. http://www.huffingtonpost.com/2013/12/09/out-of-the-furnace-ending_n_4365572.html.
Rothman, William. "Violence and Film." In *Violence and American Cinema*, edited by J. David Slocum. New York: Routledge, 2001.
Sanders, E. P. *Paul and Palestinian Judaism: A Comparison of Patterns of Religion*. Philadelphia: Fortress Press, 1977.
Sanders, E.P. "Sin and Sinners (NT)." In *The Anchor Yale Bible Dictionary, Si–Z: Volume 6*. New Haven; London: Yale University Press, 1992.
Scharlemann, Martin H. (Martin Henry). "'In the Likeness of Sinful Flesh.'" *Concordia Theological Monthly* 32, no. 3 (March 1961): 133–38.
Schleiermacher, Friedrich. *The Christian Faith*. Edited by H. R. Mackintosh and J. S. Stewart. London: T&T Clark, 1999.
Schlier, Heinrich. *Principalities and Powers in the New Testament*. New York: Herder and Herder, 1961.
Schmiechen, Peter. *Saving Power: Theories of Atonement and Forms of the Church*. Grand Rapids: Eerdmans, 2005.
Schnackenburg, Rudolf. *The Gospel According to St. John: Volume 3*. London: Crossroad/Herder & Herder, 1983.
Schnelle, Udo. *Apostle Paul: His Life and Theology*. Translated by M. Boring. Baker, 2012.

Schrader, Paul. *Transcendental Style In Film*. New York, NY: Da Capo Press, 1988.

Schwager, Raymund. *Must There Be Scapegoats?: Violence and Redemption in the Bible*. San Francisco: Harper & Row, 1987.

Schüssler Fiorenza, Elizabeth. *Jesus: Miriam's Child, Sophia's Prophet: Critical Issues in Feminist Christology*. New York: Continuum, 1994.

Scott, Bernard Brandon. *Hollywood Dreams and Biblical Stories*. Minneapolis: Fortress Press, 2000.

Sison, Antonio. *World Cinema, Theology, and the Human: Humanity in Deep Focus*. New York: Routledge, 2012.

S.J, Lloyd Baugh. *Imaging the Divine: Jesus and Christ-Figures in Film*. Kansas City, MO: Sheed & Ward, 1997.

Slocum, J. David. "Film Violence and the Institutionalization of the Cinema." *Social Research* 67, no. 3 (2000): 649–81.

Snaith, Norman, ed. *Leviticus and Numbers*. New Century Bible. Greenwood, S.C.: Attic Press, 1967.

Song, Choan-Seng. *Jesus, the Crucified People*. New York: Crossroad, 1990.

Soskice, Janet Martin. *Metaphor and Religious Language*. Oxford: Clarendon Press, 1987.

Stendahl, Krister. *Paul Among Jews and Gentiles*. Philadelphia: Fortress Press, 1976.

Sternberg, Meir. *The Poetics of Biblical Narrative: Ideological Literature and the Drama of Reading*. Reprint edition. Bloomington, IN: Indiana University Press, 1987.

Stott, John R. W. *The Cross of Christ*. Inter-Varsity Press, 1986.

Streufert, Mary J. "Maternal Sacrifice as a Hermeneutics of the Cross." In *Cross Examinations: Readings on the Meaning of the Cross Today*. Edited by Marit Trelstad. Minneapolis, MN: Augsburg Fortress, 2006.

Swartley, Willard M., ed. *Violence Renounced*. Telford, PA: Pandora Press U. S., 2000.

Taylor, Barry. Entertainment Theology: New-Edge Spirituality in a Digital Democracy. Grand Rapids, Baker, 2008.

Thielman, Frank. *From Plight to Solution: A Jewish Framework for Understanding Paul's View of the Law in Galatians and Romans*. Eugene, OR: Wipf & Stock, 2008.

Thiselton, Anthony C. *The Two Horizons: New Testament Hermeneutics and Philosophical Description*. Grand Rapids: Eerdmans, 1980.

Tidball, Derek, David Hilborn, and Justin Thacker, eds. *The Atonement Debate: Papers from the London Symposium on the Theology of Atonement*. Grand Rapids: Zondervan, 2009.

Tillich, Paul. *Boundaries of Our Being*. London: Fontana, 1973.

———. *The Religious Situation*. Meridian Books, 1956.

———. *What Is Religion?* Translated by James Luther Adams. New York: Harper & Row, 1969.

Treat, Jeremy R. *The Crucified King: Atonement and Kingdom in Biblical and Systematic Theology*. Grand Rapids: Zondervan, 2014.

Trompf, G. W. *Payback: The Logic of Retribution in Melanesian Religions*. Cambridge: Cambridge University Press, 1994.

Turnau, Ted. Popologetics: Popular Culture in Christian Perspective. Phillipsburg, NJ: P&R, 2012.

Turretin, Francis. *Institutes of Elenctic Theology, Vol. 2*. Edited by James T. Dennison, Jr. Translated by George Musgrave Giger. Phillipsburg, NJ: P & R Publishing, 1994.

Twitchell, James B. *Preposterous Violence: Fables of Aggression in Modern Culture.* New York: Oxford University Press, 1989.
Venema, Cornelis P. "Violence, Hospitality, and the Cross: Reappropriating the Atonement Tradition." *Mid-America Journal of Theology* 16 (2005): 183–85.
Venter, Dirk J. "Romans 8:3–4 and God's Resolution of the Threefold Problems of Sin, the Incapability of the Law and the Weakness of the Flesh." *In Die Skriflig* 48, no. 1 (September 2014): 7. doi:doi:10.4102/ids.v48i1.1687.
Via, Dan O. *The Parables: Their Literary and Existential Dimension.* Eugene, OR: Wipf & Stock Pub, 2007.
Viladesau, Richard. *Theology and the Arts: Encountering God Through Music, Art and Rhetoric.* New York: Paulist Press, 2000.
Weaver, J. Denny. "Narrative Christus Victor: The Answer to Anselmian Atonement Violence." In *Atonement and Violence: A Theological Conversation*, edited by John Sanders. Nashville: Abingdon Press, 2006.
———. *The Nonviolent Atonement.* 2nd ed. Grand Rapids: Eerdmans, 2011.
Weinandy, Thomas G. *In the Likeness of Sinful Flesh: An Essay on the Humanity of Christ.* Edinburgh: T & T Clark, 1993.
"Westminster Confession of Faith (1647) Chapter VIII: Of Christ the Mediator." Center for Reformed Theology and Apologetics. http://www.reformed.org/documents/wcf_with_proofs/.
Willard, Samuel. *The Doctrine of the Covenant of Redemption In Which Is Laid the Foundation of All Our Hopes and Happiness, Briefly Opened and Improved.* Edited by Therese B. McMahon. Coconut Creek, FL: Puritan Publications, 2014.
Williams, Carol A. "The Decree of Redemption Is in Effect a Covenant: David Dickson and the Covenant of Redemption." Unpublished Ph.D Dissertation, Calvin Theological Seminary, 2005.
Williams, Delores S. "Black Women's Surrogacy Experience and the Christian Notion of Redemption." In *After Patriarchy: Feminist Transformations of the World Religions*, edited by Paula M. Cooey, William R. Eakin, and Jay B. McDaniel. Maryknoll, NY: Orbis Books, 1991.
Williams, James G. *Bible, Violence, and the Sacred: Liberation from the Myth of Sanctioned Violence.* San Francisco: HarperCollins, 1991.
Wilson, Joshua Lacy. *Imputation of Sin and Righteousness: A Sermon from Rom. 5:18,19.* Hanover College Press, 1835.
Wink, Walter. *Engaging the Powers: Discernment and Resistance in a World of Domination.* Minneapolis: Fortress Press, 1992.
———. *Unmasking the Powers.* Philadelphia: Fortress Press, 1986.
Wolterstorff, Nicholas. *Art in Action: Toward a Christian Aesthetic.* Grand Rapids: Eerdmans, 1980.
———. *Art Rethought: The Social Practices of Art.* Oxford University Press, 2015.
———. *Works and Worlds of Art.* Oxford : New York: Clarendon Press, 1980.
Wright, David P. "Azazel." Edited by David Noel Freedman. *The Anchor Bible Dictionary*, Vol. 1: A–C. New Haven; London: Yale University Press, June 1, 1992.
Wright, Melanie J. *Religion and Film: An Introduction.* London; New York: I. B. Tauris, 2006.
Wright, N. T. "On Becoming the Righteousness of God: 2 Corinthians 5:21." In *Pauline Theology*, edited by David M. Hay, 2:200–208. Minneapolis: Augsburg Fortress, 1993.

———. *The Climax of the Covenant: Christ and the Law in Pauline Theology.* Minneapolis: Fortress, 1993.

Zillman, Dolf. "The Psychology of the Appeal of Portrayals of Violence." In *Why We Watch: The Attractions of Violent Entertainment,* edited by Jeffrey Goldstein. New York: Oxford University Press, 1998.

CPSIA information can be obtained
at www.ICGtesting.com
Printed in the USA
LVOW10*2354010418
571926LV00006B/30/P